The Applied Linguistic Individual

Studies in Applied Linguistics

Series Editors: Srikant Sarangi & Christopher N. Candlin

This series publishes books that are innovative applications of language and communication research. It is a companion series to the recently launched *Journal of Applied Linguistics.*

Published

Applied Linguistics: Towards a New Integration?
Lars Sigfred Evensen

Language, Identity and Study Abroad: Sociocultural Perspectives
Jane Jackson

Metaphor Analysis: Research Practice in Applied Linguistics, Social Sciences and the Humanities
Edited by Lynne Cameron and Robert Maslen

Sociocultural Theory and the Teaching of Second Languages
Edited by James P. Lantolf and Matthew E. Poehner

The Applied Linguistic Individual:

Sociocultural Approaches to Identity, Agency and Autonomy

Edited by Phil Benson and Lucy Cooker

SHEFFIELD UK BRISTOL CT

Published by Equinox Publishing Ltd.

UK: Kelham House, 3 Lancaster Street, Sheffield, S3 8AF
USA: ISD, 70 Enterprise Drive, Bristol, CT 06010

www.equinoxpub.com

First published 2013

ISBN 978-1908049-38-4 (hardback)
978-1-908049-39-1 (paperback)

British Library Cataloguing-in-Publication Data

A catalogue record for this book is available from the British Library.

Library of Congress Cataloging-in-Publication Data

The applied linguistic individual : sociocultural approaches to identity, agency and autonomy / edited by Phil Benson and Lucy Cooker.
p. cm. -- (Studies in applied linguistics)
Includes bibliographical references and index.
ISBN 978-1-908049-38-4 -- ISBN 978-1-908049-39-1 (pbk.)
1. Applied linguistics--Research. 2. Autonomy (Psychology)--Cross-cultural studies. 3. Literacy--Social aspects--Cross-cultural studies. 4. Language and languages--Study and teaching. 5. Sociolinguistics--Research. I. Benson, Phil, 1955- II. Cooker, Lucy, 1970-
P129.A65 2012
418.0072--dc23

2012011567

Printed and bound in Great Britain by Lightning Source UK Ltd., Milton Keynes and Lightning Source Inc., La Vergne, TN

Contents

Contributors vii
Preface xi

I: INTRODUCTION

1 The social and the individual in Applied Linguistics research 1
Phil Benson and Lucy Cooker

II: THEORETICAL PERSPECTIVES

2 Sociocultural Theory and the dialectics of L2 learner autonomy/agency 17
James P. Lantolf

3 The struggle to belong: individual language learners in Situated Learning Theory 32
Martin Lamb

4 Individuality, imagination and community in a globalizing world: an Asian EFL perspective 46
Tomoko Yashima

5 Chaos and the complexity of second language acquisition 59
Vera Menezes

6 Drifting in and out of view: autonomy and the social individual 75
Phil Benson

III: THE INDIVIDUAL IN RESEARCH

7 A social-ecological exploration of autonomy, beliefs and identity 90
Jane Kehrwald

8 Teenagers making sense of their foreign language practices: individual accounts indexing social discourses 104
Anne Pitkänen-Huhta and Tarja Nikula

9 Individuality in L2 identity construction: the stories of two Chinese learners of English 119
Mingyue (Michelle) Gu

10 The ideal sexual self: the motivational investments of Japanese gay male learners of English 135
Ashley R. Moore

11 Using Dynamic Systems/Complexity Theory in linguistic data analysis: a language ecology approach to the study of individual and social process 152
Anne Whiteside

12 A tale of two teachers: teacher identity and the care of the self in an era of accountability 164
Matthew Clarke

IV: CONCLUSION

13 The Applied Linguistic individual: gaining perspective 178
Phil Benson and Lucy Cooker

References 187
Index 207

Contributors

Phil Benson is a Professor in the Department of Linguistics and Modern Language Studies at the Hong Kong Institute of Education. He has published widely on the topic of autonomy in language teaching and learning and is currently especially interested in informal language learning and the development of second language identity and the use of narrative research methods in Applied Linguistics. pbenson@ied.edu.hk

Lucy Cooker is a Lecturer in Education at the University of Nottingham. Her PhD thesis was on the formative assessment of language learner autonomy. Previously, Lucy was a Senior Lecturer at Kanda University of International Studies in Japan where she established the award winning self-access learning centre. lucy.cooker@nottingham.ac.uk

Matthew Clarke is a Senior Lecturer in the School of Education at the University of New South Wales in Sydney. His work draws on social and political theory to explore a range of issues in education, including teacher formation and teacher professional identities, education policy, and language and literacy education. m.clarke@unsw.edu.au

Mingyue (Michelle) Gu is Assistant Professor in the Faculty of Education at the Chinese University of Hong Kong. Her research interests include language and identity, language ideology, discourse theory and analysis, second language learning motivation, communities of practice in language education, and teacher education. She has published in journals such as *Journal of Pragmatics*, *International Journal of Multilingual and Multicultural Development*, *Computer Assisted Language Learning, System, Critical Inquiry in Language Studies, Journal of Education for Teaching*, *Language and Education* and *Teacher Education Quarterly.* mygu@cuhk.edu.hk

Jane Kehrwald is currently a Language & Learning Coordinator in the Learning & Teaching Unit at the University of South Australia. In her 16 years' experience in the field, Jane has worked as an EFL/ESL teacher, teacher-educator and manager of language and academic bridging programmes in Australia, New Zealand, Japan and Thailand. Jane is in the final stages of her doctoral studies with the School of Linguistics and International Languages, Massey University, New Zealand. Jane.Kehrwald@unisa.edu.au

Martin Lamb is a Senior Lecturer in TESOL at the University of Leeds where he teaches undergraduate and postgraduate courses on aspects of language learning and teaching. He previously taught in Sweden, Indonesia and Bulgaria. His main research interest is in language learner motivation, both as a traditional psychological construct and a dynamic, contingent social phenomenon closely related to identity. M.V.Lamb@education.leeds.ac.uk

James P. Lantolf is the Greer Professor in Language Acquisition & Applied Linguistics at The Pennsylvania State University. His research focus is on sociocultural theory and second language learning and teaching. He has been co-editor of *Applied Linguistics*, President of the American Association for Applied Linguistics, and is co-author of *Sociocultural theory and the genesis of second language development* (with Steven Thorne, Oxford University Press, 2006). jpl7@psu.edu

Vera Menezes has a PhD in Linguistics and is a full Professor of Applied Linguistics at Universidade Federal de Minas Gerais, one of the most important universities in Brazil. She is a former president of ALAB (Brazilian Association of Applied Linguistics) and of APLIEMGE (Teachers of English Association of Minas Gerais State). She has edited several books and published papers in Brazil and abroad. vlmop@veramenezes.com

Ashley R. Moore is Director of the Language Learning Center at Osaka Institute of Technology in Japan. His teaching and research interests include language learning motivation, identity, sociocultural theory, curriculum design and assessment. moore@rsh.oit.ac.jp

Tarja Nikula is Professor in the Centre for Applied Language Studies (CALS) at the University of Jyväskylä, Finland. Her research interests include classroom discourse in content and language integrated learning (CLIL) settings, pragmatics of foreign language learning and use, English–Finnish language contact phenomena, and language education policies. Her current research focuses on conceptual challenges that CLIL poses for some key concepts within applied linguistics. Her publications have appeared in a number of international journals and edited volumes, recent publications include a co-edited book (with Christiane Dalton-Puffer and Ute Smit) *Language Use and Language Learning in CLIL Classrooms* (2010). tarja.nikula@jyu.fi

Anne Pitkänen-Huhta received her academic training at the universities of Jyväskylä and Lancaster. She received her PhD in English from the University of Jyväskylä in 2003. She works currently as a professor of English at the Department of Languages, University of Jyväskylä. She is also the Head of the Department of Languages. Her research focuses on literacy and discourse practices of young people, foreign language learning in formal and informal contexts, and the role of English in Finnish society. Her research employs ethnographic and discourse analytic methods. anne.pitkanen-huhta@jyu.fi

Anne Whiteside (PhD. U.C. Berkeley in Educational Linguistics) teaches at City College of San Francisco, where she recently completed a study of adult immigrant ESL students. She has taught linguistics in Mexico, and has worked with language teachers in Europe and Algeria. Research interests include second language acquisition, early adult L1 and L2 literacy development, language practices of transnational migrants, and cognitive linguistics. awhitesi@ccsf.edu

Tomoko Yashima is Professor of Applied Linguistics and Intercultural Communication at Kansai University. Major publications include: *Motivation and Affect in Foreign Language Communication* (a book published in Japanese); The influence of attitude and affect on willingness to communicate and second language communication. Language Learning, 54, 2004; The effects of international volunteer work experiences on intercultural competence of Japanese youth. *International Journal of Intercultural Relations*, 34, 2010. yashima@ipcku.kansai-u.ac.jp

Preface

This idea for this book emerged during a conversation between the editors over a sushi dinner at the Independent Learning Association Conference in Tokyo in October 2007. Throwing around ideas about possible publications, one of us mentioned a theme that had cropped up in several of the presentations we had attended, which had not yet been widely discussed in the context of independent learning. The theme was 'identity'. We agreed that the presentations that had touched on this theme were among the most interesting that we had heard. We also agreed that we were still a long way from understanding exactly how identity factored into independent learning. We knew, however, that it was being placed on the floor by researchers who took a broadly social view of language teaching and learning. We also noticed that, when the topic of identity came up, agency and autonomy were never far behind. But wait a moment, we thought! When they address issues of identity, agency and autonomy, aren't these researchers sailing close to the wind of 'individualism' against which social approaches to Applied Linguistics are perpetually struggling? A few judicious questions produced an answer. Yes, they said, we *are* concerned with individuals and individuality, but not in an *individualistic* way. What we are concerned with, in fact, is the *social construction* of identity, agency and autonomy – not with individuals, as such, but with *social* individuals.

A little the wiser (but only a little!) we came up with the idea that the best way to understand the issue would be to edit a book, in which we would ask socially-oriented researchers to explain exactly how they conceptualized individuals and individuality in their research. The issue is, after all, an important one. Some of us believe that the practice of language teaching and learning must be grounded in an appreciation of individual difference; others believe, to the contrary, that it must be grounded in an appreciation of the fundamentally social nature of the individual. Are these beliefs as contradictory as they seem? Can they be reconciled in theory and research?

An invitation went out to researchers who we thought would have something interesting to say on these issues. Some had presented at the Independent Learning Association Conference and some had not. There followed a protracted process of negotiating areas of focus, of drafting and redrafting, which has brought the book to its present shape. We are now more than a little wiser and profoundly grateful to our contributors for putting up with and responding to what must have seemed like an endless series of requests for clarifications. The final product is, we believe, a book that not only clarifies complex issues concerning the social and the individual in Applied Linguistics research, but also makes an important contribution to debates that are likely to be crucial to the future of Applied Linguistics research for many years to come.

Acknowledgements

We would like to thank the contributors to the this book for their enthusiasm for this project and their patience in waiting for it to come to fruition; Chris Candlin and Srikant Sarangi for their enthusiasm, patience and wise editorial comments; Valerie Hall and George Moore at Equinox; and Nikita Chan and Ada Wong at the Hong Kong Institute of Education, for their considerable help in preparing the manuscript for publication.

We would also like to thank Sara Cotterall and Garold Murray, co-conveners (with Lucy Cooker) of the Independent Learning Association Conference 2007.

Phil Benson and Lucy Cooker, September 2012

1 The social and the individual in Applied Linguistics research

Phil Benson and Lucy Cooker

Introduction

In recent years, Applied Linguistics has come under the sway of two apparently contradictory views: one emphasizing the social and the other the individual. The social view argues that language learning is a *social* process in the double sense that it is grounded in social interaction and conditioned by social, cultural and historical contexts. This view dates back to the rise of Sociolinguistics, Pragmatics and Discourse Analysis in the 1960s, if not further, and was central to the communicative perspectives on language education of the early 1980s (Breen and Candlin 1980; Canale and Swain 1980). Later, the 'social turn' in Applied Linguistics was articulated in a critique of 'universalist' accounts of second language learning and in the adoption and adaptation of research frameworks from the social sciences (Firth and Wagner 1997; Coupland *et al.* 2001; Block 2003), including Vygotskyan Sociocultural Theory (Lantolf and Thorne 2006), Situated Learning Theory and Communities of Practice (Norton 2000), Second Language Identities and Imagined Communities (Kanno and Norton 2003; Block 2007b), Complexity Theory (Larsen-Freeman and Cameron 2008a), Social-Ecological Theory (van Lier 2004) and Social Realism (Sealey and Carter 2004).

An alternative to this social view argues that language learning is a uniquely *individual* process. This view can be traced back to the rise of psycholinguistics in the 1960s and is associated with the rise of learner-centredness in language teaching, from which interest in concepts such as individual differences, autonomy, and learning styles, strategies and beliefs emerged in the 1970s (Gremmo and Riley 1995; Wenden 2002). Most recently, this view has also been fostered by narrative studies of language learning experiences, in which the individuality of learners and learning experiences is particularly brought to the fore (Benson and Nunan 2002, 2005; Kalaja *et al.* 2008; Barkhuizen 2011).

At present, social approaches to Applied Linguistics research are in the ascendancy and they are often defined in terms of their opposition to outdated 'individualist' approaches. In this context, the term 'individualist' has three distinct meanings, which can be illustrated by citations from work by Kelleen Toohey and Bonnie Norton, in which they have critically engaged with the idea of autonomy. The first sense is illustrated by Toohey and Norton's (2003: 58) observation that language learners are often represented as 'individuals who act, think, and learn in accordance with innate, specifiable characteristics, independently of the social, historical, cultural and political-economic situations in which they live'. Here, individualism refers to a belief in an atomistic and unitary individual self that is prior to and somehow remains within the socialized self. The second sense is illustrated by Toohey's (2007: 232) observation that two learners that she observed were 'not agentive or autonomous on their own', because 'the social settings in which they participated both imposed constraints on, and enabled their agency'. Here, individualism refers to a tendency to treat individual agency as causal, while failing to recognize that agency itself is socially constituted. The third sense is illustrated by Toohey and Norton's (2003: 58) suggestion that autonomy should be understood 'not so much as individualized performance but as socially oriented agency'. Here, individualism involves the representation of constructs such as autonomy, motivation and learning strategies as attributes of the individual. From a social perspective, such constructs need to be reconceptualized as socially constituted, situated and dynamic relationships between learners and their social contexts, as Norton (2000), for example, reconceptualized motivation as 'investment'.

There are, however, a number of paradoxes to be observed in the opposition between social and individual views of Applied Linguistics. While some socially oriented researchers charge Second Language Acquisition (SLA) research with individualism, Larsen-Freeman (2001: 12) argues that SLA research has, in fact, paid too little attention to 'individual learner factors' and too much to identifying 'an acquisition process that is common to all learners'. Williams *et al.* (2001: 172), on the other hand, are critical of research on individual learner factors for its focus on groups with particular sets of attributes. They argue instead for small-scale, personally orientated investigations of 'the ways in which individuals' thoughts and feelings about themselves as learners affect their approaches to and success in learning'. This kind of research, moreover, turns out to be most characteristic of socially oriented approaches, which have tended to favour fine-grained, qualitative case studies of individual learners. At times, socially oriented researchers also allow considerable space for individual agency. As Norton and Toohey (2001b: 308) suggest, social approaches to Applied Linguistics do not aim to erase the individual from the picture, but are rather concerned with 'the dialectic between the individual and the social; between the human agency of these learners and the social practices of their communities'. This volume sets out to explore some of the theoretical and empirical challenges of working within this dialectic.

Conceptions of the individual

The key issue addressed in this volume is the conceptualization of the individual in social approaches to Applied Linguistics and, in particular, the sense in which individuality, in the context of language learning and use, should be considered as socially constituted. Lave (1988: 16), for example, tells us that individual agency is 'partially determined, partially determining'. If this is the case, how do we articulate the relationship between its determined and determining sides? If individual agency is entirely socially constituted, what space remains for the dialectic between the individual and the social? If, on the other hand, agency is partially determining, how do social approaches to Applied Linguistics avoid becoming enmeshed in the very individualism that they seek to avoid?

Although these questions are yet to be addressed in depth by Applied Linguists, they are familiar, if unresolved, questions in the wider literature. In an especially insightful discussion of the 'problem of the subject' in western thought, Lemke (1995) locates individualism in the social sciences in a tendency to work with a common sense notion of the human individual that is obtained by 'mapping the social-biographical person onto the physical-biological organism' (p. 81). The discourses that identify the embodied biological individual are, however, quite different to those that identify the social individual and, in many non-western cultures, the assumption of 'one body one person' does not hold. The individual who constitutes the unit of analysis in western thought is, therefore, an ideological construction, which is replaced in socially oriented research by 'a larger system including the informational pathways and social interactions linking "us" with the artefacts and tools we use and with the whole of our non-human and inanimate environment as well as the social dyads and groups in which we participate' (p. 92).

Critics of individualism in Applied Linguistics are, thus, essentially objecting to the use of the 'biological' individual as the unit of analysis in research. Yet as socially oriented research abandons this unit of analysis, in favour of the language learner/user-in-context, it faces several tensions. On the surface, Lemke argues, the difficulty is 'how to have an active, creative human subject which constructs social meanings, at the same time that this subject must itself be a social construction' (p. 80). At a deeper level, however, there is the difficulty of giving up 'the moral comfort that the traditional liberal discourse of human individuality provides'. The active human subject becomes an 'object of desire' that is often re-created within social theory and represented as 'the problem of the subject' (p. 80). A related difficulty concerns the subjectivity of the researcher. According to Lemke:

> what we are taught in our culture to call our own minds, our own subjective sense of experiencing and being, is a projection onto the complex, interactive, self-organizing system of an organism-in-its-environment of a cultural model of what it is to think of ourselves according to one community's view of being human. (p. 89)

It is evidently much easier to see and represent the subjectivities of others as being socially constructed, than it is to see our own subjectivities as researchers in the same way, and to incorporate such a view of ourselves into our research.

The problem of the individual in social approaches to Applied Linguistics, then, is essentially one of understanding and representing the embodied individuals who are so often the subjects of research as 'social individuals'. To abandon the embodied individual entirely would mean giving up much of the conceptual language we are accustomed to work with. Riley (2003: 97), for example, observes that basic concepts such as memory, needs and motivation 'clearly entail the existence of an individual person, an identity, someone real who has those memories, needs and motivations'. This would also apply to many other concepts that are currently central to Applied Linguistics, including the fundamental idea that language learning is a matter of individuals 'acquiring' languages, and making them 'their own'. The social turn in Applied Linguistics may eventually lead to a comprehensive shift in the focus of research from processes that take place within the brains of individuals to the social 'activities' or 'practices' (Gee 1992; Cole 1995) through which people learn and use languages. We may also, eventually, see a much wider application of notions such as 'socially shared' or 'distributed' cognition (Resnick *et al.* 1991; Salomon 1993), which view cognition as being 'stretched across mind, body, activity and setting' (Lave 1988: 18). But as Cole (1995: 105) demonstrates, the task of finding a 'unit of analysis larger than, but inclusive of, the individual' is not an easy one, because there is no shared conception across social theories of the meaning of constructs such as 'activity' and 'practice'. It is also worth noting here that the unit Cole is aiming at incorporates the individual, which again raises the question that is central to this volume. Does the social turn in Applied Linguistics simply imply a widening of the investigative lens, such that individual language learners are always studied within a social context of some kind, or does it imply a radical reconceptualization of the individual as subject of research and practice?

Individual differences, identity, agency and autonomy

Although Individual Differences emerged as a recognized sub-field of SLA research in the late 1970s, current approaches have much in common with the 'personality psychology' of the 1930s, which explored the influence of various psychological traits on individual behaviour (McAdams 2007). As noted above, an overwhelming preference for quantitative methods and an emphasis on psychological and social categorizations means that Individual Differences research has, paradoxically, failed to engage with the uniqueness of each individual's experiences of language learning and use (Larsen-Freeman 2001; Williams *et al.* 2001). Ellis (1994: 534) concluded his review of the field by reiterating Skehan's (1991) call for naturalistic studies that 'can shed light on the individuality of single learners'. Ten years later, Ellis (2004) observed that qualitative methodologies were still infrequently used. Benson (2005) also argued that the more holistic sense in which individual learners *become* different from each other as a consequence of engagement in differently situated learning experiences has been largely unacknowledged. But again we see a paradox. Although social approaches to Applied Linguistics have for the most part ignored Individual Differences as a relevant concept, socially oriented empirical studies have come closest to providing the kinds of accounts of learner individuality that Skehan and Ellis have called for. At the same time as they have rejected individualist approaches to research, they have also constructively engaged with three key constructs that have much to do with individuality: identity, agency and autonomy.

Identity

Identity has long been a topic of interest in Sociolinguistics, although language identities were until recently understood as more or less direct reflections of the kinds of social and psychological variables discussed in Individual Differences research. Social approaches to language education research have reconceptualized language identities as multiple, dynamic and contested, and it is often the interactions between language and identities that is of interest in research that views identity development as an important outcome of language learning (Block 2007b: 864).

Social approaches also tend to reject the largely unreflective use of the 'language learner' identity in much Applied Linguistics research, which Riley (2003: 96) describes as 'an abstraction, a simplified representation or personification of *the learning process*, devoid of any truly individual and social dimension'. Lantolf and Pavlenko's (2001) proposal that we view language learners as 'people' also signals a rejection of this view. From this perspective, the sense in which a person who is learning a language is a 'language learner' should always be treated as problematic and not simply inferred, for example, from the person's presence in a language classroom.

Recent research on identity in language learning has focused on two main, overlapping areas. First, social approaches assume that the identities that individuals bring to the task of learning a language will have an impact on their language learning and use and be modified in the process. Much of the research on identity, therefore, uses ethnographic methods to examine experiences of language learning and use in particular social and situational contexts. A second area of research focuses more on longer-term developments within individuals, or the ways in which 'individuals narrativise language learning as an identity project' (Coffey and Street 2008: 452). Research in this area often follows Giddens' (1991) argument that, in a mobile world in which the force of identities established at birth is diminished, individuals are increasingly obliged to take on the responsibility for the construction of their own personal identities, a task that involves the construction of narratives of the self. From this perspective, learning a new language can destabilize personal identities, and narratives of language learning can be a form of identity work through which feelings of 'ambivalence' are addressed and potentially resolved (Block 2007b). Block links this perspective to individual agency by asking whether 'identity is, at least to some extent, a self-conscious, reflexive project of individual agency, created and maintained by individuals' (p. 865).

It is mainly through these two kinds of research on identity that social approaches to Applied Linguistics have begun, as Lemke (1995) proposes, to separate the social individual from the embodied individual. From the perspective of identity research, language learning does not necessarily produce a change in the embodied individual, but it does have considerable impact on the identities that are attached to and enacted by it. The idea of multiple identities also helps us understand how the same body can be inhabited by more than one social individual at the same time. Yet, the concept of identity remains problematic. Though identity is clearly a social process, identities are also fundamentally individual. An 'identity card', for example, fixes our individuality as a social category. While we can speak of group and individual identities, group identity often depends on ongoing self-identification of individuals with the group. In this sense, although identity (together with constructs such as the 'subject' and the 'self') can be viewed as socially constructed and constrained, it also has much to do with agency and autonomy.

Agency

The term agency entered Applied Linguistics around the turn of the twenty-first century in conjunction with Sociocultural Theory. One of the earliest references to it that we have found is by Lantolf and Pavlenko (2001), who suggested that rather than viewing language learners as devices for processing linguistic input, we should appreciate their 'human agency'. 'As agents,' they argued, 'learners actively engage in constructing the terms and conditions of their learning' (145). Used in this way, agency could mean much the same thing as autonomy, but it also often appears as a socially oriented alternative in work where autonomy is perceived to imply individualism. In the social sciences, agency often refers to the human capacity to act on informed choices: the capacity 'to have acted otherwise' (Giddens 1976: 11) or, more strongly, 'the power to maintain or modify the world' (Sealey and Carter 2004: 11). For socially oriented researchers, agency also implies social mediation and Ahearn's (2001: 112) definition of agency as 'the socioculturally mediated capacity to act' is often cited. This is also apparent in Toohey and Norton's (2003: 59) proposal to reconceptualize autonomy as 'socially oriented agency'.

Autonomy

The term autonomy has the longest history of the three in the field of language education and there is now a broad consensus that it is best used to refer to learners' capacity to take control of their own language learning (Benson 2011a: 58). Autonomy is constituted by a variety of abilities and dispositions and is liable to vary from person to person and, within the same person, from context to context and time to time. In this sense, autonomy is doubly concerned with the individual, because it implies an assertion of individual identity that is itself variable according to the individual concerned. For some socially oriented researchers, autonomy is strongly associated with the idea of the atomistic, unitary individual to which their approaches are opposed. These researchers also associate autonomy with modes of language teaching and learning in which individual students are required or encouraged to work 'on their own'. For the most part, however, learner autonomy is now understood to be a social capacity that develops through 'interdependence' rather than 'independence'. A number of socially oriented researchers have also engaged with the concept on these terms, seeking to reconstruct it as a social construct rather than dismiss it out of hand (e.g. Pennycook 1997; Holliday 2003; Toohey and Norton 2003; Schmenk 2005).

Structure and agency

Much of what this volume has to say about identity, agency and autonomy relates to the well-known 'structure versus agency' debate discussed by Sealey and Carter (2004: 5–12). Positions in this debate range along a continuum from the view that individual agency determines social structure to the view that, on the contrary, it is social structure that determines individual agency. As Sealey and Carter point out, however, the extremes of the continuum have few adherents and social theorists are most often to be found in the middle ground; Giddens' (1984) 'structurationist' position, for example, sees structure and agency as being mutually constitutive within social practice, while Layder's (1990) 'realist' position treats them as opposing and ontologically real forces. Having persisted for several centuries, the structure versus agency debate is unlikely to be resolved soon and may be best left to social theorists. Yet when Applied Linguists adopt social approaches to research, it seems important that they identify their positions in relation to this debate and how they map on to the domain of language learning and use. The conceptions of the individual language learner and user that underlie our use of terms such as identity, agency and autonomy are crucial in this respect. Do we emphasize, for example, the ways in which individual language behaviours are socially conditioned or constrained, or do we emphasize the role of self-determination? In regard to self-determination, do we view the individual as a linguistically 'free' agent, or do we view linguistic agency itself as being conditioned by preconstituted identities and pathways for language learning and use? Situating broader issues of personal identity within the domain of Applied Linguistics, if language learning involves destabilization and reconstruction of language identities, as Block (2007b) suggests, do these identities also become more 'individual' as learning a new language progresses?

This last question points to the importance of situating discussion of the individual in Applied Linguistics within contemporary contexts of language learning and use. An emphasis on individual agency is typically associated with elitism, while an emphasis on social determination often signals an approach that claims to address inequalities in power and access to resources. In eighteenth- and nineteenth-century western thought, concepts of individuality evolved in conjunction with private property rights. Individuality was held to grow out of the cultivation of the mind and implied an intellectuality that was opposed to the physicality of 'the masses'. In this sense, individual identity was not a universal attribute, but one that people acquired along with membership of the elite. The robust, male, self-made, autonomous individual of the nineteenth century was the epitome of this mode of individuality, and was often linked to self-educational processes that allowed selected individuals to rise out of the 'masses'. In general, however, individual agency was denied to the masses, whose agency could only be made effective through collective action. This history largely explains why post-Marxist approaches to socially oriented theory, in particular, are mistrustful of the idea of individual agency. There is a clear historical association between individualism and elitism in western thought. One of the characteristic social processes of the late twentieth and early twenty-first centuries, however, has been the acceleration of an 'individualization' of a different kind, in the loosening of traditional frames of social identity, such that more and more people are required to act as individuals in more and more contexts of their lives (Bauman 2001; Beck and Beck-Gersheim 2002). In many parts of the world, the possession of an individual identity remains a matter of social privilege that is often bound up with the ability to use a locally dominant second language or an international foreign language. The idea that a person might become more 'individual' through second or foreign language learning is, in other words, a distinctively modern idea related to the growing role of second and foreign language learning in social and geographical mobility in many parts of the world.

Finally, our thoughts on structure and agency in Applied Linguistics might take more account of the ways in which modern forms of urban and technological life produce distinctive types of social individuality. Writing in the early years of the twentieth century, Simmel (1997: 183–4) pointed to a particularly modern conception of individualism. This conception differed from the eighteenth-century notion of individual independence, or 'full freedom of movement in all social and intellectual relationships' and consisted instead in 'the elaboration of individuality itself'. The most significant characteristic of the metropolis, Simmel argued, is its 'functional extension beyond its physical boundaries' through trade and social interactions with other towns and cities. Correspondingly, the metropolitan citizen 'does not end with the limits of his body or the area comprising his immediate activity', but is constituted 'by the sum of effects emanating from him temporally and spatially'. From this derives a conception of individual freedom, based on the particularity and incomparability that comes from 'the working out of a way of life'. Many years later, White and Siegel (1984: 239) made a similar observation when they criticized the superficiality of the idea that socialization is a 'universal process through which all children in a society acquire a common stock of knowledge, attitudes, beliefs, and customs'. Because children occupy only a fractional part of the contexts of the towns and cities in which they live, socialization is also 'negotiation to find a viable and unique set of social contexts to be used and lived in by the individuals', and a process that 'makes children not alike as it makes them alike'. Here, then, we have a concept of individuality, in which independence is constituted through difference and the functional extension of the self in time and space as individuals seek out spaces in which to live their lives. For both young people and adults, language may also be implicated in this process of seeking out individualized spaces. A great deal of second and foreign language learning now takes places in the context of internal and international migration to increasingly multilingual urban areas and, increasingly, in the context of globalized online communication.

The image of young people drawing on social resources to construct identities in globalized spaces of which they have only a fractional knowledge resonates with Ryan's (2006) idea of an 'imagined global community' of English speakers, consisting of like-minded individuals who are learning and using English while accessing a shared body of English language resources. Ryan emphasizes that this imagined community is 'specific to the individual' and that membership and participation 'occur in the imagination'. New technologies for globalized communication are, however, creating contexts in which such imagined communities are potentially actualized. Gee (1998) has used the term 'affinity spaces' to describe online areas (such as collaborative role-play games) in which people are drawn together in common endeavours, which presumably include many that involve second and foreign language learning and use. While 'affinity spaces' are essentially social spaces, they presuppose a high degree of individual agency and autonomy as participation in them is not a matter of location or socially determined identity, but of individual choice and motivation. Wellman (2002: 16) takes this view somewhat further when he uses the term 'networked individualism' to refer to a new network paradigm, in which the nodes are individuals operating multiple devices, rather than physically located workstations, and in which each individual 'separately operates his networks to obtain information, collaboration, orders, support, sociability, and a sense of belonging'. Within this paradigm, Wellman argues, 'individual autonomy and agency become more important, as each person becomes the responsible operator of her own personal network' (p. 19). Again, this has a strong relevance to second and foreign language use, as the globalized online spaces for social networking, video and image sharing, shopping and gaming that have sprung up in the last few years have become important sites for second and foreign language use (Benson and Chik 2010). In the ongoing debate over the influence of structure and agency, therefore, modernity appears to favour agency, or at least to demand understanding of the ways in which the exercise of individual agency has become a pervasive characteristic of increasingly complex social structures.

The social and the individual in Applied Linguistics theory

There are, of course, no straightforward answers to the questions raised in this chapter. Or perhaps it would be better to say that there can be no straightforward resolution to the dialectic between the social and individual, precisely because dialectics are constituted by a dynamic tension between opposing forces. Such tensions are, rather, productive sites for inquiry and debate. With this in mind, we set out to commission contributions to a volume that would offer multiple perspectives on the Applied Linguistic individual and reflect both theoretical and empirical concerns. Our starting point was the observation that social approaches have tended to define themselves in opposition to the individualistic 'Other' of mainstream SLA research. We therefore invited a number of researchers who have adopted social approaches in their research to take this opposition as their starting point, and articulate and reflect on the sense in which individuals and the concept of individuality may remain important to their work. The range of approaches touched upon in this volume is considerable, but here we would like to highlight three of the more prominent approaches in Applied Linguistics at the present time, which also recur throughout this volume: Sociocultural Theory; Situated Learning Theory; and Complexity Theory, in order to clarify what we aim to achieve through this book.

Sociocultural Theory has become the term of choice within Applied Linguistics to refer to a body of theoretical work, centred on Vygotskyan theories of learning, which places social interaction at the heart of all learning involving higher mental processes (Lantolf and Thorne 2006). In Sociocultural Theory, Vygotsky's work on the psychology of learning is often represented as the primary 'social' alternative to earlier 'individualistic' accounts. Evensen (2007), however, initiated a discussion in recent issues of the *Journal of Applied Linguistics*, which calls this assumption into question. Evensen observes that the relationship between social and individual aspects of learning is, in fact, a controversial issue in Vygotskyan theory and asks whether Vygotsky's emphasis on social context excludes the role of individual learners. He suggests that interest in Vygotsky stemmed from a view that SLA research had not sufficiently recognized the central role of social interaction, but in the course of the turn to Vygotsky 'the learning individual was toned down by focusing one-sidedly on the social aspect of learning' (p. 334). Arguing that Vygotskyian theory is essentially concerned with how *individuals* learn through social interaction, Evensen maintains that it is through 'a mediating process of increasing individual control' that 'learning moves from the *inter*mental to the *intra*mental, from *between* persons to *within* persons' (p. 336). Commenting on Evensen's paper, Cazden (2008: 210) shares his view, arguing that 'what can be internalized, or appropriated, from other people still requires significant mental work on the part of the learner'. In the context of a discussion of the terminological shift from 'language acquisition' to 'language socialization', she also cautions against forgetting that 'regardless of our naming habits, ultimate agents are the individual learners' minds' (p. 211).

Some Applied Linguistics researchers have, thus, begun to question the assumption that Sociocultural Theory is an *exclusively* social theory of learning, to which questions of individuality are largely irrelevant. The problem they raise, however, is to understand who the 'individual' at the heart of socially oriented theories of learning actually is. In his response to Evensen, Lantolf (2008) takes a strong view on this point, which he develops in Chapter 2 of this volume. For Lantolf, individuals are 'formed on the basis of their relations with other human beings and culturally constructed artefacts, including language' and 'the source of the individual is situated not in biological genes but in the sociocultural world created by objective purposive activity' (p. 215). 'Individuals', in other words, are created by socialization, and do not exist independently of it. The problem with SLA, from this perspective, is that it acknowledges the *influence* of social interaction on learning, but fails to perceive 'the necessary dialectic unity between individual development and social relations' (p. 216) within which individuality is created. In response to this view, Evensen (2008: 225) asks: 'But are individuals only *formed*. Is the *source* of the individual only an external one?' Following Mead (1934), he suggests an alternative view, according to which individuals are '*formed* by our primary socialization' through the discourse of significant others, but also '*influence* that very formative context through our individual utterances' (*ibid.*). At the same time, Evensen questions what we might call the 'separation' of individual minds from each other that Lantolf's argument seems to assume and suggests that the premises of mediation and *inter*mental learning indicate that 'learning somehow transcends any individual's central nervous system' (Evensen 2007: 346). This is supported, he argues, by numerous instances in which professional competence is distributed among individuals, rather than held within any one individual's mind.

Situated Learning Theory was developed by Lave and Wenger (1991), based on anthropological observations of apprenticeship systems. Like Sociocultural Theory, it foregrounds social interaction as the site and cause of learning, but differs from it in several important respects, notably in its emphasis on learning as the development of identities that arise from 'participation' in 'communities of practice', and in the wider scope it allows for individual agency. The larger systems of socialization that condition individual agency in Sociocultural Theory are largely absent from Situated Learning Theory. Wenger (1998) examined the notion of communities of practice in much greater depth than Lave and Wenger (1991), invoking Anderson's (1983) notion of 'imagined communities' to describe communities beyond the immediate face-to-face settings studied in apprenticeship research. These notions have subsequently had a considerable influence on Applied Linguistics research as frameworks for describing the various kinds of social relationships that language learners engage in, both inside and outside the classroom. The roles of individuality in applications of the idea of communities of practice in Applied Linguistics are examined in more detail by Lamb in Chapter 3, while Yashima discusses applications of the idea of imagined communities in Chapter 4.

Gee (2005: 215) is critical of the term 'community of practice', mainly because it appears to 'label a group of people', which creates problems of determining the boundaries of the 'community' in question and of deciding who is and who is not a 'member' of it. It is for this reason that Gee prefers the concept of 'affinity space', which 'focuses on the idea of a *space* in which people interact, rather than *membership* in a community' (p. 214). In the context of discussions of the nursing profession as a community of practice, Candlin and Candlin (2007) also find the idea of 'membership' problematic, because sites of engagement for the practice of nursing typically involve other specialists as well as patients and their significant others. In contrast to Gee's focus on 'space', they suggest a shift of focus towards the people who participate in communities of practice and the replacement of the idea of 'membership' with one of 'subscription', or 'a highly dynamic practice of subscribing to a range of communities, while retaining a personal centre – albeit one accommodating multiple and changing identities' (p. 264). This shift is also evident in Keating's (2005) work on Portuguese migrants in the United Kingdom, in which she proposes a distinction between *practice*, involving 'sedimented ways of doing, talking, reading, writing and being … sustaining and sustained by social organisations and structures', and *activity*, which 'brings in the person's engagement in a focussed and microscopic way, involving the person in the doing, her own history and her own processes of negotiating the aims, the tools and artefacts used in the doing' (p. 114). In this context, she suggests that the focus in research should shift from communities to 'individual's *activities* as they happen in *events*' and the exploration of 'participation in *practices* and the *communities* that these practices imply' (p. 112). Similar problems can be observed in research using the concept of 'imagined communities', in which the communities at issue are even more difficult to define, simply because they are 'imagined'. Again, research in this area tends to focus less on the 'imagined communities' themselves, which are often ill-defined, than it does on the individuals who participate (or fail to participate) in them through the medium of imagination.

What these comments illustrate is the tendency for Applied Linguistics work that draws on the ideas of Lave and Wenger to emphasize the idea of 'communities of practice' over that of 'situated learning'. It could be argued, however, that Lave and Wenger's (1991: 29) understanding of learning as 'the process of becoming a full participant in a sociocultural practice' has largely survived the critique of Communities of Practice theory, because it focuses on the participation of individuals in sociocultural practices, without necessarily specifying the nature of the social arrangements in which these practices occur. Although Gee, for example, finds the concept of community of practice inadequate to describe many contemporary patterns of social interaction, he remains a strong advocate of situated learning (Gee 2004). Like Vygotskyan theory, Situated Learning Theory is perhaps best understood as a theory of the ways in which individuals learn through social practice, which does not stand or fall on any particular conceptualization of the social organization of this practice. As Barton and Tusting (2005b: 3) put it, Situated Learning Theory represents 'a significant rethink of value to anyone wanting to take learning beyond the individual', which is 'attractive as a middle level theory between structure and agency'. The same might well be said of Vygotskyan and other socially oriented theories of learning. It is becoming increasingly apparent, however, that in order to move forward, such theories need 'to look more closely at the relation between learning individuals and their social embedding' (Evensen 2007: 334).

A third approach that is gaining ground in Applied Linguistics at the present time draws on a diffuse body of interconnected theories (including Chaos Theory, Dynamic Systems Theory and Social-Ecological Theory) that we place under the heading of Complexity Theory), which is discussed in more detail by Menezes in Chapter 5. In terms of the 'social turn', research that draws on this body of work perhaps represents a view that relationships between the social processes of language education and the social structures that condition them (if this is the right terminology) are far too complex to be accommodated within simple models of causality. There is, thus, both a critique of the search for causality that has characterized much SLA research and an acknowledgement that there is a good deal about language learning that we cannot know, given the current limitations of our ability to build predictive models of social behaviour (Larsen-Freeman and Cameron 2008a). At the same time, there is also a more 'open' view of socialization, in which learning is viewed as a process of interaction between the individual learner and affordances in the environment, and both the individual and the environment are subject to change (van Lier 2004). This point of view, which essentially rejects the idea of an *entirely* socialized individual, clearly allows more scope for individual agency and autonomy in models that view individuals as one of many agentive elements in complex and dynamic systems (see, for example, van Lier 2007).

As editors of this book, we began, therefore, from a sense that social approaches to Applied Linguistics research are beginning to move away from an unexamined rejection of 'individualism' to more nuanced views of the dialectic between the social and the individual. We also began from our particular interest in the idea of autonomy in language teaching and learning, which has often been an equally unexamined target of the charge of individualism, and a sense that a certain rapprochement was under way between these two ends of the social-individual continuum. Yet again there is a paradox in the view of autonomy that we often find in social approaches to language education, because autonomy was, in fact, one of the first areas of language education to take on Vygotskyan theory through the work of Little (1991) and Ushioda (1996). From this perspective Autonomy Theory, is itself thematized as a social approach within Applied Linguistics, which is discussed in terms of its concerns with the social and the individual by Benson in Chapter 6.

Structure of the book

The remainder of this volume is divided into two main sections. Chapters 2–6 are mainly theoretical and based on re-interpretations of previously published work in terms of its treatment of individuality in social context. As we have noted above, the approaches covered in these chapters are Sociocultural Theory (Lantolf, Chapter 2), Situated Learning Theory (Lamb, Chapter 3), Imagined Communities (Yashima, Chapter 4), Complexity Theory (Menezes, Chapter 5) and Autonomy Theory (Benson, Chapter 6). In planning the book, we were also keen to include chapters that show how socially oriented research frameworks are applied 'on the ground', as it were, by researchers engaged in empirical work. Chapters 7–12, therefore, have an empirical focus and report the authors' original research. At first, we thought that the approaches adopted in the second half of the book might neatly match those discussed in the first half, but this thought was soon revised for the very good reason that many Applied Linguistics researchers adopt an eclectic approach to the use of socially oriented frameworks for research. Although they may set out to conduct a study within a certain framework, they often end up by drawing on more than one established framework or by exploring new theoretical ground. In this book, Kehrwald (Chapter 7) draws on both Sociocultural Theory and Autonomy Theory, Pitkänen-Huhta and Nikula (Chapter 8) on Sociocultural Theory and Critical Discourse Theory (Blommaert 2005), Gu (Chapter 9) on Communities of Practice, Moore (Chapter 10) on Imagined Communities and Social Realism, Whiteside (Chapter 11) on Complexity Theory, and Clarke (Chapter 12) on Foucauldian ethics. The common factor in these chapters is their use of one or more socially oriented research frameworks to interpret data that primarily relates to individual language learners or teachers. In these chapters, the authors not only report their research, but also reflect on some of the tensions between the social and the individual levels in their work. Finally, in Chapter 13, we return as editors to the main themes of the book in the light of what we have learned from working with these authors on their contributions to the book.

2 Sociocultural Theory and the dialectics of L2 learner autonomy/agency

James P. Lantolf

Introduction

Although I have not assiduously followed developments in the area of learner autonomy from the time of Holec's (1981) introduction of the concept, I have noted with considerable interest that at least three autonomy researchers, Little (1994, 2007a, b), Oxford (2003) and Palfreyman (2003), have discussed the potential contribution of Sociocultural Theory (SCT, henceforth) to autonomous learner research (ALR, henceforth). This is a most welcome circumstance, particularly given the intense focus on schooling and its role in development that has formed a major component of SCT research. Having said this, I am a little concerned by some of the proposals and recommendations made in the name of SCT. My goal in the present chapter, therefore, is to address some of the concerns I have regarding these matters and to suggest some modifications based on a fuller understanding of Vygotskian theory.

To set the stage, I will first discuss the concept of agency as it has been interpreted within SCT. I will then consider those SCT concepts borrowed into ALR, which I believe appropriately reflect the theory. Next, I will discuss those concepts that in my view have been problematically integrated into ALR. Finally, I will discuss those SCT principles that I see as relevant to classroom instruction and learning that aims to develop the learners' agency. The discussion to follow is not intended to disparage the value of learner autonomy in school. It is rather intended as an attempt to reshape the claims made on the basis of SCT. There is no question that SCT supports learner autonomy but not precisely in the ways that it has been so far discussed in the ALR literature.

Autonomy/agency

With the exception of a recent, and controversial, discussion by Bakhurst (2007), the term 'autonomy' is not referenced in the SCT literature and it is certainly not a central concept of the theory. On the other hand, 'agency' is very much featured with regularity in the writings of SCT scholars (e.g. Wertsch *et al.* 1993; Stetsenko and Arievitch 2004). Although autonomy in the ALR literature is generally defined as incorporating aspects of agency, there are, as I hope will become clear, significant differences between how the two frameworks conceptualize agency. I am also quite sympathetic to Toohey's (2007) view that agency is a more liberating and flexible concept than autonomy.

The concept of agency in western social sciences is rooted in Locke's notion of the individual as a solipsistic and sovereign entity capable of acting 'without interference or subordination to outside authority' and who is 'developmentally prior to social life' (Wertsch *et al.* 1993: 338). The person for Locke is an autonomous being. The individual agent in SCT, on the other hand, is anything but the atomistic entity described by Locke. He or she is above all a social being whose very individuality rests on, and is derived from, social relationships, culturally organized activities, and use of artefacts (Vygotsky 1978). Leontiev (1978: 32) states that the social does not influence the individual, but is in fact the 'source' of the individual. According to Vygotsky (1987), although we are biological beings endowed with specific mental capacities (memory, attention, perception, reflexes) passed on through the genetic endowment inherited from our ancestors, we also inherit a cultural endowment from our ancestors passed on (i.e. internalized) through participation in social relationships and cultural activities (e.g. play, labour, family life, education, religious and political practices, etc.). Indeed, as Leontiev (1959/2004: 85) cogently states: 'In the course of history, humans, governed by social laws, have developed higher mental features. Thousands of years of social history have produced more, in this regard, than millions of years of biological evolution' (translated from Spanish by JPL). Our cultural inheritance endows us with the capacity to organize and control our biological inheritance (Yaroshevsky 1989: 230). On this view, mental and physical functioning are mediated, thus making us fundamentally sociocultural beings. This is so irrespective of whether we are alone or engaged in interaction with other human beings. Said in another way, just as our biological history remains with us at all times, so does our sociocultural history.

The two branches of our humanity – natural and cultural – do not operate independently of each other; rather they mingle and interpenetrate one another (Lee 1985). This happens largely through language, the 'means through which society converts the principles of cognitive development from biological to social dialectical' (Lee 1985: 86). The ability to create and use symbols, in particular linguistic symbols, enables humans to mentally plan their activity ideally and in advance of objectifying that activity in concrete action. Thus, semiotic mediation not only imbues humans with the means to control, organize and resignify their own behaviour (Holland and Lachicotte 2007: 109) but also to regulate and change the world and in so doing regulate and change themselves.

From the SCT perspective, agency, and by implication, autonomy, is most appropriately understood as 'the socioculturally mediated capacity to act' (Ahearn 2001: 112), or as Wertsch *et al.* (1993) argue, a human agent is an-individual-that-operates-with-mediational-means. Although this definition includes the term 'individual,' the authors' intent is not to imply that there can be individuals that operate without mediation. In the absence of mediation there would in fact be no human individuals, although there might be human organisms, as for instance occurs in cases of feral children. Thus, mediation is a necessary condition for human agentive individuals to develop. To this, Lantolf and Thorne (2006: 143) add that agency also 'entails the ability to assign relevance and significance to things and events', and as van Lier (2008: 172) further adds, it 'includes an awareness of the responsibility for one's own actions'. Hence, agency is understood as the human ability to act through mediation, with awareness of one's actions, and to understand their significance and relevance.

Van Lier (2008: 163) also suggests agency is not the same always and everywhere, but how it plays out is dependent on the circumstances of specific contexts. As an example, it is helpful to consider Vygotsky's writings on the method of 'double stimulation'. Consider the experiment carried out by Kurt Lewin as discussed in Vygotsky (1987: 356). A researcher invites a participant into a room ostensibly to conduct an experiment, whereupon the experimenter promptly exits without explaining the set-up for the experiment. After about ten minutes of solitude the participant invariably searches for some external point of support (e.g. looks at a clock on the wall and tells himself that when 2:30 strikes he will leave the room). According to Vygotsky, the participant created a new 'psychological field' by converting the clock from a situationally neutral object into one that was saturated with relevance (i.e. a second stimulus) for the given circumstance, which enabled him to deal with the uncertainty arising from the initial stimulus created by the experimenter's exit (Engeström 2007: 373). Through the second stimulus, the clock, the participant created his own agency. This then is what we mean by agents as human-entities-acting-with-mediational-means.

ALR and SCT: points of convergence

Zone of proximal development

The discussion to follow takes as its starting point Little's (1994: 431) definition of learner autonomy as 'accepting the responsibility for one's own learning' that entails 'taking some of the initiatives that shape the learning process, and developing a capacity to evaluate the extent and success of one's learning'. According to Little (2007a: 4), the definition reflects Holec's original motivation for bringing autonomy to the attention of researchers and educators: the need for education to promote the development of individuals with the capacity to behave responsibly and to contribute to the well-being of the communities in which they live. Little cautions, and rightly so, that autonomy does not mean that someone learns 'spontaneously' on the basis of factors situated within the individual; rather it is a process that 'develops out of the learner's dialogue with the world to which he or she belongs' (*ibid.*). He explains that autonomy results not from independent but from interdependent performance (Little 1994: 435). Here we note the first, and clearest point of contact with Vygotsky's theory and his concept of the 'Zone of Proximal Development' (ZPD) (see also Oxford 2003; Palfreyman 2003).

The ZPD, although often discussed in terms of a spatial metaphor, is in fact not a space at all, but the activity in which instruction leads development. In other words, what matters is the process through which individuals (e.g. teacher/students) negotiate mediation that gives rise to development. This means that education is not expected to wait until learners are developmentally ready to learn; rather, instruction itself, understood as a special kind of mediation that must be systematic and contingent (i.e. handing over responsibility for the activity to learners at the appropriate time) in order to create the conditions for development to occur. The crucial feature of mediation in the ZPD that promotes agency is its contingent quality. The mediator, usually, but not always, the teacher, must not only prepare the learners to take responsibility for their behaviour in particular activities, but must also encourage them to seek out new activities where their abilities can be brought to bear. Thus, I concur with ALR that the ZPD is one of the most important mechanisms through which autonomy, or agency, to use the preferred SCT term, can be promoted.

I want to make it clear that according to SCT, individuals become independent agents 'toward the very end of the formal learning experience' in opposition to the Piagetian perspective whereby individuals are presumed to be true agents from the outset of the educational process (Kozulin 1998: 3). It seems to me that there is something of a divide within the ALR literature on this matter, with some, such as Holec, supporting a fairly strong

Piagetian view, and others, such as Little. leaning more towards Vygotsky's way of seeing things.

Products to producers

Another area of convergence relates to Holec's (1981) argument that one of the goals of autonomous learning is to shift educational focus from learners as products of society to learners as producers of society. In Vygotsky's theory the two ways of conceptualizing individuals is seen not in terms of a shift from product to producer but in terms of a dialectic unity whereby individuals actively transform and create new environments through collaboration with others and with artefacts. Stetsenko and Arievitch (2004: 65) describe this important theoretical principle as follows:

> human activity – material, practical, and always, by necessity, social collaborative processes aimed at transforming the world and people themselves – is the basic form of human life that lies at the very foundation and is formative of everything that is human in humans, including knowledge produced by them.

This means that through their agency humans not only internalize features of the social world but at the same time they contribute to it (Stetsenko and Arievitch 2004: 68). The two processes are in fact different sides of the same developmental coin. The authors make the important point that even individuals who do not change the environment contribute to it by maintaining the status quo and thereby blocking change. Grabois (2008) carried out an extended study of university students of Spanish as a foreign language engaged in a service-learning programme. He shows how learners not only improved their language proficiency (i.e. internalized the affordances available in the Hispanic community in which they worked) but also developed a better understanding of the community culture and an awareness of their own agency to contribute to the community through the work they carried out.

Learner reflection

A third area where ALR and SCT mesh well is the importance assigned to learner reflection in the development of agency/autonomy. Borrowing from Bruner, Little (2007b: 20) sees 'reflective intervention' as a 'defining characteristic' of autonomous learners. This process is different from incidental reflection that normally occurs during 'planning, monitoring and evaluating learning'; it is instead 'detached reflection on the process and content of learning (Little 2007b: 24).

Piotr Gal'perin (see Haenen 1996; Stetsenko and Arievitch 2000), one of the most influential interpreters of Vygotsky's educational theory, argues that reflection plays a dual role in developmental education. It induces learners to fully understand a given scientific concept relevant to their learning and at the same time it contributes to the internalization of that knowledge. Gal'perin proposes that the optimal way of stimulating reflection is self-dialogue, or private speech. Through private speech learners verbalize to themselves their understanding of the object of study. According to Feigenbaum (2009: 105), 'verbalizing brings ideas into awareness by making them explicit'. In particular he suggests that private speech:

> creates the very special psycholinguistic conditions that enable her [the individual] to practice, explore, discover, and consciously comprehend the cognitive, pragmatic, and communicative skills that she has been developing implicitly since infancy. (p. 105)

Negueruela (2003) traces how, over time, verbalization as private speech leads to increasingly deeper understanding of linguistic concepts (e.g. temporal aspect and modality) and to learners' ability to use these concepts in their own performance. As learners gain greater control over knowledge and performance the private speech disappears, an indication that control has been internalized. Some SCT-L2 researchers such as Swain (2006) argue that internalization can take place through social dialogue between peers because, following Vygotsky, speech has a reflexive function in that it can be simultaneously directed outwardly towards others and inwardly towards the self. Yáñez-Prieto (2008) offered a third possibility whereby social dialogue is carried out between the instructor and individual learners. Little (1995: 178) argued that pedagogical dialogue between teachers and learners is perhaps the decisive means for convincing learners 'to accept responsibility for their learning.' In my view, although the necessary comparative research is still to be carried out, teacher-learner dialogue is preferable to peer mediation because it increases the chances of pushing learners to be as explicit as possible.

Knowledge

A fourth area of (partial) convergence has to do with the status of knowledge in the educational setting. ALR situates itself within the constructivist epistemology (see Little 2007b: 18), where truth, if it exists at all, is local rather than universal. While some have detected an affinity between Vygotsky and Dewey and therefore have situated SCT within the constructivist camp (see Lave and Wenger 1991; Rogoff 1995), this is a clearly mistaken reading of the theory. This is not the place to delve into this complex matter in great detail; nevertheless, it needs to be made clear that SCT is without question a realist theory (see Langford 2005). The fact that we are able to understand how the world is organized through 'scientific thinking, theory construction, procuring and analyzing evidence' and the fact that scientific knowledge is socially generated does not mean that the world, physical, social and psychological, is not real and that research does not result in objective truth (Ratner 2006: 229). We use our senses, aided by scientific instruments and procedures, to 'infer and deduce unobservable properties of reality' and we gradually compile the bits and pieces of information that we collect from different perspectives into the 'right way' of understanding that 'corresponds to the real features of the world, which have one definite nature' (Ratner 2006: 230).

According to Little (2007b: 18) constructivism in education 'casts doubt on the efficacy of transmission models of teaching and learning, preferring instead exploration and interpretation to recitation'. Even though transmission models have received a perhaps well-deserved rap, transmission is at the heart of cultural survival. As Bruner (1966: 101) states: 'culture ... is not discovered; it is passed on or forgotten' (cited in Karpov 2003: 75). Whether we like it or not, education, as with all cultural institutions, is a site for the transmission of knowledge. What matters, of course, is how transmission takes place. Clearly, 'effective learning is more than a matter of memorizing what one is told' (Little 2007b: 18). SCT proposes that scientific knowledge (i.e. knowledge in any discipline, including humanities, that emerges as a consequence of rigorous systematic research) must be the unit of instruction (Negueruela 2008). The goal of instruction, however, is not memorization but to make the knowledge functional. That is, what learners construct is ways of making the knowledge relevant to their evolving history as individuals. It is not likely that they are able to do this without guidance from someone else—the teacher. Given how agency is defined in SCT, school is where new and more powerful types of agency emerge as students internalize new forms of mediation (i.e. scientific knowledge) and extend these to contexts that matter to them, including other domains of schooling as well as the outside world. The argument then is that we can reject the transmission-passive reception model of knowledge without rejecting transmission altogether. In fact, SCT proposes what I have called, following Ausubel (1970), a transmission-active reception model of instruction (Lantolf 2011).

ALR and SCT: points of divergence

There are several points where. in my view, at least ALR has either misinterpreted SCT or has made some claims with regard to language learning that are not readily supported by existing SCT-L2 research. Since most of these claims have appeared in the writings of Little, I will rely on his work as the basis for the ensuing discussion. Again, I want to be clear that my discussion is not intended to subvert integration of SCT into ALR; rather it is to try to modulate what is integrated into it.

Inner speech

One of the sharpest distinctions between ALR and SCT is on the nature and role of inner speech in the process of developing learner autonomy. This is an exceptionally complex topic that I will not be able to discuss in the depth that it merits. Little (2007b: 24) notes that SLA research has not paid much attention to the 'dialectical unity of thinking and speech'. Although this is an accurate appraisal of mainstream SLA research, SCT-L2 research has made this topic one of the central concerns of its research agenda (see Lantolf and Thorne 2006). The disagreement, however, is not so much about whether research has been carried out on the connection between thinking and speaking in a second language but it has to do with the nature of the connection.

Reflecting Vygotsky's position, Little (2007b: 24) points out that thinking and speaking unite in inner speech, which is the basis for the formation of higher psychological functions, including voluntary memory and attention, logical thinking, concept formation, planning, monitoring and so on. He states that 'the capacity for inner speech must be an integral part of any worthwhile second or foreign language proficiency' as it supports all manner of L2 performance (p. 24). He then asks: 'how do we develop this capacity for inner speech in the language classroom?'; an interesting question! It is, however, his answer that is problematic from the SCT perspective. Little strongly intimates that by using the L2 for communicative activities and for reflective intervention, learners will develop inner speech in their new language. This in turn is 'the essential characteristic of *language* [italics in original] learner autonomy' (p. 24), as the language becomes 'part of the individual learner's internalized mental resources' (p. 25). Tomlinson (2000) argues for a similar course of development, although from a somewhat different theoretical perspective. In fact, Tomlinson proposes that teachers should externalize their thinking process in the L2 for learners to imitate in generating their own inner speech. It is important to make a distinction between inner and private speech. While inner and private speech have the same psychological function – to mediate thinking – they do not share the same formal properties. Private speech has real linguistic substance (i.e. it looks like communicative speech even though it is self- rather than other-directed). Inner speech has no linguistic substance and therefore ceases to be vocal, consisting instead of 'pure meaning' (Vygotsky 1987: 263). Thus, to model inner speech for learners, as Tomlinson suggests, is impossible. What can be modelled is private speech. However, the real problem is not about modelling private speech as linguistic substance; rather it is about internalizing L2 meanings that serve to mediate thinking.

As appealing as the idea of developing L2 inner speech may be, actually developing a second way of mediating one's mental activity is not so easily achieved. It must be kept in mind that inner speech is meaning and not structure based. That is, higher mental functions are mediated not by linguistic form, per se, but by the meanings carried by linguistic forms. As form dies away in the transition from social to inner speech, meaning remains; and it is this that we use to mediate thinking. Meaning for its part is not universal but is very much culturally and socially created. To develop inner speech in a second language therefore entails creating a new way of making and deploying meaning and this is not so easily accomplished. For one thing, the meanings laid down in our first language are deeply rooted in our histories as social and psychological beings. By the time we reach adulthood, we have spent hundreds of thousands of hours using these meanings to mediate our thinking. To expect someone to give up, or even modify, this entrenched system of mental life is asking a great deal. Indeed, the research evidence shows that it takes much more than using the language for communicative and reflective tasks in a classroom setting to produce a functional inner speech in a new language. A great deal of experimental research was conducted in the former Soviet Union on the question of whether or not adult L2 learners are able to develop inner speech in the new language. This work is reviewed by Ushakova (1994), who concludes that the L2 learning process 'consists of incorporating and plugging the newly established structures into the ones worked out earlier' for the first language (p. 155). More recent work by Centeno-Cortés and Jiménez-Jiménez (2004) corroborates Ushakova's conclusion. Their research shows that even very advanced speakers of L2 Spanish (i.e. students enrolled in a Spanish graduate programme and who had spent considerable time living and studying in Spanish-speaking countries) were unable to deploy private speech (the externalized manifestation of inner speech) to successfully mediate their own thinking during complex problem-solving tasks. Research informed by Slobin's (1996) thinking for speaking framework and McNeill's (2005) model of speech-gesture synchronization grounded in Vygotsky's notion of inner speech has uncovered very little evidence that L2 learners, even at advanced levels, are able to appropriate new meanings to mediate their thinking process.

To appreciate the kind of sea change involved in developing a functional inner speech in a new language, consider the case of Eva Hoffman (1989), who emigrated from Poland to Canada as a teenager and was confronted with the daunting task of constructing a new identity through a different semiotic system. Hoffman provides several penetrating insights that reveal the importance of inner speech in this process. She laments the loss of her 'inner language, which used to be my nighttime talk with myself' (p. 107). Polish meanings no longer relate to the experiences she encounters in her new cultural milieu, while at the same time, English has 'not penetrated to those layers of my psyche from which a private connection could proceed' (*ibid.*). Only after intensive immersion in US culture (she eventually moved to the US) does she even begin to develop a new inner speech as she matures into adulthood. She writes that she felt herself surrounded by different voices all tinged with different emotional overtones, 'modulation, intonation, rhythms' (p. 219), some of which were appealing and some of which were not. From these voices she rebuilds her own inner voice: 'But some of them satisfy a need; some of them stick to my ribs … Eventually, the voices enter me; by assuming them, I gradually make them mine' (p. 220).

Given the complexity and emotional intensity of Hoffman's experience one has to wonder what the chances are for promoting a reorganization of an individual's inner order through educational activity alone, or whether language education should even worry about this issue. Clearly, one can develop a wide array of communicative abilities in a new language without using the language as a tool for thinking. Nevertheless, it is an intriguing topic.

The acquisition process

Another area of divergence between ALR and SCT, not completely unrelated to the previous topic, has to do with the process through which first languages are acquired in the everyday world and how second languages are acquired in a classroom context. Little (2007b: 21) observes that children acquire their first language through interaction with their parents and siblings. He also points out that adults, in everyday settings, pick up the language by interacting with others in their social contexts. From this, Little infers that classrooms should be organized in ways that allow students to pick up the L2 by using it. On this view, given that first language acquisition is by and large an experientially based and unconscious process (see Paradis 2009), L2 acquisition at school should occur, to the extent possible, in the same way (Little 1994: 434). Little's position resonates with many mainstream SLA researchers who support the notion that the mental process of acquiring an L2 is the same no matter where it occurs (see Long 2007).

According to Little (1994) experiential learning is advantageous because it is efficient, durative and 'naturally autonomous' (p. 435). On his view, schooling does not easily lend itself to experiential learning and therefore it must be deliberately and carefully orchestrated to bring about such learning. Little fleshes out his proposal with recommendations from Tharp and Gallimore's (1988) often-cited work on instruction, which relies heavily on their reading of Vygotsky's theory. Clearly, there is much to recommend in Tharp and Gallimore's perspective, but it does not reflect the fundamental distinction that Vygotsky makes between everyday, spontaneous non-conscious development and educational, theoretically grounded, development (see Davydov 2004).

Education is one of the central components of the sociocultural world. It is not merely the site where we acquire knowledge. Vygotsky theorized education as a unique type of developmental activity, which contrasts sharply with everyday learning. Instead of inserting the everyday world into the educational setting, Vygotsky and neo-Vygotskian scholars (e.g. Kozulin 1998; Karpov 2005) inject educational activity into the everyday world. The aim is to develop a fully agentive being; one that is maximally able to not only adapt to the world but to change it through conscious intentional activity. Vygotsky's educational theory develops learner agency through carefully orchestrated activities that promote the internalization of highly systematic knowledge that is connected to life activity of the learners. In the next section I briefly sketch out what language instruction framed by SCT is like.

Education as artificial development

Given that Vygotsky grounded his psychological theory in Marx's philosophy, he insisted that the goal of scientific research is not to merely observe existing psychological processes but to promote the formation of individual agency and ultimately 'that set individuals free' (Stetsenko and Arievitch 2004: 77) and ultimately give rise to individual agency. Vygotsky proposed a praxis-based approach to research in which theory and practice form a dialectical unity. Stetsenko and Arievitch (2004: 78) capture Vygotsky's approach to theory and practice in the following comment: 'Kurt Lewin's famous expression that there is nothing more practical than a good theory could thus be expanded, in the spirit of Vygotskian approach, by the mirror expression – that there is nothing more theoretically rich than a good practice.'

To appreciate Vygotsky's approach to education, we need to understand the essential distinction he makes between everyday, empirically grounded development and educational, theoretically grounded, development (see Davydov 2004). The former, also called spontaneous development, is largely non-conscious and depends heavily on inductive inferencing based on empirical evidence of the object of attention. It is a slow trial-and-error process of pattern recognition, not unlike the models of language acquisition proposed by Tomasello (2003) or Nick Ellis (2007). Even in this case, however, mediation by representatives of the individual's sociocultural community plays a central role in the process (see Speidel and Nelson 1989; Tomasello 2003). Formal education, on the other hand, is a very special type of cultural activity understood as 'the artificial development' of the person, which if properly organized 'not only influences certain processes of development, but restructures all functions of behaviour in a most essential manner' (Vygotsky 1997: 88). Education is the intentional introduction of explicit knowledge as a mediational artefact into goal-directed activity (Wertsch 2007).

Although Vygotsky did not propose a fully fleshed-out approach to education, he did lay down its foundation. At its core is mediation through scientific concepts, which 'represent the generalizations of the experience of humankind that is fixed in science, understood in the broadest sense of the term to include both natural and social science as well as the humanities' (Karpov 2003: 66). These concepts are explicit, and therefore accessible to conscious inspection, domain specific, and 'aimed at selecting the *essential* [italics added] characteristics of objects or events of a certain class and presenting these characteristics in the form of symbolic and graphic models' (Karpov 2003: 71). They are generalizable across contexts and bring to light otherwise hidden properties of entities and events and require intentional, rigorous and systematic scientific investigation to uncover. They result in far more efficient development than leaving learners to figure out deep and hidden patterns of the object of study even if assisted by their teacher as is supposed to occur in discovery learning (Karpov 2003: 75). Equally important for Karpov is that in discovery learning the '"relaxed" attitude toward scientific knowledge' (p. 75) teachers are encouraged to promote in their students undermines the value of such knowledge for development. Kirschner *et al.* (2006) raise significant doubts about the effectiveness of discover-based education, even if it is accompanied by a modicum of teacher guidance. They contend that the evidence supports 'strong instructional guidance' over 'constructivist-based minimal guidance' programmes (p. 83), especially at novice and intermediate levels of education.

To illustrate the difference between everyday and scientific knowledge consider the everyday concept of 'circle', understood as 'things that are round' as derived from our experience with objects such as coins, cakes, wheels and so on. The scientific concept of a circle, on the other hand, is the figure that emerges as the result of a line with one fixed and one moving end (Kozulin 2003). Scientific knowledge, as in the case of circle, Kozulin (1998: 55) points out 'is generative because it provides a procedure for the generation of circles, it is universal because all possible circles can be generated in such a way, and it is theoretical because it requires no previous knowledge of round objects' (Kozulin 1998: 55).

This distinction is also relevant to language. The grammatical rules of thumb included in a wide variety of language instructional programmes are similar to everyday concepts in that they are empirically based descriptions of features of the target language. Hammerly (1982: 421) characterizes these as '*simple, nontechnical, close to popular/traditional notions* [italics in original] of grammar'. He sees value in such explanations because they are 'short and to the point' and are therefore not too complex 'for the students to absorb' (p. 421). The problem is that rules of thumb are not always complete, coherent or accurate. They generally describe what is typical in a specific context rather than an abstract principle that promotes a deep understanding of the concept that allows learners to use the language in a flexible way across an array of contexts. That is, they lack the generativity of scientific concepts.

Spanish language textbooks often describe the use of past tense, which entails an overtly marked distinction between perfective and imperfective aspect, as follows: preterit 'reports, records, narrates' and imperfect 'tells what was happening, recalls what used to happen, describes a physical or mental emotion, tells time in the past, describes the background and sets the stage upon which another action occurred' (Whitley 1986: 108). As with most empirically based rules, it is not fully accurate, because while one encounters instances where use of verbal aspect accords with the rule, one also easily finds exceptions, as for instance where preterit is used to describe emotions. Moreover, rules of thumb give the impression that language study is about learning to produce correct while avoiding incorrect forms, rather than understanding language as a cultural artefact for creating meanings that reflect the user's communicative intentions. As a result the real object of study 'remains outside the classroom door, beyond the boundaries of the academic subject' (Ilyenkov 1974).

Space does not permit a full exegesis of the scientific concept of verbal aspect. Instead, I will briefly summarize the three-phase procedure that has been followed in previous pedagogical projects. First the concept of temporal aspect is related to spatial perspective. Talking about events or states can be accomplished from different perspectives just as physical objects can be looked from different visual perspectives (e.g. from the top, the bottom, the side, near, far, etc.). The observer or the speaker has the option of profiling the object or the event as he or she wishes. Aspect serves the profiling function with regard to the time dimension. The next phase is to explain lexical aspect whereby events and states have inherent temporal qualities that are encoded in the lexicon of a language. For example, an action such as jump is inherently punctual, in that has a natural beginning and end point. This is implicitly reflected in the English verb 'jump' and the Spanish verb *saltar*. An activity such as talk, on the other hand, is inherently continuous in that once begun it could in theory continue for an indefinite time span. This information is implicitly reflected in the English verb 'talk' and the Spanish verb *hablar*. Grammatical tense allows a speaker to profile an activity such as talk not as continuous but with an end point. English and Spanish can mark the profile shift through verb endings (i.e. 'he talked' and *habló*). The third phase visually models the concept as a SCOBA (i.e. SChema for the Orientating Basis of Action). Such models have the advantage of representing a concept holistically, which avoids the tendency for learners to rotely memorize verbal explanations without genuine understanding. The SCOBA is then used to guide learners as they connect the concept to concrete communicative (oral and written) activities designed to provide them with the experience of expressing their own meanings through the L2. For two extensive studies where a concept-based approach was implemented in regular L2 courses see Negueruela (2003); Yáñez-Prieto (2008). Additional studies, including those with focus on writing and pragmatics, can be found in Lantolf and Poehner (2008). The goal of the concept-based approach to instruction is not merely to teach grammar more effectively but to do so in a way that allows learners to make the grammar work for them and in so doing enhance the manifestation of their agency through the new language.

Conclusion

In this chapter I have discussed learner autonomy/agency from the perspective of Sociocultural Theory and have considered those areas where I believe the theory has been appropriately and less appropriately brought into contact with ALR. There is certainly much more that can be said about both projects as they relate to language education than I have been able to say in this chapter. SCT and ALR clearly share the common goal of educating students to become independent and agentive individuals. They differ on the specifics of how to attain the goal. SCT because of its commitment to praxis argues that individuals are created and emerge from socialization processes mediated by cultural artefacts and social relationships. It further argues that everyday development, due to its largely spontaneous and unconscious nature, is likely to constrain the freedom individuals have to fully regulate their mental and physical activity. According to Vygotsky (1987), it is difficult for people to regulate their behaviour when it is outside of their awareness; consequently, their knowledge of the world that guides their activity in it is derived by and large from empirical observations. Educational activity, as a special type of cultural development, is expected to bring students into direct contact with rigorous scientific knowledge – knowledge which, unlike everyday knowledge, is explicit and generative and therefore not linked to specific contextual constraints. For this reason education develops a different kind of agency than arises in everyday life. It instils greater freedom and flexibility precisely because it allows individuals enhanced options for dealing with circumstances that they confront throughout their lives.

3 The struggle to belong: individual language learners in Situated Learning Theory

Martin Lamb

Introduction

It has been said that the paradox of research into individual differences in second language acquisition (SLA) is that it often loses sight of the individual language learner (Ushioda 2009; Benson and Cooker, Chapter 1, this volume). Paradoxical but perhaps not surprising, since Individual Differences research has usually been conducted in parallel with the dominant 'cognitive science' view of SLA, which seeks to identify universal processes within the human mind that can account for language acquisition and, as Gregg (2006) explains in his vigorous defence of the approach, 'tries to set aside individual differences that might accidentally differentiate members of the same category [i.e. human beings]' (p. 431). The only individual differences of interest, in this view, are those that systematically identify particular categories of learners and can be hypothesized to have specific effects on the learning process and outcome, such as age, language aptitude or type of motivation (e.g. Larsen-Freeman 2001; Ellis 2004).

A wave of theoretical developments over the past decade, however, collectively known as the 'social turn' in SLA (Block 2003), have encouraged many researchers to attend to individual learners in all their daunting complexity. Where language is viewed as a form of social practice, rather than an abstract code, study of its acquisition by individuals cannot so easily be confined to language modules in the brain but implicates their social behaviour, motives and relations. Where learning is conceived as identity development – as becoming a different kind of person, whose enhanced knowledge and skills gradually transform their relations with other people and their position in the community – it demands attention to individual growth, implicating the person's unique history and future aspirations. And where the context is viewed not as a 'container' for the acquisition process but as a complex eco-system in which human beings are agents in constant dynamic interplay with each other, it is no longer easy to treat the individual learner as a theoretical abstraction to which acquisition 'happens'.

Incorporating to some degree each of these perspectives on language, learning and context, Situated Learning Theory (SLT) (Lave and Wenger 1991; Wenger 1998) has become a popular lens through which to view the endeavours of language learners and teachers. In this chapter I will first describe the theory, demonstrating in the process how SLT accounts for the relationship between individuals and the communities in which they learn. I will do this with particular reference to two recent research studies that have utilized the theory in Applied Linguistics research. John Hellerman (2008) used state-of-the-art audio-visual recording devices to track the learning of adult immigrants engaged in paired speaking tasks as part of a long-term American English as a Second Language (ESL) course; his focus is not on their individual acquisition of language structures or lexis but rather on changes in the *way* they do the tasks, how they begin them, how they tell incidental stories within them, and how they end them. In other words, his interest is in the students' changing participation in the practices of their particular community (the ESL classroom). Matthew Clarke (2008) researched the development of EFL student teachers during two years of a new B.Ed (Teaching English to Young Learners) degree offered by the Higher Colleges of Technology (HCT) in the United Arab Emirates (UAE); informed by SLT and discourse theory, his study conceptualizes their learning in terms of developing a teaching identity, as evidenced in their changing participation in the discourse practices of their community (the teacher training institution). Both researchers use SLT in combination with tools of linguistic analysis (Conversation Analysis and Discourse Analysis respectively) as a heuristic to help explain aspects of the learning process.

The second part of the chapter will draw more widely on studies of situated learning to reflect on what the theory tells us about the sub-themes of this book: identity, agency and autonomy in language learning. I will conclude by assessing some of the strengths and weaknesses of the theory for understanding the Applied Linguistic individual.

The theory

Situated learning

In common with other social approaches (e.g. Rogoff 1998; Atkinson 2002; Lantolf, Chapter 2, this volume), SLT views learning as an integral part of living and as intrinsically social in nature. What makes SLT distinctive, perhaps, is its emphasis on the ways in which individual learning occurs through participation in communities. Informed by their anthropological studies of various kinds of apprenticeship, Lave and Wenger (1991) proposed that learning be viewed as gradual change in a person's way of participating in a particular community, and accordingly in their social relations with other members of it. Change occurs as the newcomer to a community observes and interacts with more experienced 'old timers', 'gradually becoming able to be involved in new activities, to perform new task and functions, to master new understandings' (Lave and Wenger 1991: 53), and thus being enabled to move, on an 'inbound trajectory', from 'peripheral' to core participation in the community. Their preferred term for learning, therefore, is 'legitimate peripheral participation' (LPP), acknowledging that newcomers have to be allowed access ('legitimated') by old timers and that in many communities there are people whose participation is marginal because they are denied such opportunities. Conversely, we may *prefer* to remain on the periphery of some communities, while struggling to belong to others. As Boylan (2010) points out, an immediate problem with this conceptualization of learning is that it apparently fails to account for the continued learning of 'core' members – '[f]ull participation would appear to lead to completion of learning' (p. 63). However, no community is static; meanings and practices are constantly renegotiated with each 'generation' of newcomer, and old timers themselves are often on trajectories of learning in relation to other communities.

All learning is situated in a very broad sense, that is, it happens in a context: an institution, a neighbourhood, a country. In the terms of SLT, however, situated learning happens in a particular type of community, what Lave and Wenger call a 'community of practice' (CoP) (Wenger 1998). CoPs have three essential features. Firstly, members have regular *mutual engagement* – they interact, negotiate meanings and engage in practices together. Second, though their practices may differ, and conflict may characterize some of their interactions, members of a CoP have a *joint enterprise*, a shared sense of direction for their mutual engagement. Finally, as a result of persistent engagement in their joint enterprise, members of a CoP build up a *shared repertoire* of resources for negotiating meaning. Such resources include patterns of participation like routine meetings and ritual acts; and reifications like key documents, qualifications and motifs. Crucially, a shared repertoire may also be linguistic – the jargon of a profession, the pragmatic rules of a social club, the regular jokes that characterize happy families.

CoPs cited in the Applied Linguistics literature have varied widely in scale and nature, from small groups within language classes (Leki 2001) to 'imagined' global communities of English language users, as discussed in more detail by Yashima (Chapter 4, this volume). Critics have argued that researchers' very broad interpretations of the concept of CoPs have weakened its value (Gee 2005; Haneda 2006; Candlin and Candlin 2007; Boylan 2010), although this criticism does not necessarily undermine the broader concept of situated learning (Benson and Cooker, Chapter 1, this volume). Even if the communities described do not meet all the criteria by which Wenger defines a CoP, the concept appears to answer some need among contemporary Applied Linguists to link the personal and the social and to find ways of explaining individual language learning behaviour with reference both to a person's own preferences and concerns and their social contexts of learning.

Ways of belonging to communities

Individuals belong to CoPs in various ways. The research of Hellerman (2008) and Clarke (2008) catalogues extensively these modes of belonging, the way they change as their subjects learn, and the way this process of change itself shapes the evolution of the CoP. The first way that people belong to CoPs is through their *engagement* in the practices of the community. Hellerman (2008), for example, describes how adult ESL learners engage in paired teacher-assigned tasks in their classroom, and focuses on the 'practices that learners use for opening interactions, engaging in extended [story]telling, and doing disengagements from interactions' (p. 19). In other words, his interest is not in the overt language teaching/learning process but in the way learners negotiate their participation in classroom events, making use of the linguistic affordances of the classroom such as teacher language, peer models and texts. While each individual's engagement varies, the long-term effect of multiple simultaneous pairwork activities is to establish the shared repertoire of talk and action for the whole classroom CoP. Meanwhile the UAE student teachers also had a range of common experiences on their B.Ed course – attending the same lectures, encountering the same educational discourses, doing similar assignments – which builds a shared history that is constitutive of their social relationships, and contributes to the 'cumulative development of issues and questions between community members' (p. 87) apparent in the focus group and online discussions that Clarke (2008) monitors. These discussions contribute in turn to the development of common understandings of their joint enterprise, and a shared repertoire of meanings and routines within the CoP. So rather like openings and closings of classroom tasks in Hellerman's study, the informal interactions of students in Clarke's study are not the formal substance of the educational provision, but they are where much of the learning happens.

Another mode of belonging to CoPs is through the *imagination* – the 'process of expanding our self by transcending our time and space and creating new images of the world and ourselves' (Wenger 1998: 176). Perhaps because of his focus on linguistic interaction in the classroom, this mode of belonging is not salient in Hellerman's (2008) study. But in teacher training, Clarke (2008) points out, the now well-established practice of professional reflection 'can be seen as another form of imagination in the sense of stepping back, even if briefly, from immediate concerns and realities' (p. 100). He provides evidence of the UAE student teachers regularly doing this in their discussions, and sometimes explicitly imagining alternative educational scenarios.

The final way in which members belong to a CoP is through *alignment*, or 'coordinating our energy and activities in order to fit within broader structures and contribute to broader enterprises' (Wenger 1998: 174). The purchase of a brown corduroy jacket by a young man may be an act of alignment with an academic CoP; the regular wearing of a tie by a senior academic may signal alignment with a different business-oriented CoP (though we would need evidence of engagement and imagination to be sure that these did represent aspirational acts of belonging – the three modes do not necessarily entail each other). The adoption of discourses is a prototypical form of alignment (*ibid.*), and so it is not surprising that this aspect of the theory has been readily transferred to the field of language learning and in particular investigations of the microgenesis of interactional competence (e.g. Mondada and Pekarek Doehler 2004; Atkinson *et al.* 2007; Cekaite 2007). Hellerman's (2008) study is an example of (indeed, an alignment with) this emerging line of research. He shows how individual learners move from peripheral to fuller participation in the classroom CoP through appropriating the language of their interactants – teachers, peers and classroom texts – while engaged in teacher-assigned communication tasks. Using Conversation Analysis, he demonstrates for example how novices in beginners' classes tended initially to launch their tasks only through physical orientation (e.g. turning towards each other); after a while they adopted teacher-provided language for assigning roles (e.g. 'you teacher I student'); still later, even when there was no explicit modelling of a task, the students were able to use this language autonomously together to start their interactions.

In language teacher education, Clarke (2008) shows how the students' alignment is both with peers and also with practices and discourses beyond their own CoP. For example, they appropriate materials from the wider ELT community and negotiate lesson plans with their college teacher supervisors and actual lessons with their school mentors. Clarke argues that 'much of their learning to teach will be achieved in this arena of boundary-crossing practices through participation in the college and the school communities' where they do their practicum, though it is 'clearly the community of college teachers that the students value most highly and who play the most significant role in shaping their practices' (p. 94); in fact, Clarke musters considerable evidence to demonstrate how the student CoP defined itself *in opposition to* the existing professional teacher CoP, establishing discourses and common practices that consciously countered those of more 'traditional' teachers (e.g. favouring learner-centred education over teacher-centred, equality over hierarchy, active learning over passive learning). For individual students this 'boundary-crossing' could be stressful – working in schools demanded alignment to certain established practices (e.g. arriving on time, attending assembly) but other practices like lesson planning offered scope for negotiating meanings, and enacting their emerging identities as 'new generation' teachers.

It is precisely these kinds of individual tensions, sometimes energizing and sometimes frustrating learning, which an SLT perspective can bring to light in specific contexts of language learning and use. As it does so, it implicates the constructs of identity, agency and autonomy which contemporary researchers have found useful in understanding and explaining individual language learning. In the remainder of this chapter I will discuss what SLT has to say about these three constructs, with reference to a wider selection of literature.

Identity

Identity has a central place in SLT – learning is ultimately about becoming somebody new, with new patterns of participation in a CoP and new social relations with other members. Identity is both how we view ourselves and how others view us; but also, significantly, something that we live day-to-day. As Solsken (1993, cited in Toohey *et al.* 2007: 626) writes in relation to literacy learning, 'each and every literacy transaction is a moment of self-definition in which people take action within and upon their relations with other people' (p. 8). Identity, therefore, is something 'performed' in our practices. Intentional change in our patterns of participation – as when we decide to learn something – entails 'identity work' on our part. Further, because we belong to multiple CoPs, we have multiple identities; because these overlapping CoPs pull us in various ways, our identities may be contradictory and are never entirely stable; because our position in CoPs is partly determined by the configuration of power relations within them, our identities are also sites of struggle, and we may be denied the identities we most value and have unwanted identities thrust upon us.

This conception of identity is closely aligned with that in most post-structuralist accounts of language learning, and not surprisingly SLT has been drawn upon in many contemporary studies of language learner identity (Norton 2001; Block 2007a). It is also proving useful in theorizing L2 learner motivation (e.g. Dörnyei 2005: Lamb 2009). Block (2007a) has argued that second language identity construction is much more likely to happen in migrant or study abroad contexts of learning, rather than the EFL classroom, because they are more likely to provide those 'critical experiences' which challenge the individual's sense of self, whereas classrooms position learners mainly as 'pupils' with narrower academic concerns. It is nevertheless true that for the majority of foreign language learners, the classroom is the primary site for learning and it is the affordances and constraints of this CoP for individual learners which I will discuss next.

Identities of participation in the L2 classroom

Studies of younger language learners in the classroom have tended to focus on their struggle to adopt desirable academic identities. In a pioneering work Toohey (2000) followed six young ESL learners over three years in a Canadian elementary school, and showed how their identities were 'produced' by their participation in classroom events. Some, by virtue of being able to demonstrate competencies in assessments or in informal social activities, were able to appropriate identities of full participation in the class while others became hamstrung by having the label 'ESL learner' attached to them, which ironically restricted their access to useful interaction practices with local children. Similarly Hawkins' (2005) year-long ethnographic study of a kindergarten classroom showed how its relational dynamics contributed over time to the construction of pupils' identities; some became 'school-affiliated' – seeing themselves and being recognized by others as 'a person who belongs in, and can be successful in, this sort of community' (p. 67) – while others were 'non-school affiliated', in other words not feeling a sense of belonging. Both these studies emphasize how the child needs to recognize and develop an identity of competence in new forms of practice, for the classroom CoP has norms and values distinct from those of the family CoP; by the same token, each child's response to the classroom CoP is shaped by expectations and preferences developed during participation in activities at home. Even at the very earliest stage, then, a child's orientation to learning will be both deeply social and uniquely individual.

SLT has also been used to illuminate the development of academic literacy at higher levels of the education system. The struggles of L1 students to align their study practices with the expectations of academic communities have been explored in some depth (e.g. Ivanic 1998; Lea 2005). The particular difficulties of L2 speakers are exemplified in Morita (2004), who studied the experiences of six Japanese female students over the first year of their Master's degree course at a Canadian university. Just as for the primary school children discussed above, the challenge for the students is to negotiate the discourses, competencies and power relations of their specific classroom CoP; and the challenge is always unique as each individual brings their own personal history, values and aspirations to the situation. Morita points out, for example, how the participation of several students was characterized by 'silence'. From a traditional cognitive science perspective this might be interpreted as a product of anxiety, and attributed to personality or a cultural tendency, but from a CoP perspective it was seen to be a response to a variety of novel practices. In fact 'the students were actively negotiating their multiple roles and identities in the classroom even when they appeared passive or withdrawn' (p. 587). Like the primary school pupils, however, the students' changing identity positions were co-constructed, produced *through* their classroom participation and not only through their own volition. While one learner was able to employ a variety of strategies (e.g. eliciting help from peers) to overcome an identity as a less competent participant, another, with a less open-minded instructor and more judgemental peers, struggled to escape this identity, in turn further inhibiting her participation and reinforcing the unwanted identity.

Identities of non-participation and marginality

Norton (2001) has argued that one of the most valuable aspects of SLT is the way it can illuminate *failure* to learn, which is after all the experience of many second language learners. Wenger (1998) reminds us that '[w]e not only produce our identities through the practices we engage in, but we also define ourselves through the practices we do not engage in' (p. 164). As we have already seen, 'non-participation' in our CoPs *may* be a form of legitimate peripheral participation, for example when we decide strategically to direct our energies to certain practices rather than others (like when Morita's students decided to remain silent during some class activities) but this is viewed both by ourselves and others in the community as only a temporary phase in the 'inbound' trajectory towards full participation. At other times non-participation may be part of an 'outbound' trajectory, in other words

LPP is being either denied (by others) or resisted (by ourselves), leading eventually to a position of marginality.

In Norton's (2001) study of adult immigrants to Canada, some learners eventually rejected an ESL course because they felt that the classroom CoP, and in particular the teacher/'master practitioner', did not validate their emerging identities; both resisted the ascribed classroom identity of 'immigrant' because it clashed with their aspirations to belong to other communities, for one a profession similar to the one she had left behind in her country of origin, for another the wealthy expatriate community that was quite distinct from the poor immigrant community which the class ostensibly served. In my own study of an EFL school context in Indonesia (Lamb 2009), one school pupil who by conventional measures would be regarded as highly motivated was a reluctant participant in her school English classes, and highly critical of her teacher; by contrast she was an enthusiastic interactant with myself, attended a local private language school in her spare time and read English language magazines aimed at young teens. Following Norton (2001), I interpret her apparently contradictory behaviour in terms of conflict between the classroom CoP – and its dry teacher-led language practices – and the largely imagined (though made momentarily real by my presence) CoP of global English users. In the same school context there were also many cases of marginalization on display – those who, for lack of resources, felt marginalized from any 'live' community of English users, and others who were being marginalized within the classroom because they failed to exhibit the required competency in the restricted range of practices of that community.

From the perspective of SLT, schools will always be problematic sites of learning, not least because attendance in class is involuntary and thus not a 'joint enterprise' (this issue is discussed more fully below). Like all of us, teenagers are also aspiring to membership of multiple CoPs. As Stroud and Wee (2007) exemplify in their study of multilingual practices in Singapore school classrooms, allegiance to one's peer group may inhibit full participation in classroom practices and lead to avoidance, in this context, of the legitimate language of the classroom (English). Likewise in my Indonesian study, learners reported that the use of English outside of class – on the one hand signalling membership of their imagined CoP of global English users, on the other hand signalling distance from local CoPs – could provoke admiration or derision depending on the particular context (Lamb 2007). And as in most schools, there were pupils who identified more strongly with practices in alternative youth CoPs and were happy to be on an outbound trajectory; ironically, the headmaster's nephew was one of them.

Agency

A particular strength of SLT, it has been argued, is that it can help to uncover the extent to which individuals are shaping their own futures (Swain and Deters 2007). All CoPs are ultimately made up of individuals with their own unique pasts and present agendas. The different experiences that individuals bring to a CoP (from their other CoPs) are in fact essential to the continued dynamism of the community (Wenger 1998). But their coming together inevitably impacts on the individuals too. Classroom or other relevant CoPs have the potential to empower language learner agency by reinforcing pupil identities as current or future L2 speakers. As Murphey and Carpenter (2008) argue, a teacher who works to engage all learners in class activities, establishes a sense of joint enterprise and encourages positive attributions for their successes and failures is likely to heighten their individual and collective sense of agency, in turn reinforcing their emerging identities. Involvement in more ephemeral CoPs may also serve to strengthen agency, as when an Indonesian school pupil (in my own data) gets involved in an 'English Speech Contest' and finds that the excitement of the rehearsals, and the event itself, reignite her desire to learn English.

Other studies have focused on the way CoPs can suppress learner agency, by challenging existing or hoped-for identities. As we have already seen from the discussion of learner identity above, questions of 'access' and 'legitimacy' are central to the theory, and learning trajectories are as much subject to the constraints of the environment and the intentions of others as any literal journey. An individual may exercise agency to become a peripheral participant in a community, like when Morita's (2004) Japanese students chose to take a Master's course in Canada. But when access becomes problematic, as when a student felt she was being positioned as linguistically deficient in the class, she could exercise agency only through non-participation in oral class activities, a strategic response to her relative lack of power within the class CoP. While this was probably a temporary setback to the student's long-term learning project, DePalma (2008) uses SLT to explain a more critical case of academic failure, where a nine-year-old Mexican girl, whose working-class family had recently moved to the USA, unwittingly complies with her own marginalization. As a well-motivated immigrant child keen to participate in her public school environment and to please the teachers, she developed competencies in several key school practices, such as completing worksheets quietly and neatly, but then reproduced these behaviours in inappropriate settings – she did not realize, for instance, that in the ESL class silence and diligence were not valued practices and instead she needed to be talkative and active; as a result the teacher underestimated her language abilities, and interpreted the long time that the girl spent reading English books as evidence of difficulty and passivity. The intertwining of learner and teacher agency led eventually to a designation of failure. DePalma argues that this kind of close situated analysis, revealing the 'collective and socially mediated nature of agency' (p. 158), demonstrates the danger of blaming individuals (whether learner or teacher) and instead directs attention to features of the CoP, in this case the need to provide for more explicit negotiation of learning practices between members (staff, pupils and parents).

Micro-analyses of interactions within CoPs have been criticized for lacking attention to 'more remote, less visible forms of power and control, located in wider social relations' (Trent 2006: 432), which also constrain individual agency. As Varghese *et al.* (2005) remark, 'issues of access, participation, and social engagement are always reflections of larger institutional, national and global ideologies, which are not the focus of exploration in situated learning and CoPs' (p. 31). In the context described by Morita, for example, we might ask what institutional policies are influencing the practices of instructors in their dealings with international students. In DePalma's study we might consider what the broader economic or political imperatives were which were shaping the assessment system that categorized nine-year-old immigrant girls as failed language learners. However, Trent (2006) acknowledges that 'it is not possible … for all empirical work to devote equal attention to all aspects of social life' (p. 434). As Layder (1993) has argued, social science research projects will always need to focus on one or possibly two levels of social life, from the self through situated activity, organizational setting and broader social context, but these levels are experientially linked and thus all are always part of the explanation for social behaviour (for a discussion of Layder's Social Realist approach, see Moore, Chapter 10, this volume).

Autonomy

In their original formulation of SLT, Lave and Wenger (1991) deliberately avoided a direct focus on schools, because 'learning through legitimate peripheral participation takes place no matter which educational form provides the context for learning, or whether there is any intentional educational form at all' (p. 40). Schools unquestionably play a large role in the learning of young people, but what is learned there *is* questionable. If learning is conceived as LPP, school itself is comprised of many CoPs, from different subject classrooms to the playground and sports field, each with their own particular forms of engagement, joint enterprise and shared repertoire of activity and discourse. School pupils need to negotiate their way along 'inbound' trajectories in each of these CoPs, yet as Wenger (1998) points out, we need to remember that education as a whole is about placing students on 'an outbound trajectory toward a broad field of possible identities' (p. 263). Then there is the question of educational content. The transmission of decontextualized subject knowledge is, Lave and Wenger (1991) argue, 'a circumscribed form of participation, preempting participation in ongoing practice as the legitimate source of learning opportunities' (p. 97). Thus, students in a physics class are not actually learning to become physicists but to become members of the 'community of schooled adults', with some awareness of the reified knowledge of the community of physicists but probably little awareness of their practices (Lave and Wenger 1991). Learning, in short, bears little direct relation to teaching, which is but one of its 'structuring resources' (Wenger 1998: 267).

While there is still debate about how far the tenets of SLT can or should be applied to formal learning contexts (see Boylan 2010, for a recent discussion), language educators in many contexts have already gone some way towards addressing Lave and Wenger's concerns about educational institutions by redesigning traditional classroom settings and practices. Communicative and task-based learning offer promising approaches to making the language classroom a reproduction of a 'community of English-users', with the teacher as an authentic master practitioner, to which pupils can belong through acts of engagement, imagination and alignment. But as Hellerman's (2008) study shows, the language learning that occurs will not only be what is intended by the teacher, but also what emerges through learner participation in classroom activities, for example ways of beginning and ending tasks and telling diverting stories within them. More important, if pupils are truly to develop identities as L2 users, the classroom has to be seen by all concerned as only one of several possible 'situated opportunities … for the improvisational development of new practices' (Lave and Wenger 1991: 97).

Such a view of learning has clear relevance to the concept of learner autonomy. First, the autonomous learner could be said to be the one who is travelling along the trajectories that (s)he wants to (see Little's comment that '[r]elative to schooling in general, the autonomous learner is one whose learning gradually enlarges his or her sense of identity' (1996: 210)). Schools potentially circumscribe learner autonomy by making the learning of specific subjects the primary object of their existence, substituting institutional goals for personal goals. This resonates with Holliday's

(2005) notion of 'social autonomy', 'which students bring with them from their own worlds outside the classroom, but which ESOL educators often fail to see because of their preoccupation with their own professionalism' (p. 85). As Holliday discusses, and as we saw in our discussion of learner agency, because teachers have their own agendas, learners may express their autonomy through resistance, such as silence or actually disruptive behaviour, and this may occur even when the teacher is explicitly trying to enhance learner autonomy through forms of 'learner training'. This view, therefore, supports what Smith (2003) calls 'strong pedagogies' for autonomy, which focus on 'co-creating with students optimal conditions for the exercise of their own autonomy' (p. 131), and implies honest engagement with learners about the nature of their 'joint enterprise' and acceptance of learners' other trajectories, in other communities of practice. The contemporary teacher of English as a foreign language is fortunate that there are often youth-oriented communities of practice, in which their pupils may peripherally participate, whose discoursal repertoire includes some use of English (e.g. pop music fan clubs, online social networks, computer gaming).

From a research point of view, SLT argues for the need to seek evidence for autonomous learning in all areas of an individual's life, and to recognize the limited role that formal institutions can have in its development. In light of this discussion it is ironic that, as Benson (2008) has written, 'the bulk of the literature on autonomy in language learning is concerned with institutional settings and pays very little attention to non-institutional learning' (p. 15). In my own research with Indonesian teenage learners of English, I found I could only gain an understanding of learners' behaviour *in class* by trying to view the experience from their perspective, as one site for learning the language with its own distinct set of practices (Lamb 2004). Likewise, researchers need to look beyond the teacher as the main social influence on the learner's autonomy. As Atkinson *et al.* (2007) remark, 'teachers have decidedly important roles to play … [but] the world is full of teachers – family members, friends, peers, colleagues, lovers, and so on – basically anyone a person can align with in meaningful interaction' (p. 184). Learner autonomy, like learning itself, emerges from the individual's participation in social practices distributed across numerous overlapping communities; evidence for it will similarly be found in changes in their patterns of participation. For example, evidence for language learner autonomy might be sought in changes in the people they use the target language with, the purposes they use it for, and the tools and materials they use to access it. There seems to be no alternative to studying individuals, in context, over time.

Conclusion

SLT has been subject to several criticisms, some of which have already been alluded to. The definition of a CoP is problematic; Edwards (2005) points out that a group of drivers regularly stuck in a traffic jam on their commute home would seem to satisfy the joint criteria of mutual engagement, joint enterprise and shared repertoire, but do not evidently constitute a community of learners. It has been suggested that Lave and Wenger provide little guidance on how language is used in the formation and maintenance of CoPs (Barton and Tusting 2005a), though this is now being addressed by studies such as Hellerman's (2008) and Clarke's (2008) that use the tools of Conversation Analysis and Discourse Analysis. There is a need to look at social structures and political configurations at a more macro-contextual level (Barton and Tusting 2005a; Trent 2006). And there is the more profound issue, which Edwards (2005) argues is common to many theories which come under the 'participation metaphor', of accounting for the generalization of learning from one context to another.

Despite these shortcomings, and those discussed earlier in this chapter, SLT has proved useful to Applied Linguistics researchers interested in exploring the social origins, processes and outcomes of second language acquisition. As Barton and Tusting (2005a) discuss, part of its popularity comes from it being a 'middle-level theory between structure and agency' (p. 3). In articulating the various ways that community membership produces the desire and capacity to learn, as well as the content of learning, SLT has already contributed much to our understanding of the sociocultural nature of language acquisition. It should be clear by now, though, that it is also helping us to understand individual learners, just as the study of individual learners helps us understand the communities they participate in. The individual always carries with them into each CoP a personal history of community membership, as well as personal identities forged elsewhere and built on competence in other practices and other meanings. A full account of language learning in any particular context has to consider *actual* individual differences. This is not to say that the generalizations produced by traditional cognitive and social psychological Individual Difference research cannot help. One way of working towards a synthesis is researching how the characterizations of individuals produced by such research – for example, learners with certain 'kinds' of motivation or learning styles – play out in specific individuals in specific sets of circumstances. This is beginning to happen in general motivation research (e.g. Bempechat and Boulay 2001; Turner and Patrick 2008), and a recent volume of work (Dörnyei and Ushioda 2009) linking language learning motivation and identity from both quantitative and qualitative perspectives is perhaps a sign of rapprochement in our field too.

4 Individuality, imagination and community in a globalizing world: an Asian EFL perspective

Tomoko Yashima

Introduction

The social turn in Applied Linguistics (Block 2003) has introduced two major sociocultural perspectives on research and practice: (1) the cultural historical/Vygotskian perspective, and (2) the post-structuralist/critical perspective. Although these perspectives are based on completely different theoretical backgrounds, they share a common critique of traditional Second Language Acquisition (SLA) research as an approach that focuses on individuals' cognitive processes as they gain abstract second or additional language (L2) competence. SLA research on individual differences, including aptitude, personality and motivation, has also been criticized for its preference for methodologies in which a sum (or mean) of individuals' characteristics represents the group's tendency. In contrast, sociocultural approaches see language learning as being embedded in social contexts and, therefore, as not amenable to being studied in isolation (i.e. in a laboratory, or via a questionnaire). Since the context is different for each individual, researchers are required to look at how individuals experience learning, to listen to each individual's story (Benson and Nunan 2005), and to pay attention to how learning takes place through interaction between individuals and their environments.

Vygotskian Sociocultural Theory (Lantolf, Chapter 2, this volume) focuses on the development of cognitive capacities that are socioculturally mediated and individually internalized to gain self-regulation. Initially assisted by more capable others, individuals also internalize the capacity to mediate their own learning to become more independent learners often by creating new forms of mediation. This perspective suggests that humans have both the capacity and agency to remediate themselves in order to cope with unknown situations (Lantolf and Thorne 2006). From the post-structuralist perspective, on the other hand, while human beings are constrained by social structures and forces, they are not entirely controlled or structured by them. SLA research that is informed by post-structuralist critiques considers the power relations embedded in situations in which people learn an L2 as well as the agency that learners exercise to overcome the challenges they face. To be critical of the discursive positioning of L2 learners in certain social categories (e.g. as members of a minority group or as non-native speakers) and to empower those who are marginalized have become important goals of post-structuralist Applied Linguistics (e.g. Pennycook 1997; Canagarajah 1999).

Both the cultural historical and post-structuralist perspectives characterizing the social turn help us to understand the complexities of L2 learning in a globalizing world, because they reveal how humans cope with new and unknown situations instead of being at the mercy of environmental forces. An important question related to sociocultural perspectives on learning, however, is whether or not competence, skills and knowledge acquired in one historical and sociocultural context are transferable to new contexts. In her discussion of two metaphors of learning, Sfard (1998) attempts to answer this question by suggesting that a new metaphor of learning as participation in communities should complement the traditional metaphor of learning as acquisition. In Asian English language teaching (ELT) contexts, the acquisition metaphor is predominant and should, perhaps, be replaced by a metaphor of participation. But as Sfard notes, the participation and the acquisition metaphors are complementary to each other and we cannot (or should not) simply choose one over the other. In contrast to second language (SL) learning contexts, where newcomers learn the L2 to participate in the L2 communities in which they live, in foreign language (FL) contexts that are typical of Asian ELT, we need to educate learners to use the L2 in situations they are yet to experience. Thus, we need to see learning as being both acquired and transferable as well as participatory.

In this chapter, I argue that the idea of participation in *imagined* communities can help us bridge the gap between acquisition and participation in Asian EFL settings. In this chapter, I will therefore use the participation metaphor together with the concepts of imagined communities and imagined selves to explore the issues of identity and agency among Asian EFL learners, with a particular focus on Japan. In the course of this discussion, I will review research on imagined communities. I will also revisit several studies that I have conducted within the Individual Differences research tradition, with an expanded focus on imagination and participation in L2 learning. This process inevitably involves mixing different research paradigms, including the two metaphors just discussed. Although learning is socially structured, humans have a capacity for creating new ways of mediation (using artefacts) to cope with difficult circumstances. Learning a new language should equip individuals with a greater cognitive, behavioural and affective repertoire, which will help them when they need to counter social constraints. In other words it should equip them with additional tools that can help them become 'authors of their own worlds' (Pennycook 1997: 45).

Imagination and imagined communities for L2 learners

Anderson's (1983) conceptualization of 'imagined community' captures the socioculturally constructed nature of nation as something that resides in people's minds. People who have never been in face-to face contact believe that they belong to the same community. Nation, therefore, is a result of collective imagination. Based on this idea, all communities larger than a local community where members know each other are imagined. For Appadurai (1996), in his attempt to capture the structure of globalization, imagination is something that every one of us deploys in the world of mass-media and mass migrations. He states that imaginations are 'resources for self-making' for more people in more parts of the world than ever before (p. 3). In globalizing societies, the imagination is 'a staging ground for action, not only for escape' (p. 7), in search of new life possibilities.

To the best of my knowledge, Norton (2001) was the first researcher to use imagined communities in the Applied Linguistics literature in her study of immigrant women in Canada. However, she draws the idea not from Anderson (1983) but from Wenger's (1998) work on Communities of Practice (CoPs), and in particular his idea that 'imagination' (alongside 'engagement' and 'alignment') constitutes an important mode of 'belonging' to a community. Norton used imagined communities to refer to certain host communities that two women in her study wished to participate in as they invested in learning the target language (a community of professionals for one and that of wealthy immigrants from the same origin for the other). Norton tries to show that when learners engage in L2 learning, they also envision their imagined communities outside of the ESL classroom, and that ESL teachers' lack of understanding of these visions can discourage learners from investing in the language.

For many foreign language learners, on the other hand, a target community is a more abstract concept that refers to a country or region where the target language is used or to a group of people who use the language. It is somewhat similar to Anderson's (1983) 'imagined community' in the sense that it is a collective belief that we can point to a country on a map and say: 'We are learning the language of this country.' While migrant learners are often trying to participate in specific L2 communities, in FL contexts, a target community is not as clearly defined. This is particularly true when the target language is English, which is a de facto lingua franca spoken in various parts of the world.

In addition to this vague sense of imagined community that refers to the target discourse community for FL learners, I also draw in this chapter on Wenger's (1998) CoPs, just as Norton did. According to Wenger, imagination 'concerns the production of images of the self and images of the world that transcend engagement' (p. 177). It is a 'process of expanding our self by transcending our time and space and creating new images of the world and ourselves' (p. 176). Meanwhile, Appadurai's (1996) discussion of imagination encourages us to contemplate the significance of L2 learning, including both ESL and EFL, in a globalizing world that is characterized by trans-border movements not only of people but of media images and voices.

If we accept that imagination does have such power, then what specific role can it play in FL learning? When you are writing a sentence as part of a speech, you are seeing yourself saying that sentence in the speech, to a certain audience on a certain occasion, and you are conscious of the purpose of the speech and its impact on the audience. Imagination allows you to foresee the consequences of the task you are engaging in. Imagination is, therefore, essential to agentive action as it allows you to be aware of the possible changes you can make in your environment. In this sense, the vision of yourself as an L2 user needs to be one of participating in communities, not just memorizing words by yourself, but being involved with others in a joint enterprise using the L2 in personally meaningful activities.

The imaginative capacity of humans is also at the core of the recent and influential movement towards 'possible selves' in L2 motivation research, which draws on theories of the self in psychology (Dörnyei 2005; 2009). 'Possible selves' concern 'how people conceptualize their as-yet unrealized potential' and act as 'future self-guides' (Dörnyei 2009: 11) and account for the dynamic process of how someone moves from the present towards the future. In this theory, two types of possible, or imagined, selves are distinguished: the *ideal* self representing the person one would like to become, and the *ought-to* self that a person believes he or she ought to become. These concepts help us see how individuals' visions of self guide their actions in imagined communities. Learners need to envision imagined selves using an L2 in imagined communities in order for the visions to really motivate learners to work towards them. If a learner is writing a sentence to address someone in his or her imagined community, the experience can be more personally meaningful than just writing a sentence for its own sake. Individuals can also have their own imagined communities, which they wish to participate in (e.g., an international community of soccer players, Applied Linguists, or cardiac surgeons). Imagined communities can thus provide insight into relationships between the individual and the social in EFL teaching practices.

In the following section, I will explore how FL teaching practices can be linked to imagined communities in a number of significant ways. First, by creating CoPs in L2 learning linked to activities in imagined communities, some realistic values can be attached to engagement in L2 learning in the classroom. Second, I review study-abroad reports in which learners, urged on by a desire to participate in their imagined L2 communities, choose to visit the target community. Many studies have shown that real-life participation in study-abroad contexts involves identity negotiations, or what Block (2007a) calls 'identity work'. This may involve pain but possibly also a crucial process through which learners construct L2 identities. Third, when learners who visited the target community are back in their home country, the visions of individualized imagined communities may continue to help them sustain motivation and engagement in learning the language.

After exploring the three possibilities of linking FL teaching to imagined communities, in the section that follows, I will go back to the acquisition/participation metaphors and discuss the way imagination connects these two metaphors. Finally, I will conclude this chapter with two examples in which imagination leads people to participate in an international CoP to expand their life options.

FL teaching and imagined communities

Engagement in EFL classrooms linked to imagined communities

A problem in many EFL contexts is that there is not much target-language mediated identity work in schools, as Block (2007a) points out. In classroom communities of practice in Japan, for example, English is a school subject, tested, and evaluated within the school. It is not a means for learners to participate in communities outside the classroom and imagined L2 selves do not therefore often leave the four walls of the classroom. If classroom engagement is tied to the outside world, where learners can be guided to see their possible selves in ways that will help expand their life opportunities and career options, the knowledge and skills they have acquired in school can be situated in their imagined communities and thus English might retain its meaningfulness through their lives.

One example of an attempt to create an imagined community is reported in Yashima and Zenuk-Nishide (2008). In the Model United Nations (MUN), a theme-based EFL learning experience based in a Japanese high school, students learn to form and express opinions from the perspective of the country they are representing in order to negotiate and reach genuine agreements that represent the country's interests to the maximum. They imagine themselves as delegates, making speeches, speaking and negotiating on behalf of the country they represent, where problems (e.g. child labour) are particularly severe. They try to persuade other delegates that wordings that represent their ideas (e.g. in the child labour case, about protecting children) will be included in the final resolution, or they imagine themselves as chairs and secretaries coordinating discussions. Through realistic L2 experiences of this type, they may well begin to visualize their future ideal L2 selves as linked to what they do in the here and now. As the students negotiate in the interests of the country they represent, they experience situations in which their performance affects the future course and destiny of the country. While some students report feeling frustrated by not being able to express what they want to say, others feel exhilarated at devoting their energy to a cause they find important. This negotiation process creates spaces where learners' L2 mediated identities are located in real-world international affairs, albeit in the imagination. In this way, learners experience 'socially, culturally, and politically engaged forms of L2 teaching' (Pennycook 1997: 49).

McMahill (1997) also describes how imagined communities had a liberating effect within feminist English adult education classes in Japan. In these classes, Japanese women participated in a local community of EFL learners with an imagined link to the international feminist community. Although the influence of the linguistic features of gendered language use on identity was not a central issue, some participants reported that it was a somewhat different experience to express themselves in English as opposed to Japanese. One member said that it was easier to express opinions and beliefs in English because she felt a sense of equality with the people she was talking to, while another found it more difficult because she could not be as ambiguous in English as she might have been in Japanese, for example, by dropping the subject and/or object in a sentence. McMahill characterizes the learning that takes place in these classes as feminist consciousness-raising that acts as a 'launching pad for actions outside of the class' (p. 619). She also shows how women emotionally support each other's struggles to fight institutional sexism as well as 'internalized sexism' (p. 619). In a sense, the English classes where participants learned about feminism in English were classroom CoPs linked to an imagined L2 community in which participants were liberated from fixed gender roles tied to the hierarchical social system of their L1 world.

Identity work in study-abroad contexts

Imagination and the desire to participate in imagined communities may also bring foreign language learners to the target L2 community through study abroad (SA). The SA experience often activates identity work for foreign language learners in a way that can seldom be experienced at home.

Participation in a community requires alignment with its cultural norms. Through learning a second language, the learner gradually acculturates into the sociolinguistic and cultural conventions of the host community, which triggers identity work, often accompanied by resistance. Siegal's (1996) study reports that western women studying Japanese in Japan often feel resistant to gendered social positioning imposed upon them. A woman in her study was under constant pressure to behave politely by being humble and formal in interactions with her superior. However, despite her efforts, her positioning as 'foreign other' was discursively co-constructed. An example of non-participation is reported in Deguchi and Yashima's (2008) study of international students living in a dormitory on a Japanese university campus, where the majority of the residents are Japanese and traditional norms and strict rules based on hierarchical interpersonal relationships govern the community's cultural practices. From the analyses of interviews conducted twice during their stay on campus, the researchers learned that international students' refusal to adapt to the traditional cultural practice mirroring Japanese corporate culture prevented them from participating fully in the students' community in the dormitory and consequently their voices, which argued for changes in the rules, were lost. Yet, some people find L2 norms more acceptable than L1 norms. In Mori (1977), for example, the author adopted an American (L2) rather than a Japanese (L1) identity, because she would feel freer and true to herself in English, as she found certain Japanese linguistic behaviours (e.g. vagueness and formality) to be polite but insincere and remote.

The paradox of the need to use the L2 in order to improve proficiency and the difficulty of actually finding opportunities to use the language, which Norton (2000) drew attention to, is also relevant to EFL learners in SA contexts. A study of Japanese high school learners' SA experience in the United States (Yashima 2004) demonstrated the problem of students' adaptation to a new community using the language they are trying to learn. Many students found it particularly vital, but difficult, to initiate interactions to make friends in school, as the following comments indicate: 'They [the American peer group] will not talk to me unless I take the initiative. But I could not as my English was poor.' 'I tried to talk, but maybe she [an American classmate] got bored and went away. It was a sad experience.' The identity of these learners in the new community rested on whatever competency they could demonstrate in the L2, which made them keenly aware of the fact that they were being evaluated based on their L2 selves in interactions with their hosts. Without a willingness to communicate in the language, they were invisible, as one of the participants commented: 'If I talk they are friendly, but if I'm quiet I'm the air [i.e. I'm invisible and inaudible].' Another student who was told by his host father that his use of polite forms was not as good as that of his four-year-old niece commented: 'I'm more than full-fledged in Japan, but I'm not a full-fledged person in America,' revealing both his realization and frustration that his L2 self was deficient. Morita's (2004) study focusing on the academic socialization of international graduate students from Japan used the CoP framework to illustrate identity negotiation by the students in an academic community in Canada. Using ethnography and in-depth interviews with her participants, Morita shows that the degree of their participation in class discussions was not determined by individual factors such as personality traits but situated in each classroom context within embedded power relations, and therefore socially structured. She showed that the same student can be an active participant in one class but totally silent in other classes, for many different reasons. In one class, a student asked the instructor to change the class discussion format so as to make it more inclusive of L2 speakers. However, the instructor would not change her way of teaching. In this case, the structure of the class and the power of the old timers and more experienced group members did not allow for participation by the novice. Self-reports documented the profound struggle of these international graduate students to 'negotiate their roles and identities' as non-native speakers, less competent group members, and non-white females (p. 596).

In brief, embodied experiences of using the L2 in SA contexts trigger identity work and L2 identities. I have focused more on negative experiences through which learners became conscious of their L1 and L2 identities. Benson *et al.*'s (2012) narrative study on Hong Kong EFL learners' SA experiences gives us insight into how L2 identities are also mediated by positive experiences using the L2. They clarified the process by showing how learners' L2 identities develop through improvements in language competence that enable learners to function as a person in the L2, enhanced self-confidence as L2 users, and L2 mediated personal development via for example, resolving problems through the use of L2. SA experiences thus make learners' imagined L2 selves lucid and real.

Visions of imagined communities sustaining engagement

Other studies show that the SA experience helps learners visualize the imagined communities in which they participate after they return to their home countries and resume their study of EFL. In her longitudinal study following Japanese EFL learners' writing development, Sasaki (2004, 2007) demonstrated that those who went through an SA experience not only improved their writing ability but maintained the motivation to write better, while those without SA experience did not. Sasaki (2007) attributed this difference to both the alienation and the social support they experienced during their SA experience. After returning home, such experience may have helped them imagine the overseas communities where they once lived and visualize an authentic audience when they wrote and this may have further motivated them to write better.

My own recent study (Yashima 2010) also indicates the possibility that international SA experience helps Japanese EFL learners gain visions of imagined communities, which can motivate their L2 learning. Semi-structured interviews with participants on short-term international volunteer projects revealed that joining an international youth community in collaborative work helped Japanese participants become more self-reliant, self-confident and willing to communicate. At the same time, the Japanese students felt that they were positioned somewhat peripherally or even marginally in international communities. Their comments include: 'We were just like obedient kids'; 'People in other countries are much more mature and have their own opinions on many things'; 'I felt Japanese people don't have opinions to express'; and 'We were out of the picture when it comes to discussion.' Some participants attributed this to their relatively low competency in English in comparison with European participants. Many came to the realization that they needed to empower themselves by improving their English and becoming more self-expressive in order to become full-fledged participants in international youth communities. At least their experience helped them relate to imagined communities that can positively affect their motivation to learn English as well as their attitude towards English. As one student stated: 'If you ask me what the world is, it is these ten people I met in the project.' Now they can see their faces in the community, and they can participate through the mediation of English. Hopefully, these young learners will even find ways to connect their learning of English to some career options.

These images of selves using English created through SA will guide their efforts to expand their skills, knowledge and competence, which will allow them to cope with future encounters more effectively. In the following section, I will discuss how the two metaphors for learning – acquisition and participation – are at work for individuals participating in imagined communities.

Two metaphors at work in participating in imagined L2 communities

For Wenger, learning is participating in a CoP through three modes of belonging, that is engagement, alignment and imagination (Wenger 1998). Knowledge and skills are regarded as situated in practice and they are learned as people engage in day-to-day activities in the community. On the other hand, L2 learning is more complex because the language is the medium used for acquiring the knowledge and skills to do the work in the community. For this reason, a certain amount of knowledge of grammar and vocabulary that is more abstract than situated, and transferable to a new situation in which the learner is to be placed, may be necessary to initiate the full process of participation. Without imagination, abstract L2 knowledge learned in L2 classrooms cannot find its place in an L2 CoP outside of the classroom, yet the acquisition of L2 knowledge is also mandatory for learners to engage in and align with the activities in the imagined community.

One of the five immigrant women in Norton's (2000) study, Eva, was characterized as a more successful learner than the others. As Toohey and Norton (2003) show, Eva exercised her agency to resist social pressures that marginalized and silenced her, in order to access the social networks of an English-speaking host group in her workplace. In the beginning, she was treated as someone who did the most menial type of work, requiring no command of English, but she tactfully utilized her resources (her European background and Italian language skills) to position herself as a person 'worth talking/listening to' in her L2 (p. 70). Although Sfard's (1998) participation metaphor is predominant in Eva's story, the acquisition metaphor helps us see how growing L2 competence mediated her progress from peripheral towards fuller participation. When asked how she was able to join a conversation of English speakers, she told the researcher: 'I don't wait for when they are completely quiet, but when it's the moment when I can say something about what they are talking about' (Norton 2000: 69). This shows how Eva developed a communicative repertoire in the L2 (including the skill of joining a conversation) as she began to participate legitimately in the community. Here we see the dialectic of participation and acquisition of competence. Similarly, in Yashima's (2004) study of Japanese SA students in the United States cited earlier, as part of their struggle to participate in peer CoPs, some high school students withdrew into themselves while others at least attempted to do something to expand their opportunities for interaction, as their comments show: 'I was taking lunch and eating alone, but once I stopped taking lunch and instead went to the cafeteria and said "Can I sit here?"'; 'I ask my friend to teach me a phrase that I can use to talk to girls.' The use of the modal auxiliary, 'Can I ~' and a request such as 'Could you teach me ~?' are precisely what they had learned in their EFL classrooms back in Japan. These learners show agency, however modestly, in using the language they had learned in order to try to adapt their own behaviours in the hope of changing their environment.

This study of high school students led me to do research on willingness to communicate, and I introduce this concept here as it is a way to look at the same phenomena focusing on individuals rather than on the society using the participation metaphor. Willingness to communicate in the L2 (MacIntyre *et al.* 1998; Yashima 2002) was introduced as a new psychological construct to account for individual differences in the readiness to initiate interactions in situations such as those shown above. The underlying assumption is that if students acquire the necessary linguistic skills and the willingness to communicate, it will help them 'change the dynamism of interactions by themselves rather than leaving it to the empathy and/or control' of others in intercultural interactions (Yashima *et al.* 2004: 122). Again, the sociocultural approach informs us that the willingness (or the unwillingness) to communicate is socially structured within inequitable power relations, as Morita's (2004) work cited earlier demonstrates.

In the struggle to participate in the L2 community, learners feel frustrated as participation is socially structured. Yet, with imagination and an L2 behavioural repertoire, they can exercise agency to change the environment. The behavioural repertoire, in turn, can be enhanced as they participate in the community. This perspective on L2 learning can help us see how we can prepare EFL learners before their SA adventure. For example, as reported in Yashima and Tanaka (1996), we designed a social skills training programme for high school students departing for a year's study in the USA in the hope that students would learn to develop confidence in using specific skills in the L2 – for example, initiating interactions or introducing particular topics into conversation. The emphasis was on how students can utilize these skills to take the first step towards participation in their imagined communities.

I have shown that EFL teaching can utilize the imaginative powers of individuals to create realistic learning situations in classrooms and through SA experiences in order to sustain their learning. Finally, I will discuss through examples how imagination can be deployed and imagined communities can become resources for self-authoring.

English for expanding life opportunities and means of articulation

While it is important to keep a critical eye on the symbolic domination (Pavlenko and Blackledge 2004) of users of powerful languages in the international linguistic market, it is also true that competency in such languages allows fuller participation in various activities and access to a wider range of opportunities. Without voice in English, we may even be excluded from the public critique of its symbolic dominance. As Pennycook (1997) notes, learning a language is a matter of 'struggling to find means of articulation amid the cultures, discourses, and ideologies within which we live our lives' (p. 49). The following examples illustrate this point.

Sabatini (2007) reports a longitudinal case study of a Japanese woman, Haruko, who gave up her traditional role as housewife to establish herself as a successful fitness instructor, well-versed in American fitness methods, which she achieved by attending seminars in the United States. Through the course of her life (first as a housewife, later divorced from a husband who was conservative about gender roles as well as through her experience abroad), the meaning of English changed from something she had to learn to a way to connect with an international community of fitness instructors from whom she could access 'cutting edge research and information' (p. 39). Drawing on Foucault, Sabatini observes the transformation of Haruko's gendered and professional identity, albeit not entirely free from the power of the discourse, as she 're-crafted her subjectivity as a work of art in her struggles, which [was] always open to change as she [participated] in different discourses' (p. 42). For Haruko, English was a tool that she could use to mediate her access to knowledge she could only gain in English. Having found the community in which she wanted to participate, she succeeded in acquiring the specific skills that enabled her to do so, which in turn helped her along the way to a new career. The imagined community opened up possibilities for her, enabling her to begin to self-author her life.

Another example is a Japanese story teller, Kaishi, and his venture to introduce the Japanese traditional art of comic story telling called *rakugo* to international English discourse communities. His ambitious undertaking was made possible by his imagination, which helped him go beyond the national and linguistic borders to imagined communities of would-be *rakugo* lovers. Unlike *kabuki*, *noh*, and some other traditional performing arts, *rakugo* is predominantly linguistic as the teller by himself plays the role of all the participants without using any props except for a towel and a small fan. Given the demands that performing and understanding the *rakugo* makes on linguistic competency, it is a popular belief that this art form cannot be appreciated by non-Japanese speakers. To perform *rakugo* in English, the teller needs to be highly proficient in the language. Torikai (2011) analyses how Kaishi became interested in the outside world using 'international posture' (Yashima 2002) as an individual tendency that distinguished him from people who prefer to stay within Japanese communities. She also cites from his homepage that he liked English as a school subject and dreamed of having a career in which he would use English. His interest and proficiency in English were the driving force that created his imagined community beyond the audience within Japan to access the far greater number of people who understand English all over the world. (According to Torikai, Kaishi had made 320 *rakugo* performances in English in 83 cities around the world as of January 2010.) By doing that, Kaishi crafted his L2 self as a successful international story teller, who can bring the breeze of laughter to wider communities of *rakugo* fans.

Conclusion: individuals and Applied Linguistics

In a globalizing world, people deploy imagination to access alternative ways of life (Appadurai 1996), even though it does not necessarily promise easier options. As we have seen in this chapter, L2 learning can aid learners in crafting new identities, if imagination functions to connect what they have acquired in classrooms to the communities they can participate in using the L2. Although participation (or non-participation) in an L2 community is socially structured, it also depends on individual characteristics represented in different forms of agency. A greater cognitive, behavioural and affective repertoire will provide an individual with more options to choose from when he or she needs to challenge and overcome constraints. Second language education can thus make a contribution to empowering individuals in this regard.

According to Giddens (1999), as well as Sato and Yoshitani (2005), in a globalizing world, where traditional social organizations are enfeebled, individuals need agency more than ever to self-direct and be self-reliant. This places a tremendous amount of demand on individuals. Often, anxiety and uncertainty drive people to seek connections. When people connect themselves and create new CoPs, they also create new artefacts, norms and values through dialogues. Hopefully, L2 teaching can help expand not only individuals' communicative repertoires, but also the collective power of dialogues to bridge differences, so that we can deal with problems globalization potentially imposes on us, and thus have greater control over our environment.

5 Chaos and the complexity of second language acquisition

Vera Menezes

Chaos in the world brings uneasiness, but it also allows the opportunity for creativity and growth. (Tom Barrett n.d.)

Introduction

The objective of this chapter is to discuss the role of identity, autonomy and agency in second language acquisition (SLA). I argue that science and myth have much in common and whatever theory we use to try to understand any phenomenon, in our case SLA, we will be offering a metaphor, a way of seeing something in terms of another. My metaphor will be one of 'chaos', a term used in Chaos Theory (Gleick 1987; Lorenz 2001; Smith 2007), which has been discussed in the field of Applied Linguistics under the headings of Chaos/Complexity Science and second language (Larsen-Freeman 1997), Complex Systems Theory (Larsen-Freeman and Cameron 2008a) and Dynamic Systems Theory (de Bot 2008). Taking the assumption that SLA is a chaotic complex system, I will demonstrate that identity construction is in intimate relation with agency and that identity, autonomy and agency can move SLA chaotic systems to the edge of chaos, understood as an overwhelming experience that changes the learners' behaviours. Some examples taken from a corpus of language learning histories will be used to exemplify the theoretical assumptions.

Myths and science

Human beings have tried to explain the universe and the different phenomena around them, first by way of myths and then by science. As Armstrong (2005: 3) puts it, '[M]ythology and science both extend the scope of human beings.' Among scientists, there is a dispute between those who defend the objectivity of science and those who deny it, positioning themselves in favour of subjectivity. Lakoff and Johnson claim that both objectivism and subjectivism are myths. They explain:

> Myths provide ways of comprehending experience; they give order to our lives. Like metaphors, myths are necessary for making sense of what goes on around us. All cultures have myths, and people cannot function without myth any more than they can function without metaphor.
>
> (Lakoff and Johnson 1980: 185–6)

Lakoff and Johnson advocate the myth of 'Experientialism', which does not oppose external and internal aspects of understanding. For them, there is neither absolute truth nor totally unrestricted imagination.

> The experientialist myth takes the perspective of man as part of the environment, not as separate from it. It focuses on constant interaction with the physical environment and with other people. It views this interaction with the environment as involving mutual change. You cannot function within the environment without changing it or being changed by it.
>
> (Lakoff and Johnson 1980: 230–31)

The Experientialist perspective is coherent with the complexity paradigm, a new way of knowing that highlights the dynamic interrelations among the elements of a phenomenon nested in the physical environment. This new paradigm brings together a series of approaches to complexity, including Chaos Theory. Complexity approaches encompass all the theories which see the object of study as a dynamic system made up of interconnected components. Among these theories, we can mention the ecological approach which highlights the relationship between humans and their environment in terms of affordance (see van Lier 2002; also Menezes 2011) and Chaos Theory (see Gleick 1987) that emphasizes that there is order underlying disorder and that the systems are sensitive dependent on initial conditions. In the Applied Linguistics field, researchers usually do not make a distinction between chaos and complexity and refer to them as chaos/complexity (see Larsen-Freeman 1997; van Lier 2002; Larsen-Freeman and Cameron 2008a). Both Experientialism and Chaos Theory see their objects of study as inseparable from physical reality.

Curiously enough, Chaos Theory borrowed its name from Greek mythology, offering a new metaphor which radically changes the way we view the world and everything in it. Chaos is a substitute for the Newtonian metaphor of clockwork predictability. Instead of explaining the world as a clock governed by simple rules, the Chaos Theory metaphor describes it as 'a kaleidoscope:

the world is a matter of patterns that change, that partly repeat, but never quite repeat, that are always new and different' Waldrop (1993: 330). Chaos Theory and its shifting kaleidoscope metaphor have been used to describe different phenomena in different research fields, including knowledge dynamics (see Massen and Weingart 2000) and SLA (see Larsen-Freeman and Cameron 2008a). Researchers have attempted to explain SLA through many different theories, models and hypotheses, but no consensus has been reached so far. Could there be any similarity between creation myths and SLA theories?

Creation myths in different cultures often begin with an initial emptiness, or chaos, and opposing forces which give birth to the universe. So do SLA theories. As in the Jewish/Christian *Genesis* which tells us that the world was created from a formless state through the addition of elements, the structuralists, for example, defend that SLA develops from a formless state through the addition of structures in an ordered sequence. From that perspective, first language was considered an opposing force to the birth of the new language. On the other hand, in the Chinese creation myth, the universe is described as a black egg where Pangu, the creator of the universe, was mixed together with heaven and earth. Feeling suffocated, Pangu splits open the egg, holding the top and the bottom as the sky and earth. As in the Pangu myth, the mentalists in Applied Linguistics believe in the existence of a previous innate structure from which language develops. It seems that both structuralists and mentalists would agree that in the beginning there was chaos, not understood as disorder, but as described in the *Oxford Dictionary of English Etymology* as 'the primordial formless void'.

In the creation myths, the universe comes into existence through the agency of the gods. In the Jewish/Christian *Genesis*, agency was exerted by means of language when God said, '"Let there be light"; and there was light'. Linguistic agency is also crucial in SLA no matter what the concept of language is. Whether it is understood as a set of syntactic structures, as a social system of human communication or as a tool for thinking and acting, linguistic agency is the initial condition in all theories which try to explain SLA. If the concept of language is that of a set of syntactic structures, one believes that language is acquired if one repeats those structures *ad nausaum*; if language is conceived as a communication tool, it is acquired by means of meaningful communicative activities; and if it is considered as a tool for thinking and acting, it is acquired if the learner is engaged in authentic linguistic social practices which enable him or her to think and make decisions in order to act, to do things with the language in communities of practice.

One of the crucial debates in the SLA research field centres on the initial conditions of acquisition, and two points of view – 'language innateness' and 'environmentalism' – divide researchers into opposing theory groups. This is also called the nature-nurture debate and involves those who believe that language is something innate, a genetic predisposition, and those who argue that language is learned from the environment.

Although both ideas are still very influential, a third perspective arose when some Applied Linguists started thinking of SLA as a chaotic/complex (Larsen-Freeman 1997) or ecological system (van Lier 1997). In her seminal article, Larsen-Freeman (1997: 141) saw 'many striking similarities between the new science of chaos/complexity and language and SLA' and some months later van Lier (1997: 783), on the same track, advocated the replacement of body-mind dualism with:

> a conception of the learning environment as a complex adaptive system, of the mind as the totality of relationships between a developing person and the surrounding world, and of learning as the result of meaningful activity in an accessible environment.

Since then, there has been an increasing interest in this kind of study, evidenced by Kramsch (2002) who gathered a distinguished team of scholars around ecological perspectives, including Larsen-Freeman and van Lier; and by the special issues on Complexity Theory in *Applied Linguistics* (Cook and Kaspar 2006) and *The Modern Language Journal* (de Bot 2008a). In Brazil, Martins and Braga (2007) have reviewed work by Brazilian researchers, which includes research on SLA, on identity in SLA, and on online learning and interaction in the light of Chaos and Complexity theories. Two books – van Lier (2002) and Larsen-Freeman and Cameron (2008a) – present a thorough discussion of the main concepts in this new approach to second language learning theory. Van Lier offers a comprehensive overview of an ecological approach to language learning and Larsen-Freeman and Cameron translate their understanding of complexity and its main concepts into Applied Linguistics.

In the next section, the reader will find a brief review of Chaos Theory and its implications for SLA. In order to make the theory more palatable, I will illustrate some key concepts by referring to language learning histories (LLHs) from the AMFALE Project (AMFALE is an acronym in Portuguese for the research project 'Learning with the memories of speakers and learners of foreign languages'. The project has a corpus of narratives written by Brazilian, Japanese, Chinese and Finn students and can be seen at http://www.veramenezes.com/amfale.htm).

Chaos Theory and Second Language Acquisition

The importance of Chaos Theory to SLA is in its potentiality to reconcile 'nature' and 'nurture' as the learner can be seen as an individual with his/her cognitive capacities and at the same time as an agent who is in interaction with the other elements in his/her environment. The interacting components in a complex system can be human (e.g. teachers, relatives) and non-human (e.g. books, films, music). It is my contention that learning initial conditions are chaotic, and two opposing forces – first and second language – give birth to a third, the individual interlanguage.

In science, 'chaos' is a technical term to name systems which are apparently disordered or, as Lorenz (2001: 4) says, processes 'whose variations are *not random but look random* [emphasis in the original]'. This technical use of the word chaos blends the notions of initial conditions (as in Greek chaos) and of disorder or randomness, although the theory states that there is an underlying order beneath this apparent randomness.

Chaos Theory deals with chaotic deterministic systems. This kind of system is defined by Lorenz (2001: 24) 'as one that is sensitively dependent on interior changes in initial conditions'. Although those systems are deterministic, or predictable in the short term, their long-term behaviour is aperiodic or chaotic and cannot be predicted. The unpredictable behaviour of deterministic systems is called chaos. As Lorenz (2001: 157) explains: '[W]e may believe that some phenomenon is governed by deterministic laws and that it responds in a regular manner, only to discover at some point that its behaviour is more irregular than suspected.' Lorenz attributed the unpredictability of the weather to a chaotic deterministic system; below I will explain why a similar argument can be made to explain the unpredictability of SLA within individual learners.

Brooks (2007) states that 'while we cannot predict the weather in a particular place and on a particular day in 100 years' time, we can be sure that on average it will be far warmer if greenhouse gases continue to rise'. Similarly, in formal traditional contexts we can predict that students will be able to memorize rules and vocabulary, but we cannot predict that they will all acquire the language, that is, if they will be able to engage themselves in linguistic social practices. While we cannot predict the amount of second language (SL) an individual learner will acquire during his or her life, we can be sure that on average he or she will be more proficient if they have the opportunity to use the language in authentic contexts. The rate of change, that is, of acquisition, is not predictable and varies according to the nature of the interactions among all the elements of the learner's system.

In the deterministic perspective, one believes that every action is the result of a preceding action, but chaotic systems are unpredictable, they are non-linear, and effects are disproportionate to causes. Smith (2007: 10) offers an interesting example to help us understand what non-linearity is. He says that 'the impact of adding a second straw to a camel's back could be much bigger (or much smaller) than the impact of the first straw'. In the SLA context, which is also constrained by individual identities, agency and autonomy, similar linguistic experiences might cause different student reactions. In an EFL context, being exposed to a certain experience may help one learner but block another one. In our corpus of LLHs, for instance, some Brazilian learners praised their teachers for speaking English only and others stated that they felt blocked because they could not understand what teachers were saying. Some displayed more autonomy and agency than others, and identity construction also contributed to the acquisition processes. Identity, agency and autonomy are important elements in the SLA chaotic system and will be further discussed in the next section.

Identity, agency and autonomy

We become what we are by means of our actions and our complex interactions with other agents in the world. Language is an essential element for agency, understood as control over life or as 'socioculturally mediated capacity to act' (Ahearn 2001). Our sense of self or identity construction is in intimate relation with agency. As argued by van Lier (2004: 108):

> when we say something we do not only provide a piece of information about something or other, we also at the same time provide information about two other important matters: Who we are ourselves, and who we think our listeners or readers are.

Using a second language is thus acting in the world and simultaneously displaying fractals of our identity.

The concept of fractal was developed by Mandelbrot (1982) to represent shapes made up of similar patterns at different scales, due to having the property of self-similarity. An example of a fractal dimension can be found in trees. They do not exhibit exactly the same structure at all scales, but the same kind of structure appears on the branches and leaves. A good example of a set of fractals is the Babushka Russian doll – a set of nested dolls. Whatever the size of the doll is, one will identify the same characteristics found in the other dolls. I understand identity as a fractal set because we do not have one identity, but a set of fractalized identities. As Sade (2009) argues: no matter which identity fractal is foregrounded – learner, son, football player and so on – the other identities will also be there, in the background. As explained by Sade,

> The 'self' is constructed via emergence of several other 'selves'; therefore, we can say it's a system once it is compounded by several parts. Each of these selves interacts with the others, influencing

> and being influenced by them. From this interaction unpredictable behaviour emerges. (Sade 2008: 6–7)

She adds that 'no matter the number of internal fragmentations, the parts are interconnected into a whole which is self-similar to the parts' (p. 15).

Some identities are pre-determined in the social groups (family, school, work, etc.) we belong to. As described by Archer (2000: 73–4):

> people are involuntaristically pre-grouped at birth in relation to the social distribution of scarce resources. For simplicity these are called the 'privileged' and the 'non-privileged' and the latter confront plenty of daily exigencies, given their poor life chances.

Identity and agency are two sides of the same coin, and the non-privileged often strive to acquire more privileged identities by learning English, which is seen as a bridge to a more successful life. As Norton (2001: 166) puts it, 'if learners invest in a second language, they do so with the understanding that they will acquire a wider range of symbolic and material resources, which will increase their value in the social world'. See, for instance, the case of the Brazilian rock band Little Joy's singer and guitarist Rodrigo Amarante (2009: 125) who said that he started learning English when he was 12 in order to understand lyrics in the songs of the English popular music band, The Smiths. English is so important for his musical identity that he composed one of his first songs in English.

But not all learners have the same linguistic affordances. As Sade (2008) points out, 'the social location of a particular individual enables him/her to have access to some linguistic and non-linguistic choices and not others' (p. 14). Affordance is exemplified by van Lier (2000) as 'demands and requirements, opportunities and limitations, rejections and invitations, enablement and constraints' (p. 253), that is 'the relationship between properties of the environment and the active learner' (p. 257). In a complex perspective, it can be explained as the dynamical interaction between a learner and the other agents in the SLA chaotic system which provides linguistic experiences. As 'non-privileged' students do not have the same affordances the 'privileged' do, they have to be more autonomous and rely more upon their agency, in order to 'relate their self to the world' (van Lier 2002: 147).

An agent is one who acts and whose actions can be motivated or constrained by other elements in the system and by other systems. One can be a self-governing agent and take control of one's own acquisition system or follow instructions of a teacher. In both cases the learner is acting upon his process of acquisition. However, in the view of complexity, learners' agency interacts with the environment and as such it may be influenced by affordances and constraints. Think for instance of learners who live in the Amazon forest without electricity: their affordances will be different from our own and no matter how much they act upon their process, their 'socioculturally mediated capacity to act' will be restricted by their environment. Likewise, one can be extremely autonomous, but environmental constraints or a given context can limit one's acts or agency. Even so, the more autonomous learners will probably seek opportunities to read in English or to speak with foreign visitors.

In Paiva (2011: 63), I argue that 'autonomy is not a state, but a non-linear process which undergoes periods of instability, variability and adaptability'. I see autonomy as a complex ecological system, subject to internal and external constraints, which manifests itself in different degrees of interdependence, control of one's own learning process, and agency. It involves affordances, capacities, abilities, attitudes, willingness, decision making, choices, planning and assessment either as a language learner or as a communicator inside or outside the classroom. Agency changes the system, but we can never predict the impact of one's autonomous choices and actions. In spite of human agency, SLA systems self-organize and transform themselves beyond the conscious intentions of the learners due to one's innate capacity to learn. Larsen-Freeman and Cameron (2008a: 8) explain that:

> it is not contradictory to state that, at the same time that humans are operating in an agentful way, the resources of the language in the individual and in the speech community are being transformed beyond the conscious intentions of the speakers.

In a SLA system, I would say that slight interferences in the system might trigger overwhelming experiences and change the learner's behaviours. That is what we call the edge of chaos.

The edge of chaos

Waldrop (1993: 147) explains that these chaotic systems are 'always unfolding, always in transition. In fact, if the system ever does reach the equilibrium, it isn't just stable. It's dead.' As argued by Larsen-Freeman and Cameron (2008a: 58), '[A] system at or near the edge of chaos changes adaptively to maintain stability, demonstrating a high level of flexibility and responsiveness.'

According to Brooks (2007): '[T]he unpredictable character of chaotic systems arises from their sensitivity to any change in the conditions that control their development.' This is known in chaos literature as sensitivity to initial conditions. According to Gleick (1987: 8), 'tiny differences in input could quickly become overwhelming differences in output'. Gleick further explains that, in weather, the sensitive dependence is translated into 'what is known as the Butterfly Effect – the notion that a butterfly stirring the air today in Peking can transform systems next month in New York' (p. 8). This hyperbolic metaphor has been used in many areas to explain how minor behaviours can cause huge effects. As Gleick (1987: 23) reminds us, it is well known that 'a chain of events can have a point of crisis that could magnify small changes'. He says that this notion is not new and exemplifies with folklore:

> For want of a nail, the shoe was lost;
> For want of a shoe, the horse was lost;
> For want of a horse, the rider was lost;
> For want of a rider, the battle was lost;
> For want of a battle, the Kingdom was lost.

The loss of a nail led to the winning of the battle by the enemy, which *destabilized* the kingdom and contributed to its loss. The same point of crisis can occur in the classroom which may also be considered a chaotic system and as such can result in unpredictable outcomes. Teachers' choices, for instance, may help one student 'win' the battle of language learning, and another one 'lose', no matter how similar the educational experiences are. In our *corpus* of LLHs, we can find narrators who felt extremely discouraged by teachers who did not believe in them and others who felt challenged by a similar attitude. While the former may have halted their attempts at learning, causing the death of the SLA system, the latter accepted their teachers' demeaning attitude as a challenge and felt more motivated to overcome SLA obstacles. This shows that small perturbations in the classroom can lead to overwhelming results, to a point of crisis. The point of crisis is also known as the critical point or as the edge of chaos.[1] It is described by Waldrop (1993: 12) as 'the ability to bring order and chaos into a special kind of balance'. It is a phase of maximum creativity where the system operates between order and chaos or randomness. The edge of chaos is a phase transition where stability gives way to creativity and transformation. For Waldrop (1993: 12), the edge of chaos is 'the constantly shifting battle zone between stagnation and anarchy, the one place where a complex system can be spontaneous, adaptive, and alive.' In Ockerman's words,

> [The] edge of chaos is a paradoxical state, a spiral chance between order and chaos, a humming oscillation between the two extremes, characterized by risk, exploration, experimentation. Here is where the system operates at its highest level of functioning, where the information processing takes place, where risks are taken and new behaviour is tried out. (Ockerman 1997: 222)

Learning systems move to the edge of chaos because the less desirable state of equilibrium would mean the death of the system. For example, for the learners described previously who felt discouraged by teachers, equilibrium would be gained by those learners ending their attempts to learn the language, but this would result in the collapse of the language learning process. In SLA, we can say that the edge of chaos is where acquisition suddenly shifts from one state to another and where the learner is faced with the greatest challenges and risks. A good example of this phenomenon can be found in two narratives by undergraduate students in a Brazilian University. In that university, prospective candidates for the position of English teacher are expected to have a basic level proficiency on the assumption that they have already studied English at high school. On the other hand, as Spanish is usually not part of every high school curriculum, students have the chance to attend classes for beginners and at the same time prepare themselves to be teachers of Spanish. Despite already having a basic level of proficiency, some students enrolled in the English Program feel challenged by its requirements and find themselves at the edge of chaos where new behaviours emerge. Some of them take risks in their search for language development and achieve good results. But, those challenges might also lead the SLA system to stagnation, as shown in Excerpt 5.1.

Excerpt 5.1

> Well, I started learning Spanish around eleven years ago and it was in a Letters course. The truth is that, at the beginning I thought that English would be an interesting language, because, historically, it is a world-wide communication language. But in the University, I soon realized that the aim of the course was not to teach the English language, but to develop English teaching skills. Then, naturally, as I had much difficulty, I changed to Spanish. At first, I did not have the intention to study Spanish, but it turned out as an alternative. And surprisingly enough, what was an alternative became a passion. I had a significant development with support of the teachers, colleagues, and other fellows.
>
> [The original Spanish text can be found at http://www.veramenezes.com/audio17e.htm.]

We can infer from Excerpt 5.1 that this student's acquisition system became stressed and unstable. The student did not run any risks to cope with the disturbance introduced by the challenges of the English programme, and did not make the necessary adjustments to cope with the acquisition instability. As Bloom (2000) explains, '[I]f these adjustments fail to work and the system does not restabilize, the continued perturbation will propel movement toward "bifurcation" – a decision point, a critical choice, Robert Frost's "two paths" diverging in a wood.'[2] This new stage is supposed to be a phase of maximum agency, autonomy, creativity and transformation. The narrator did not take the less travelled path, he chose Spanish which, as a native speaker of Portuguese, offered him fewer obstacles. His choices show agency and autonomy. He took control of his SLA and decided to learn another language.

A live acquisition system is always in movement and never reaches equilibrium, although it undergoes periods of greater or less stability. That is the case of the counter-example in Excerpt 5.2. The system of the first learner bifurcated towards the acquisition of another language, but the learner in Excerpt 5.2 took the road 'less travelled by', and faced the difficulties along her learning path.

Excerpt 5.2

> Entering university was not simple and easy as I thought ... it took me a while to adapt. I started with the famous 'integrated skills' and I can't say I have good memories of any of them. It might appear I am a bit too critical, and I am sorry for that, but my experience started quite awfully. The problem wasn't only the teachers ... it was mainly me and my English background.
>
> ... As you can imagine, my results on these tasks were never good and I started feeling highly discouraged by the course: what was I doing at FALE if I wasn't able to speak?
>
> Finally I finished 'Oral Skills 3', and I felt relieved: I started studying literature and linguistics, which were the things I really enjoyed! My demoralization towards English vanished away and I started feeling motivated again.
>
> (The whole text is available at http://www.veramenezes.com/multi2.htm.)

In Excerpt 5.2, we have an excerpt from a multimedia narrative written by a student who had a similar experience to the one reported in Excerpt 5.1. Our narrator faced identity and learning problems. She was aware she did not belong to the new community and had to reconfigure her beliefs and build up a new identity. In addition, it was not easy for her to follow a course which demanded more oral skills than she had been used to. She did not give up though and managed to cope with 'disorder' in her SLA system. 'Disorder' is represented in her text by the noun 'demoralization' – 'a state of disorder and confusion', according to Dictionary.com. Confusion was caused by the emphasis on oral skills instead of grammar and reading and also by the consequent bad marks. Although it took her 'a while to adapt', she managed to attend the three levels of the 'integrated skills' courses. She overcame the turbulence and reached a new acquisition phase, exhibiting a new linguistic behaviour or a new attractor.

Attractors

Attractors are defined by Larsen-Freeman and Cameron (2008a: 49) as 'states, or particular modes of behaviours, that the system "prefers".' When the system moves into an 'attractor basin', it reaches a moment of stability. Learning histories told by learners from different countries reveal that grammar seems to operate as an attractor basin in a great deal of SLA experiences. Murphey *et al.* (2005: 93), for example, claim that most LLHs they examined often reported an overemphasis on grammar teaching as do the ones from Brazil, exemplified in Excerpt 5.2.

The SLA process described in Excerpt 5.2, and represented in Figure 5.1, presents different acquisition phase spaces. A phase space is also called a state phase and it 'represents the "landscape of possibilities" of a system, and, as it changes and adapts over time, the system moves through this landscape' (Larsen-Freeman and Cameron 2008a: 49). In Figure 4.1 three phase spaces are represented: high school, whose attractor was grammar and reading activities, then the three first semesters in the University with a shift to oral skills and, finally, the third phase represented by the final course years and another attractor: the use of the English language in Literature and Linguistics courses.

Figure 5.1 The trajectory of a SLA system across attractors in its acquisition phase spaces (inspired by Larsen-Freeman and Cameron 2008: 51).

Other learners will be constrained by different attractors and exhibit different dynamical behaviours as each learner will follow his or her own route.

The English acquisition system of the narrator of Excerpt 5.1, for instance, did not change nor adapt itself. Observe that I refer to the system and not to the learner. The latter is one of the elements in the acquisition system as we do not separate the learner from the other human and non-human elements that make up the acquisition system. In that case, school rules and the teacher's attitudes did not contribute to the SLA development. If the initial conditions had been different, the learner would have probably felt more motivated to act and learn English. On the other hand, the system of the narrator of Excerpt 5.2 had three moments of change and adaptation: from form to oral skills and then to literature and linguistic studies. Larsen-Freeman and Cameron (2008a: 57) explain that '[I]n a *cyclic or closed loop attractor*, the system moves periodically between different attractor states, as with the pendulum'. But the system can also be attracted to a strange attractor, as explained by Larsen-Freeman and Cameron:

> A chaotic or strange attractor is a region of state space in which the system's behaviour becomes quite wild and unstable, as even the smallest perturbation causes it to move from one state to another. In visual terms, this would look like a large attractor basin that is full of hills and valleys of different shapes and sizes around which the system moves fast and unpredictably. This kind of behaviour is called 'chaos' and the attractor is labelled a chaotic attractor. We should resist the poetic imagery of the label – 'chaos' as used here is a mathematical term to describe certain modes of behaviour that are not predictable but are also not random.
>
> (Larsen-Freeman and Cameron 2008a: 57)

I will try to make this point clear by referring again to Excerpts 5.1 and 5.2. If we focus on each of those two LLHs, we will understand that they are chaotic complex systems nested in another complex system – the school, which in turn is nested in an educational system, and so on. The SLA system described in Excerpt 5.2 followed a somewhat predictable route, but the one described in Excerpt 5.1, when disturbed, moved to a chaotic attractor inside the school system. In other words, the requirements of the English programme caused a butterfly effect and the student was, unexpectedly, attracted by the Spanish programme basin. This is a story of failure in terms of the acquisition of English, but a story of success if we take Spanish acquisition into account.

Several kinds of strange attractors can change the route of SLA systems leading the learners towards the path to success. One common strange attractor is travelling to English-speaking countries. Several examples of successful experiences can be found in our corpus and also in the Applied Linguistics literature. In some stories, the learners undergo painful experiences. See, for instance, the story of a Hong Kong student and her experience in England, in Chik and Benson (2008), and also the experiences abroad lived by MM and CS, in Block (2002). Chik and Benson (2008) tell the story of a student who wanted to become a *native speaker* and the impact of her experiences abroad on her identity as Hong Kong student. In spite of facing discrimination and racism and not becoming a *native* speaker, she got the fluency she needed. Block (2002) also describes the turbulent experiences lived by MM and CS and shows how their identities were destabilized. In spite of that, he concludes that border crossings have been positive experiences for those students.

Joining specific communities where English is spoken is another example of a strange attractor. Murray (2008), for instance, tells the story of a Japanese student, Yuichi, who 'got a job at an international hotel in Tokyo where he worked for six years' in order to improve his English. Menezes (2008) provides an example of a Brazilian student who started practising *capoeira*, an African-Brazilian fight-dance and martial art, and had a chance to meet foreigners and speak in English. This learner said it was the first time he felt that he could communicate with native speakers in the target language. All these examples show us the relevance of several identities – traveller, hotel worker, sportsperson, and so on – which allow the SLA system to develop. It is interesting to observe that those learning experiences happened in settings beyond the classroom. As Benson (2011b: 13) points out, those settings are not simple locations, 'but also a particular set of circumstances within a location that offer affordances for and constraints on possibilities for language learning'.

We can find in our corpus examples of unexpected changes which were not under the students' control (the student has to move to an English-speaking country; the student starts working in a place which affords them contact with English speakers), but contributed to lead their SLA system towards the edge of chaos. Nevertheless, there is also enough evidence for me to say that autonomous learners are more aware of linguistic affordances which they do control to improve their SLA. Empowered by autonomy and agency, learners are powerful agents who lead their SLA systems to the edge of chaos, despite some obstacles such as teachers' pedagogical choices, lack of opportunities to use the language and also lack of collaboration by more proficient peers in the classroom. Some narrators register in their LLHs complaints against classmates who refuse to help them, usually the ones from the 'privileged group'. Those stories tell us that the classroom is not the idealized 'collaborative paradise' teachers dream of, but an arena where some students must struggle to protect their needs and their identities against the impositions of their teachers and partners and sometimes, against the co-adaptive patterns created in the classroom. In spite of that, whole new behaviours can emerge when they reach their edge of chaos.

Conclusion

It is my contention that in the same way men have always strived to explain the origin of the universe, offering us different myths, so do SLA researchers strive to understand how languages are learned, offering us different theories and metaphors by way of explanation. I am aware that Chaos Theory is one more metaphor for SLA, but one that I hope will enable us as researchers to shed some light on the dynamic nature of language learning, particularly with regard to the individual and the important notions of identity, agency and autonomy.

The learning histories in our corpus are all unique, and yet all of them reveal a turbulent, non-linear dynamic process of transformation of order into disorder yielding the emergence of a new order, a new language. They are not identical because the elements or agents in each system are different and so are the dynamics of individual experiences.

In spite of the powerful unexpected uncontrolled changes in the individual SLA systems, most of the learning histories show that agency, identity and autonomy can move SLA chaotic systems to the edge of chaos. As we saw in LLHs (5.1) and (5.2), a learner: 'is capable of adapting itself to the sorts of new and diverse circumstances that an active agent is likely to encounter in a dynamic world' (Davis and Sumara 2006: 14). Our corpus of LLHs shows us that autonomous students always find a way to act, to overcome obstacles and to fulfil their willingness to construct their identity as a second language speaker. As we have already seen, they reach a state phase transition or edge of chaos by going abroad, by becoming members of specific communities (e.g. at work, through sports) and by engaging themselves in imagined communities (Yashima, Chapter 4, this volume) mediated by cultural productions such as music, cinema and internet communities. The very richness of affordances allows the SLA system to go through spontaneous self-organization. Waldrop says that:

> complex, self-organizing systems are adaptive, in that they don't just passively respond to events the way a rock might roll around in an earthquake. They actively try to turn whatever happens to their advantage. Thus, the human brain constantly organizes and reorganizes its billions of neural connections so as to learn from experience (sometimes, anyway). (Waldrop 1993: 11)

Successful learners are active agents who take risks, experiment and explore the environment. People trying to learn a second language unconsciously organize themselves into a linguistic ecological environment through a myriad of individual acts of language use. Most of the time, it happens without any conscious planning through evolution.

Inspired by the initial quotation, I would like to finish this chapter by saying that chaos in the SLA process brings uneasiness, but it also allows the opportunity for individual language learners to become autonomous and aware of affordances, for creativity, for agency and for the construction of a second language speaker identity.

Acknowledgements

I am grateful to my research group colleagues Junia Braga, Liliane Sade, Rita Augusto, Valdir Silva and Valeska de Souza for their insightful comments on this text, and to Alice Chik for the tips on the Pangu Chinese Myth. I would also like to thank the editors for their good suggestions.

Notes

1. The phrase 'edge of chaos', according to Waldrop (2003: 230), was coined by Langton who also used the expressions 'transition to chaos', the 'boundary of chaos' and the 'onset of chaos'.
2. Robert Frost's poem *The Road Not Taken* is well known worldwide, mainly because of its final verses: 'Two roads diverged in a yellow wood, and I/I took the one less traveled by/And that has made all the difference'. For Brazilians, learning Spanish is easier than learning English because Portuguese and Spanish are very similar languages. Learning Spanish can be compared to a road which offers fewer obstacles to the learner. For some students, learning English might be compared to travelling along a less travelled road, full of obstacles.

6 Drifting in and out of view: autonomy and the social individual

Phil Benson

Introduction

For many socially oriented researchers, autonomy is synonymous with individualism and not a transparently social concept at all. Researchers in the field of autonomy, meanwhile, emphasize that autonomy involves interdependence and insist that the development of autonomy is consistent with, and should be part of, any socially oriented approach to language education. Over the course of its history, however, autonomy has enjoyed a somewhat difficult relationship with the individual and the social, which is described here through a metaphor of the individual 'drifting in and out of view'.

The argument of this chapter is that autonomy, and Applied Linguistics more generally, is legitimately concerned with the development of individuals, but this concern needs to be underpinned by a well-grounded view of the autonomous individual as a social being. After a brief discussion of the history of the individual in research on autonomy, I will develop this argument in two ways: first, by drawing on research in educational philosophy that has addressed the charge that autonomy is an individualist construct, and, second, by revisiting an earlier study that developed a view of autonomy as a 'sociocultural process', from the perspective of what it has to say about autonomy and the social individual (Benson *et al.* 2003).

Autonomy and individualization

The idea of learner autonomy entered Applied Linguistics in the 1970s as part of a broad shift of focus away from language and towards the individual learner. This shift was manifested in the rise of terms using the prefix 'self-', including 'self-access', 'self-directed learning', 'self-instruction' and 'self-assessment', and learner-centred concepts such as individual difference, motivation, learning styles, strategies and preferences, and learner training.

Learner-centredness 'grew out of the recognition that language learners are diverse' (Wenden 2002: 32), which in turn grew out of the rapid growth of language teaching from the early 1960s on. The rise in the number of individuals engaged in language learning led to greater diversity in learners' social and cultural backgrounds and in the settings, contexts and purposes for their learning. This diversity problematized 'one-size-fits-all' language teaching methods and drew the hitherto 'invisible learner' out of the shadows of research and practice (Benson 2005).

In many ways, however, learner-centred research and practice fell short of a true focus on the individual. In research, individual attributes became group attributes through experiments and statistical surveys that turned individual learners into the theoretical abstraction of 'the learner'. In practice, differential treatments were prescribed according to group characteristics rather than individual needs. In research based on the Gardner and Lambert (1972) 'instrumental-integrative' motivation paradigm, for example, individual students might answer a series of questionnaire items in quite different ways. Statistical methods would then be used to place these individuals into instrumental and integrative groups. A sample in which the majority exhibited instrumental orientation might then be described as instrumentally oriented and teaching methods would be applied on the premise that every individual in the group was instrumentally oriented.

Individual characteristics were reduced to group characteristics in the movement from research to practice, partly because of the need to identify methods that would work with classroom groups. On the other hand, early work on learner autonomy by-passed whole class teaching in order to develop pedagogical structures that would respond to individual diversity. Introducing one of the foundational documents in the field, Holec (1981: 1) observed that learner autonomy matched a view of social progress that stressed 'respect for the individual in society', while self-directed learning insisted on the need to 'develop the individual's freedom by developing those abilities which will enable him to act more responsibly in running the affairs of the society in which he lives'. Accounts of early experiments in autonomy show that innovations such as the self-access centre, learning contracts and counselling were designed to support individual choice and decision-making, while classroom-based experiments eschewed whole class teaching, so that individuals or small groups could make or follow their own plans (Riley 1985; Holec 1988; Dam 1995).

Early experiments in learner autonomy were thus based on a strong conception of the individual learner, which was reinforced by depictions of autonomous learners as self-confident, independent-minded and, very often, male. The relationship between autonomy and individualization was also codified in the title of Brookes and Grundy's (1988: 1) collection of papers, in which the editors suggested that within the framework of learner-centredness, 'individualization will assume greater importance, as will the recognition of the autonomy of the learner as the ultimate goal'. There were objections, however, to the association of 'individualization' with 'programmed learning', in which students were expected to work their way through pre-prepared learning materials, individually and at their own pace. The objection was not to individualization as such, however, but more to the fact that programmed learning and self-instruction discouraged the expression of individuality. At the same time, it became apparent that autonomy must mean more than treating learners as individuals. If individualized pedagogical approaches discouraged the development of learner autonomy, individualization and autonomy could not be one and the same thing.

A second concern lay in the specification of learner autonomy as a pedagogical goal. Holec's (1981: 1) definition of learner autonomy as a capacity to take charge of one's learning is widely accepted, but in an often cited passage, Dickinson (1987: 11) defined it as 'the situation in which the learner is totally responsible for all of the decisions concerned with his learning' and 'entirely independent of teachers, institutions or specially prepared materials'. Although Dickinson probably did not intend to imply that this was an ideal learning situation, his definition raised fundamental questions about the meaning of learner autonomy. If language learning is essentially a social achievement, what purpose is served by a construct that appears to idealize a capacity to learn languages in isolation from others?

Classroom autonomy

This question was directly addressed in work on classroom autonomy in the 1990s, which was strongly influenced by views of the language classroom as a 'social context' in which new teacher-student relationships were possible (Breen and Candlin 1980; Breen 1986; Dam 1995). The most important theoretical outcome of this work was the insight that learner autonomy implies interdependence within normative social frameworks. Little (1996: 211), especially, pointed to the role of interdependence in the development of autonomy as a psychological capacity, by arguing that 'the development of a capacity for reflection and analysis, central to the development of learner autonomy, depends on the development and internalization of a capacity to participate fully and critically in social interactions'.

The practical implications of this relationship between autonomy and interdependence have been construed in several ways. Little (1996) emphasized the importance of interaction among students and teachers in the target language. The idea of interdependence also informed experiments in classroom decision-making and curriculum negotiation (Voller 1997; Breen and Littlejohn 2000). Lastly, it is present in the idea that learner autonomy is dependent on teacher autonomy, or teachers' capacity to exercise professional discretion and create spaces for the exercise of learner autonomy in the classroom (Benson and Huang 2008). For Little (1995: 175), 'since learning arises from interaction and interaction is characterized by interdependence, the development of autonomy in learners presupposes the development of autonomy in teachers'. In much of the work on classroom autonomy, therefore, there is a sense of learner autonomy emerging out of collaborative processes involving both learners and teachers. At the same time, there is a tendency to focus on teaching, rather than learning, and to think from the teacher's perspective (Benson 2008). Commenting on a recent collection of papers on autonomy, Auerbach (2007: 84) observes that for many of the authors 'the source of the learner autonomy project is actually the educator, not the learner'. As the idea of classroom autonomy has gained ground, individual learners have also tended to drift out of view, often to be replaced by the abstract, non-autonomous learner, who is typically viewed as a problem in need of solutions.

The return of the individual

While ideas associated with classroom autonomy have tended to dominate the field in recent years, alternative approaches to out-of-class learning have continued to proliferate. For some researchers, these approaches are problematic because their focus on the individuals conflicts with assumptions about autonomy and interdependence. Little (2000: 28), for example, suggests that, because 'all human learning has its roots in social interaction, the requirement of many self-access, open and distance learning schemes that learners work on their own poses a fundamental problem that is all too rarely acknowledged, far less grappled with at a theoretical level'. Learners are seldom entirely isolated from others in out-of-class language learning, however, and the more successful self-access and distance schemes have also developed ways of facilitating social interaction and collaboration. The important theoretical issue, therefore, appears to concern the meaning of working 'on one's own' or 'with others'. Classroom approaches to autonomy have, in a sense, naturalized the classroom as the prime site for sociality in language learning. Yet out-of-class researchers are also beginning to pose questions about the kinds of social interaction that are really important to language learning and whether they are incompatible with pedagogical approaches that encourage learners to follow individualized pathways (Benson 2011b).

The individual has also begun to drift back into view in recent years through interest in investigating individual language learning histories as an alternative to studies of the impact of pedagogical interventions. These studies have shown how learner autonomy develops over relatively long periods of time, across settings and contexts, and often in tandem with individuality and personal autonomy. Benson *et al.*'s (2003) study of the lifelong English language learning experiences of two of its authors, discussed later in this chapter, was an early foray into this area. Related studies have since been published in collections by Benson and Nunan (2002 and 2005), Kalaja *et al.* (2008) and Lamb and Reinders (2007). While learner history research has not transformed the pedagogies associated with autonomy, it has encouraged sensitivity to individual purposes and motivations for language learning. Learning histories have also been used as pedagogical tools in, for example, the Autonomous Language Modules at the University of Helsinki, Finland (Kjisik 2007) and in informal education for older language learners at Akita University, Japan (Murray 2009). Research on autonomy has also begun to align itself with other socially oriented approaches to Applied Linguistics in a more general preference for qualitative methods. A point of interest here is, perhaps, the way in which research methods often work as focusing devices in regard to the social and the individual. While quantitative methods tend to blur or erase individuality, qualitative methods tend to bring the individual sharply into focus. Simply, while quantitative methods tend to represent the social in terms of broad, and often impersonal, forces, qualitative methods tend to represent it more as the outcome of fine-grained interactions among individuals.

One other important sense in which the individual refuses to disappear from the scene of autonomy in language learning lies in the theoretical proposition that autonomy implies divergent purposes and outcomes (Ribé 2003). It is ultimately difficult to reconcile autonomy with classroom processes that direct students to all learn the same things in more or less the same ways. Consequently, classroom autonomy is now again associated with individualized, or 'differentiated' learning (Lamb 2003). Recent definitions of learner autonomy also tend to retain something of the individual even when they are couched in social terms. The EuroPAL research group, for example, defines learner autonomy as 'the competence to develop as a self-determined, socially responsible and critically aware participant in (and beyond) educational environments, within a vision of education as (inter) personal empowerment and social transformation' (Jiménez Raya *et al.* 2007: 1). The authors of this definition explain that 'socially responsible', '(inter)personal empowerment', and 'social transformation' signal a view of autonomy as 'a collective interest oriented by democratic and emancipatory ideals', while 'self-determined' signals that autonomy also has an 'individual dimension' (p. 2). Macaro (2008: 60) also reasserts the importance of the individual within a broadly social view, arguing that 'autonomy resides in being able to say what you want to say rather than producing the language of others'. For Macaro, although 'there is no getting away from the fact that individual choice is constrained by society and its institutions', in the case of schools one measure of success 'might be the degree to which it is able to assign choice to its individuals'.

The individual in the philosophy of autonomy

Personal autonomy and its critics

The ambivalent status of the individual in autonomy in language learning is also mirrored in discussion of the legitimacy of personal autonomy as an educational goal. In response to critiques of the 'individualism' of liberal views, the defenders of autonomy have sought to conceptualize the autonomous individual in social terms. In brief, modern liberal philosophers argue that a 'good' life implies some degree of personal autonomy, which entails the absence of oppressive social constraints, the development of mental, emotional and social capacities, and access to the material and social resources that individuals need in order to 'author' their lives (Raz 1986; Young 1986). Autonomy becomes a matter for education, because, unlike the agency that lies in our capacity 'to have acted otherwise' (Giddens 1976: 11), autonomy implies a higher order, *learned* capacity for self-determination. A society that values personal autonomy should, therefore, provide educational conditions in which individuals can learn to be autonomous. Because many liberals hold that individual freedom is legitimately curtailed by considerations of paternalism, however, education for personal autonomy does not necessarily entail *learner* autonomy and, in practice, learner autonomy is often severely curtailed by paternalistic, 'teacher-knows-best' assumptions. To subscribe to the idea of learner autonomy is, therefore, to adopt the relatively strong view that autonomy must be exercised in order to develop in educational contexts (Lindley 1986; Benson 2008).

Critiques of the liberal view of autonomy typically deploy one or more of the following arguments.

1. Autonomy assumes an innate individual self and fails to recognize that the self only exists as a product of socialization.

2. Autonomy overvalues individual rights and undervalues community, interdependence and care.
3. Autonomy idealizes rational self-control and fails to value emotional attachments and unconditional commitments.

Writing from a feminist educational perspective, Stone (1990: 279) has argued that autonomy is a masculine ideal that values individualism, reflectiveness, reasoning, emotional control and detachment from emotional commitment. From a communitarian perspective, Cuypers (1992: 15) emphasizes values of care over autonomy, arguing that 'we want our children to become devoted and sociable instead of detached observers or cool manipulators'. From a Foucauldian perspective, Olssen (2005: 378) argues that, 'if we are autonomous we are not interdependent'. Put together, these arguments amount to a critique of what Christman (2004: 143) calls 'the alleged hyper-individualism' of the philosophy of autonomy. The problem that the defence of autonomy faces, then, is to mount a substantive argument that autonomy *presupposes* interdependence. One solution to this problem has been found in the idea of 'relational autonomy'.

Relational autonomy

The idea of 'relational autonomy' (Mackenzie and Stoljar 2000) emerged from concerns that, by rejecting autonomy as a 'masculine' individualist value, feminists risked throwing out the baby with the bathwater. The potential trap in a purely social view of the individual lay in the feminist objection to the defining of women in terms of their relations to others: as someone's wife, daughter or mother. Nedelsky (1989: 7) thus objected to 'the individualism characteristic of liberalism', but argued that feminists must nevertheless 'retain the value' of autonomy. Feminism's equivocal stance towards autonomy, she suggested, reflected the difficulty of building a theory 'that adequately reflects both the social and the individual nature of human beings' (p. 8). Relational autonomy responded to this problem through a conception of the individual as 'a free, self-governing agent who is also socially constituted and who possibly defines her basic value commitments in terms of interpersonal relations and mutual dependencies' (Christman 2004: 143).

In view of the intensely social character of language learning and use, relational autonomy may well be what we aim for in Applied Linguistics (Aoki 1999; Jiménez Raya 2008; Zembylas and Lamb 2008). For Christman (2004: 145), however, a conception of autonomy in which certain social relations were *essentially* part of the person would deny 'the reality of change over time, variability in self-conception, and multiplicities of identity characteristic of modern populations'. If, on the other hand, relational autonomy implies no more than the general presence of social relations, it does not seem to differ greatly from existing liberal views of personal autonomy. Raz (1986: 83), however, whose work falls squarely within modern liberalism, appears already to adopt a relational position, when he argues that autonomy 'is not the natural state that individuals are in when left to exercise free choice', but 'is socially defined in that the goals, preferences, and values of individuals, in sum the meanings of individual activities, are derived from the shared social matrix'.

Relational views of autonomy also explain with difficulty how socially constituted individuals are capable of authoring their own lives. By most accounts, autonomy is socially constrained both concurrently and historically. A language learner's autonomy is concurrently constrained, for example, when she wishes to practise by chatting to native speakers of a language, but is unable to gain access to them. She may also be historically constrained by previous experiences of socialization that have been internalized as deeply rooted aspects of identity, such as gender, ethnicity, social position or psychological disposition. Philosophically, the problem of concurrent constraints can readily be disposed of by the argument that autonomy is not a matter of free agency, but of authoring one's life within prevailing constraints. The language learner in this example will display autonomy, not by insisting on practising with unavailable native speakers, but by finding another solution to the problem of practice.

The problem of historical constraints is less easily disposed of, because it relates to the substance of the self. In this example, the learner may, as a result of the historical constitution of her self, see herself a person who is incapable of solving the problem of practice. The problem of self-determination then becomes one of understanding how this historically constituted self can somehow transcend the historical constraints under which it has been constituted. How, in other words, can this language learner, who sees herself as a person who is incapable of solving the problem of practice, become a person who sees herself as being capable of doing so? The stronger social view would be that she cannot: our lives are never truly self-determined. But a concept of socially constituted agency that allows no scope for self-determination would seem to lack substance as agency. What we need, therefore, is a way of understanding how the individual self can be both historically conditioned and self-determining at the same time. Recent contributions to the debate on educational autonomy have worked on this problem through three concepts: 'authenticity' (Bonnett and Cuypers 2003), 'flexible control' (Aviram and Yonah 2004) and 'coherence' (Morgan 1996).

Alternatives to relational autonomy

Although the Applied Linguistics literature on autonomy seldom dwells on philosophical issues concerned with autonomy, the notions of authenticity, flexible control and coherence are of interest here, because they can help us to avoid oversimplifying the dichotomy between 'independence' and 'interdependence'. The work outlined below comes from the field of educational philosophy and some of its pedagogical implications are discussed at the end of this section. The following section attempts to put the three constructs into an Applied Linguistics context.

Bonnett and Cuypers (2003) use the term 'authenticity' in the existentialist sense of being true to a self that is already constituted in terms of 'authentic concerns', or purposes, preferences and other characteristics that individuals 'cannot help having' (Frankfurt 1999: 138). Authentic concerns, they argue, give us a 'unique stance on the world' and constitute 'who we are as individuals'. From this perspective the historically conditioned self is the starting point for autonomy, and individuals self-determine their lives by acknowledging their authentic concerns and accepting responsibility for their expression. The important point about this view is that it frees autonomy from the assumption of a rational, innate individual self, and replaces it with a pre-constituted self whose authentic concerns include emotional attachments and relations of care. Similarly, self-determination does not necessarily imply rational reflection on irrational authentic concerns, but only that the individual is aware of and takes responsibility for the self that is constituted by these concerns.

The implication in Bonnett and Cuypers' (2003) view that autonomous individuals simply take responsibility for who they are and act accordingly is problematic, however, because it leaves little space for renegotiation of the attachments and relations that form part of our authentic concerns. Addressing this problem through the notion of 'flexible control', Aviram and Yonah (2004: 7) adopt a philosophical view of the autonomous individual as one who discovers his or her wants, talents and potentialities through 'experiments in living', or encounters with life that provide opportunities for self-examination. The problem they identify in this view, however, is that experiments in living necessarily involve throwing oneself into states of 'unconditional commitment' or 'self-forgetting' that preclude self-examination. They thus propose a model of autonomy based on the capacity to exercise 'flexible control' according to the time and circumstances. For Aviram and Yonah, autonomy does not require active control before, during or after states that preclude self-examination, but only that 'the autonomous person will retain *in principle* the capacity to criticize each commitment or state of self-forgetting she enters' (p. 9). In an earlier paper, Aviram (1995: 65) argues that this 'control in principle' requires the individual to be in control only when there are *prima facie* good reasons for re-evaluation. He also makes the point that 'experiments in living' actually require 'whole-hearted involvement with life's various situations and hence a certain suspension of reflection' (p. 69).

Morgan (1996: 249) argues, similarly, that autonomy does not imply 'extreme individualism or independence', but merely that one's relations with others are 'matters for self-reflection'. He also suggests that, in as much as self-reflection is directed towards the disparate elements of the self, 'personal autonomy is essentially a matter of coherence among all the aspects of one's identity' (p. 239). This is an important point, because social critiques of autonomy often appear to assume that the social constitution of the individual self somehow guarantees its coherence. Morgan's view, however, addresses the multiplicity of identities that Christman (2004) finds problematic for relational views of autonomy. From this perspective, autonomy lies in the reflective sense of coherence that people make of their multiple, fragmented and shifting identities. This conception of individual autonomy, Christman argues, also requires a social conception of the individual. Insofar as the self is socially constituted, he argues, 'one cannot be autonomous relative to those social elements unless one exists in environments that allow their full manifestation' (p. 146).

Bonnett and Cuypers (2003: 339), for example, argue for a pedagogy of authenticity that focuses 'on the *engagement* of the learners with whatever seriously occupies them', which resonates with the idea of divergent purposes and outcomes and Macaro's (2008: 60) view of autonomy as 'being able to say what you want to say rather than producing the language of others'. The idea of flexible control creates space for conceptions of learner autonomy in which individuals might, for example, commit themselves to a taught language course or a strong attachment to a particular teacher, while maintaining a self-reflective stance of 'control in principle'. The idea of autonomy as the ongoing achievement of coherence also seems highly relevant to pedagogical approaches that focus on self-awareness, metacognitive approaches and the learners' language identities. In the following section, I want to explore these connections between philosophical conceptions of individual autonomy and language learning, by revisiting a study that attempted to reconcile the idea of autonomy as a sociocultural process with ideas of individuality, agency and identity.

Autonomy as a sociocultural process revisited

Benson *et al.* (2003) was written as an experimental paper built around the English language learning histories of my two co-authors. In brief, Chik's story began in Hong Kong, where her parents encouraged her to learn and use English before she went to school. She studied English at primary school and then at an English-medium secondary school, where she became one of a small group who studied English literature. Chik attributed her high levels of proficiency in English to her family and to a decision as a teenager to read and write more or less exclusively in English, which arose from her desire to create a private intellectual space within her family. Chik studied Business Administration at a university in the United States, where she also worked for a period in a finance company after graduation. At the time the paper was written, she had been working as an English teacher in Hong Kong for eight years and was enrolled on a PhD programme in Applied Linguistics at a local university.

Lim's story began at around age ten, before she began English lessons at middle school, with a memory of seeing an English television programme and feeling a strong urge to know what the characters were talking about and to use their words. In school, where lessons were dominated by memorization, she lost some of her enthusiasm for English, finally retaining it only by 'partitioning' the goals of meeting school and examination requirements and her own goal of communication with English-speaking people. Lim studied English at a Korean university and at the same time took lessons with native speakers of English at a private institute. After graduation, she took a short trip to Australia, which convinced her that she needed to spend more time overseas in order to achieve her goal. At the time the paper was written, Lim was a PhD candidate in Foreign Language Education at a US university.

In the paper, Chik and Lim's learning histories were framed within a debate on the appropriateness of western educational methods in Asian contexts, which had come to rest on the 'individualism' of learner autonomy (Smith 2001). The problem with this debate, we argued, was that, once they are characterized as members of 'collectivist' cultures, Asian students are viewed as 'products' of their family and educational backgrounds in a way that members of 'individualist' cultures are not. Citing Ram (2002: 36), we also noted how 'quests for individual autonomy' in Asian settings are easily redefined as atypical instances of 'Westernization'. The aim of the paper, therefore, was to illuminate the sense in which individual autonomy may be a crucial aspect of 'the second language learning as a sociocultural process for many Asian learners' (p. 24). Issues of individual autonomy appeared in Chik and Lim's stories in two main ways. First, they represented themselves as individuals who 'actively engage in constructing the terms and conditions of their own learning' (Lantolf and Pavlenko 2001: 145) at a number of levels, but most notably in their decisions to move from the contexts of their home cultures to new contexts for English language learning and use in the United States. Second, they also represented themselves as people who had become 'more individual' as a consequence of their language learning careers. This aspect of the paper was succinctly expressed in the words that Chik chose to use as an epigraph to her story: 'On a personal level, as a language learner, learning English was more than merely learning a language. It was my own journey to construct individuality' (Benson *et al.* 2003: 25).

While the paper succeeded in bringing out these aspects of individual autonomy, however, it was less successful in illuminating the sense in which Chik and Lim's journeys towards autonomy represented a sociocultural process. It is for this reason that I want to revisit the paper here, by exploring how their stories might be re-interpreted in terms of authentic concerns, flexible control and coherence.

Authentic concerns

The notion of authentic concerns seems especially relevant here as both Chik and Lim described strong early motivations that were retrospectively construed as having significance for their language learning histories as a whole. Chik described how, as a result of her parents' efforts, she was already watching Sesame Street, reading Dr Seuss books and meeting her father's English-speaking business associate before she went to school. This created a 'favourable impression that English is a communicative tool to express oneself', she noted, which 'built the foundation for growth later on' (pp. 31–2). In her teenage years, through her diary and reading of English literature, 'the idea of language being a communicative tool became a more complex idea of creating a whole intellectual world'. The source of Lim's early motivation was also embedded within an anecdote about an English television programme, viewed in the family setting, through which 'the spark of curiosity was lit', leading to a strong and long-lasting desire to talk with others in English (p. 26). English had, in other words, become a part of Chik and Lim's authentic concerns from an early age as they developed strong emotional attachments to the language that were clearly constituted within social relations of interdependence and care. Recalling Bonnett and Cuypers' (2003: 331) comment that autonomy is essentially a matter of taking responsibility for one's authentic concerns, autonomy appears in Chik and Lim's stories more as a capacity to express these authentic concerns within ever-widening social contexts, than as a capacity for rational reflection and decision-making.

Flexible control

Chik and Lim's stories also pose problems for a view of autonomy as 'taking charge of one's own learning' (Holec 1981: 1), because they show quite clearly that autonomous learners are never entirely in control of their language learning. Both adapted to circumstances and pursued opportunities as they arose, without ever being fully in control. The idea of flexible control is helpful, therefore, as a tool to understand how control may be distributed across situations and events. There are numerous examples of this in the two stories and here I will focus on two episodes described by Lim. The first concerns the idea of 'partitioning' learning goals, which Lim uses to describe her response to the traditional teaching methods used in her secondary school English classes:

> I had no control over the Korean educational system with its emphasis on accuracy, grammar and memorization. Only as I rejected these emphases and constructed my own rule was I able to learn and enjoy the experience of learning English.
>
> (Benson *et al.* 2003: 35)

Having no control over the system itself, Lim created a psychological space in which she could, at least, retain control of her own conceptions of what learning English meant to her. At the same time, she worked hard within the system in order to get the grades that would allow her to pursue her own goals later in life. 'I wonder if I would have been so persistent', she wrote, 'had I not been able to separate good grades from learning English' (p. 27). The second episode relates to her decision to enrol in a private English language institute during her early years at university. The period as a whole was one in which she enjoyed English and tried out new things such as writing as a campus reporter, reading books and magazines, listening to pop music and watching TV. She considered her lessons at the private institute to be an experience of self-instruction, because she 'was the one who chose the institute' and because she could have stopped at any time she wished' (p. 28).

These two examples suggest that autonomous language learners often find themselves, or willingly place themselves, in situations where they have little direct control over their learning. What matters, however, is that they adopt a reflective stance that allows them to immerse themselves in these situations, while maintaining the 'control-in-principle' that will allow them to take control if there is good reason to do so. In the first example, Lim could not withdraw from secondary school English lessons. She could only immerse herself in the proximal goal of gaining good English grades while waiting for graduation. In the second example, Lim paid for lessons at a private institute because it offered her an opportunity to speak English with native speakers, but in the end she was frustrated because, like Korean schools, the teaching methods emphasized perfect pronunciation and grammar. Again, she immersed herself in the experience for a time, but eventually exercised her control-in-principle by giving up the lessons.

Coherence

Lastly, Chik and Lim both refer explicitly to the idea of autonomy as establishing coherence. Lim explained that, for her, language learning involves 'the creation of a new identity which bridges both the native language and target language cultures', but the sociolinguistic demands of the two cultures 'may clash and learners may be confronted with chaos' (p. 35). 'Since the new identities will be somewhat alienated from the old ones', she argued, 'learners may have to become more autonomous as they seek ways to reconcile dissonances' (p. 36). Chik put this somewhat differently, suggesting that one's cultural background provides a pool of resources to start out on a language learning journey and that 'closer involvement with the target language culture opens up more cultural resources for learners to formulate their own expression'. For Chik, this requires 'a certain degree of individuality, flexibility and openness to cultural differences'. Individual autonomy, she argues, 'involves a capacity to mobilize and merge different cultural resources to create a learner's individual identity' (p. 38). *Individual* autonomy is implicated here, it seems, for two reasons. First, in contrast to first language identities, which are typically constructed within well-established social networks of interdependence and care, much of the work of constructing second language identities falls upon the learners themselves. Second, the cultural resources that second language learners draw on are embedded in uniquely individual experiences of each individual and include, as Lim puts it, both first language resources acquired at home and resources 'rooted in the language and the culture they are acquiring' (p. 37).

Conclusion

I was recently a member of a panel in the closing session of a conference on autonomy, which was asked to identify future directions for research. One speaker mentioned a need for more research on autonomy in communities. Partly in response to this, I commented that there was, perhaps, too much research on classroom teaching in the field and that I would like to see more research focusing on individuals learning languages. The next speaker said that he agreed on the focus on learning, but not with the focus on individuals, because language learning always presupposed social interaction in communities. There is, then, no apparent consensus among researchers on the role of the individual in research on autonomy. The view developed in this chapter is an idiosyncratic view, and not that of the field as a whole, which largely retains the ambivalence towards the individual discussed earlier in this chapter.

By looking at views of the autonomous individual in the field of educational philosophy and applying them to a re-interpretation of previous work, however, I hope to open up certain areas of discussion that appear to have been closed to debate. Typically, we have tended to look at the individual and the social in autonomy as if it were a matter of the individual *or* the social. In retrospect, therefore, I could wish for the presence of mind to respond to the conference panel question by saying not 'individuals learning languages', but 'individuals learning languages in communities'. By this, I mean that autonomy in language learning legitimately foregrounds the individual dimension of language learning and the importance of individuals learning languages for their own purposes, with diverse outcomes. If this focus were to be lost, there would be little purpose in retaining the term autonomy. At the same time, we need to find ways of situating research on individual learners in its social contexts that neither treat the social context as background nor erase the individuality of the learners within assumptions of social and cultural conditioning.

In the context of this aim, a comment by David Little, who has done more than most to push research and practice on autonomy in language learning in a more social direction (see Lantolf, Chapter 2, this volume), seems particularly relevant:

> Relative to schooling in general, the autonomous learner is the one whose learning gradually enlarges his or her sense of identity; relative to second language learning in particular, the autonomous learner is the one for whom the target language gradually becomes an integral part of what he or she is. (Little 1996: 210)

This comment articulates a thoroughly *social* conception of the autonomous language learner. Yet at the same time, it clearly points to a conception of the autonomous language learner as a social *individual*, who is 'what he or she is', that deserves our attention.

7 A social-ecological exploration of autonomy, beliefs and identity

Jane Kehrwald

Introduction

Situated within the broad domain of Sociocultural Theory, this chapter examines the social and discursive construction of learner autonomy, beliefs and identity in second language learning. The research presented here represents an attempt at 'widening the investigative lens' (Benson and Cooker, Chapter 1, this volume) to understand the individual's language learning experience by simultaneously focusing on the social, cultural and historical contexts in which the learner participates. The project was aimed at developing learner autonomy within a specific language learning context, through the self-exploration of the learners' beliefs. The participants of the project were second language learners at a New Zealand tertiary institution who were enrolled in a compulsory English for Academic Purposes programme as a component of their Bachelor of International Studies. Learners created a series of visual representations of their beliefs and experiences as language learners, including their language learning history, their goals and motivations and their conceptions of their roles as language learners. After a presentation of the relevant theoretical concepts which underpinned the project, the results as they pertain to one of the participants in the project, Mayu, are presented and discussed. The results not only provide some insights into Mayu's own representations of her beliefs (her identity) and autonomy as a language learner, they allow us to see the socially mediated nature of her development as a language learner with regard to these concepts. Finally, we see that it is Mayu's vision of her imagined future self which provides the impetus for her to seek out and join particular learning communities and social contexts.

The lens: autonomy, beliefs and identity

Underpinned by sociocultural perspectives of language learning, the investigative lens, as represented in Figure 7.1, allowed the researcher to explore the individual language learner in relation to the concepts of autonomy, beliefs and identity, as situated within a greater social framework (i.e. context). These key concepts were drawn from the core objective of the research project, which was to foster learner autonomy through learners' self-exploration of their beliefs. Beliefs help individuals make sense of the world around them and make sense of themselves, thus forming their identity, and play an important role in defining behaviour, including their language learning behaviour (White 1999). In adopting van Lier's (2004: 3) term 'ecology', the study of 'organisms in their relations with the environment', the complexities of the phenomenon under investigation, in this case the individual language learner, can be observed.

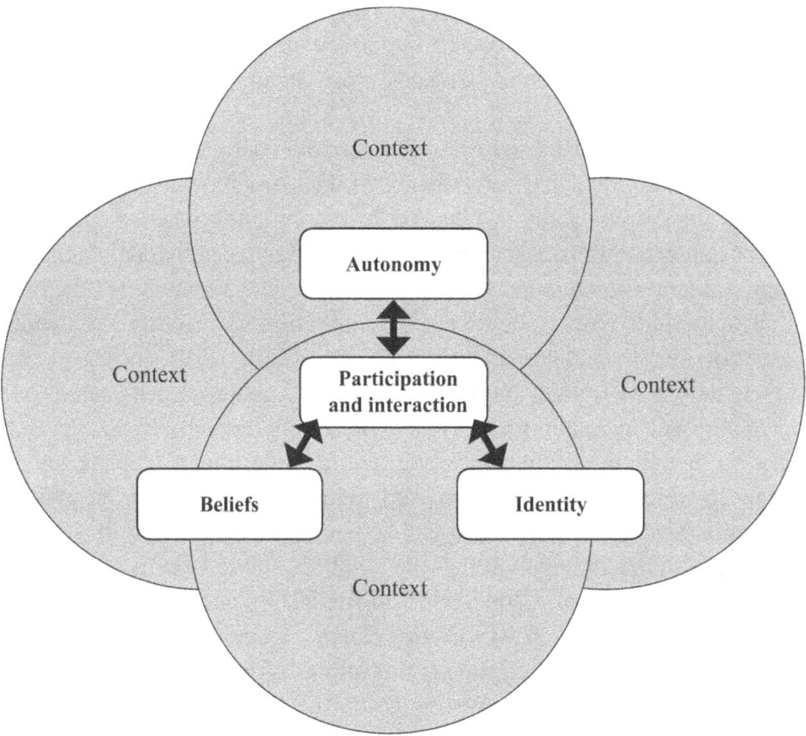

Figure 7.1 The ecology of autonomy, beliefs and identity

Sociocultural Theory 'takes into account the complex interactions between the individual acting with meditational means in the sociocultural context' (Swain and Deters 2007: 821). The concept of social mediation focuses on the tools – the physical tools such as books and technology, and socioculturally constructed symbolic artefacts, such as language – the individual is acting with. Socially situated context refers to the physical and social spaces where the action takes place, which might include 'family life and peer group interaction in institutional contexts like schooling, organised sports activities and workplaces' (Lantolf and Thorne 2007: 201).

From a sociocultural perspective, learner autonomy can be viewed as self-regulation (Oxford 2003), 'the process of planning, guiding, and monitoring one's own attention and behaviour' (Berk and Winsler 1995, as cited in Oxford 2003: 86). As represented in Figure 7.1, self-regulation develops through contextually situated and socially mediated interactions between the individual learner and more capable others, as well as interactions with physical elements, such as books and technology (Oxford 2003). Within the multitude of interconnected social settings or contexts in which an individual participates, as represented by the overlapping circles in Figure 7.1, motivation to become self-regulated intensifies as the nature of the mediated relationship becomes more meaningful to an individual (Oxford 2003).

From a more critical view of Sociocultural Theory, autonomy is not so much about individualized performance of the learner as it is about socially oriented agency (see Lantolf, Chapter 2, this volume), where cultural settings or contexts 'afford and constrain possibilities for individual and social action in them' (Toohey and Norton 2003: 59). The autonomy of the individual underpins Norton's concept of motivation as 'investment', which focuses on identity and human agency (Ushioda 2006: 155). These two conceptualizations of learner autonomy from a sociocultural perspective presented here, self-regulation and investment, are not mutually exclusive. Both focus on mediated learning; however, while 'investment' emphasizes the context in which autonomy occurs, self-regulation emphasizes the individual exercising autonomy (Oxford 2003). Learners may 'invest' in a second language with the anticipation that they will acquire a wider range of symbolic resources (language, education and friendship) and material resources (money and goods) which will in turn enhance their conceptions of themselves and further their desires for the future (Norton 2000; Toohey and Norton 2003). Learners' motivation to participate (or not participate) in social contexts to which they desire to belong (their 'imagined community', see Yashima, Chapter 4, this volume) is defined by their investment. From this perspective, social contexts are viewed as communities of practice, where participation or non-participation is mediated or constrained by existing members of the community.

Beliefs, too, are contextually situated, dynamic and socially mediated. This notion of beliefs deviates from traditional cognitivist approaches to discussing and analysing beliefs which emphasize the static or unchanging nature of mental constructs, and the 'mind as a container in which knowledge ... is memorized and stored in the form of static representations' (Dufva 2003: 131). What an individual believes or perceives is co-determined by the individual and the individual's interactions with the environment (Barab and Plucker 2002). The ecological relationship between beliefs and context is what Dewey (1938/1997, as cited in Barcelos 2003) calls the principle of interaction, which focuses on the reciprocal influence of elements within an environment. An individual's cognitive operations, of which beliefs are a part, are constructed through interaction and participation in physical and social environments, that is, through contexts, and consequently beliefs bear the mark of those contexts (Dufva 2003). Beliefs are dynamic, meaning that as an individual interacts with others and the environment, previous experiences, within current or past contexts, are drawn upon to deal with the present, and this continuous flow of input results in a constant self-reorganizing of the way an individual perceives the world (Dufva 2003). The process of giving meaning to our experiences and the connections we make between past, present and future experiences is a continuous one (Barcelos 2003).

Learning also involves the construction of identities (Lave and Wenger 1991). Identity refers to 'how a person understands his or her relationship to the world, how that relationship is constructed across time and space, and how the person understands possibilities for the future' (Norton 2000: 5). Like autonomy and beliefs, an individual's identity is conditioned or shaped by social interactions and, in turn, conditions social interactions (Block 2007b). Learning, according to Lave and Wenger (1991: 53), involves 'becoming able to be involved in new activities to perform new tasks and functions, to master new understandings' through relations among individuals within social communities or contexts and where the individuals are defined by, as well as define these relations. With the social construction of individuals' beliefs comes concurrent construction of their identity as the individuals reorganize their sense of who they are in relation to the social world (Norton 2000). As in the discussion of autonomy, above, individuals not only define themselves through the practices they engage in, but equally through what they *do not* engage in (Wenger 1998), that is, their non-participation in communities or contexts (Norton 2001).

It is with this discussion of Sociocultural Theory, as it relates to learner autonomy, beliefs and identity, as a backdrop that we move our focus to Mayu, one of the participants in the research project. This investigative lens affords us a glimpse of an individual language learner and highlights the socially mediated nature of her development as an individual language learner.

Mayu

Mayu is currently enrolled as an international student in a Bachelor of International Studies (BIS) programme at a university in New Zealand. International students enrolled in the BIS programme are required to take English for Academic Purposes (EAP) courses concurrent with their content-based courses, throughout their degree (one EAP paper per semester, over six semesters). The research took place in the EAP Level 1 course. As part of this 14-week course learners were required, through the creation of images presented in poster format, to reflect upon their learning experiences and their conceptualization of language learning through a series of Learner Development Activities (detailed in Appendix 7.1).

The images created by Mayu (and other learners in her class) essentially became a visual narrative of her language learning experience and, as such, represent her insights into her own beliefs, identity and self-regulation as a language learner. Such an approach is in line with case study methods which allow the researcher to understand 'the complex world of lived experience from the point of view of those who live it' (Schwandt 1994: 118) as well as to understand the multiple social constructions of meaning and knowledge (Mertens 2005). Through the images created by Mayu during the Learner Development Activities and subsequent interviews (one in week 7 of EAP Level 1, another in week 14 and a third at the end of EAP Level 2), the researcher and Mayu were engaged in an interactive process where meaning emerged through dialogue and negotiation (Lincoln and Guba 2003). Such an approach allowed the concepts of importance to emerge as they were constructed by the subject and not by some preconceived notions held by the researcher.

The Learner Development Activities were integrated into the EAP Level 1 course as a pedagogical response to stated outcomes of the BIS programme, which stated that upon completion of the programme students will be independent, reflective, self-directed, motivated and curious learners. In order to achieve such outcomes, it was felt that time must be dedicated to raising learners' awareness of their learning goals and objectives, resources and strategies needed to achieve goals, and of the language learning process, motivations and attitudes towards language learning (Sheerin 1997).

Given the limits of this chapter, only three of the posters will be drawn on for discussion. In her first poster, Mayu depicted her language learning journey from a junior high school student to a senior high school student in Japan with an obvious dislike for learning English. As a high school senior she travels to Denmark for a study abroad experience and depicts herself communicating with her homestay family in English and Danish. She then returns back to Japan and she presents an image of a happier looking self, where English is now 'easy!' and she has 'good pronunciation'. The final image on the poster is of Mayu studying English in New Zealand, wearing glasses and looking very studious. In the second poster, from the Learner Development Activity 6 (Appendix 7.1), Mayu presents several conceptualizations of herself as a language learner: an image of people on a journey together hiking across a 'wasteland to reach a destination', an image of a toy robot representing the repetitive nature of language learning, an image of people dressed as sheep to represent 'being part of the country' (New Zealand), and an image of a young lady relaxing in a tree reading a book because 'sometimes we need to relax and study [our] own thing'. In the final poster, Mayu presented two images of herself: one representing herself at the beginning of her Bachelor of International Studies programme and the other of herself at the end of her first year. The first image is of a baby monkey which is obviously nervous and a little frightened. The second is an image of a monkey standing upright in front of a cave with a fire burning, holding a primitive weapon. The contrasts between these two images, as can be seen in the later discussion, seem to represent Mayu's evolution as a language learner and the fire and weapon as tools she has acquired along the way.

Through the images created by Mayu, the researcher was able to gain some insight into the various contexts, past, present and future, in which Mayu has participated. These contexts (which include being a language student in Japan, an exchange student in Denmark, and an international student at a university in New Zealand) will serve as the backdrop for discussing the social-ecological nature of autonomy, beliefs and identity. The choice was made to present Mayu's voice as much as possible, to give the reader a better understanding of Mayu's emic representations of her experiences.

Autonomy

Mayu's decision to study abroad in New Zealand was initiated by a desire to communicate with others and her connection to the world as a global citizen. Her decision to place herself in an environment which she believed was conducive to achieving her language learning goals can be seen as an act of self-regulation.

> Oh because, just, I thought that now, the world is getting globalization, global. English is very useful and if I didn't English and I just speak with Japanese, but in the world there are more people ... Yeah,

> narrow. And I thought I want to know more about earth, because I am living on the earth, now … And I wanted to learn international relations, then I thought for this study I need English, because of globalization … Hopefully, I want to work in many countries. To go and report their countries, issues to Japan. (Interview 1)

Mayu's motivation to go abroad could be viewed as what Yashima (2002) has termed 'international posturing', a phrase used with particular reference to Japanese learners, and referring to a general attitudinal construct observed in learners' readiness to go overseas to study or work and an interest in developing intercultural friendships. However, Mayu's motivations can be seen as being more than simply possessing a positive attitude to an international community. Referring back to Norton Peirce's (1995) concept of 'investment', Mayu hopes to acquire symbolic resources: membership in a kiwi family and knowledge about the environment.

> Oh, just I want to use English more and I want to have a family in New Zealand … If I have a family in New Zealand I can be more New Zealand, like New Zealand, living in New Zealand. And I can have many cultures … And if I graduate [from university] and it is all finished, but if I have a family, I can visit New Zealand again, and I can think of New Zealand as like my third country. (Interview 1)

> Actually, I don't like English study and I really want to learn some subjects, like environment or IR [international relations]. (Interview 2)

However, the access to symbolic resources that Mayu hoped to acquire through this experience is, at times, constrained.

> I learned that Kiwi children are terrible. Naughty!! … So maybe, I am thinking, that I want a new family, because parents are busy to work to look after children. … It's like, my host parents are too busy to look after children, so not much time to talk to me. And food is not good. They are both working, so they are busy, so they cannot cook. (Interview 1)

Mayu would like to leave her homestay; however, for Mayu, the option of returning to the university's residential halls is not an attractive one. This type of accommodation does not offer the symbolic and material resources Mayu seeks, so she chooses not to participate in this environment. Even though she is a member of the Japanese community on campus, she chooses not to participate in that community.

> We all speak Japanese. It's like a Japanese club. So it is not good. (Interview 1)

> Because it is too much Japanese and the relationships are very complicated. And it is very noisy. I hate noisy, so, like, now I have quiet room. (Interview 2)

It appears that Mayu has acted intentionally towards achieving her goals of acquiring knowledge of the environment and international relations, working in an international context as a journalist and becoming a member of a kiwi family; though at times her participation in these 'imagined communities' is constrained.

Beliefs

As discussed earlier, an individual's beliefs are constructed through interaction and participation in physical and social environments. As an individual experiences or interacts within a physical or social environment they not only change that environment, but are also changed in the process; reciprocal influences are at force (Barcelos 2003). Mayu's beliefs about language have changed from viewing English as a dead language, as she did when she first studied English in Japan, to language as a communication tool to language as a medium through which to learn subject content, such as her environment classes.

> Then I hated to go to English class … And I didn't like class, like the way to learn English, because it was just like grammar, grammar, grammar, vocabulary, vocabulary. It is so boring. I didn't think it was learning a language … Kind of dead language. Not alive language … Yeah, so I thought I should go abroad to study English. (Interview 1)

Mayu was asked whether she felt that she is now learning 'real' language now that she is studying about the environment in New Zealand.

> Oh, I think I get more interesting study myself. Last year it was only English. And, like I feel it has no meaning, just English. Actually, I don't like English study and I really want to learn some subjects, like environment or IR. And I feel now, a little bit interested in studying. (Interview 2)

> I feel I am very happy to study. Yeah, I was excited, but I found a little bit difficulty because, um, environment class really just study environment, so I have to really understand what lecturer says. (Interview 3)

In Learner Development Activity 6 and the second interview Mayu discussed her beliefs about her role in the language learning process and that of others, such as teachers and other students. Mayu described herself as an unpolished gem and as a robot who has to wind herself up in order to be successful as a language learner.

> Like, I remember what Kanae [pseudonym] said [in her picture], which is about a stone, which has a diamond in it or something. I think it is from a movie, but I really think the same thing. And teachers, school teachers, many teachers told us that we are like stone and we can polish and we can get beautiful … So like, we have a beautiful stone inside but we have to find it. And we have to polish. Like polish means to study or improve something … Yes, I hope so. Because I already found my dreams. Something I want to do. I have goals, so I know what it is inside me. Now I am doing polishing to get the diamond. (Interview 2)

> I think the job of the teacher is to teach us the important thing and show us what we need and how to improve or something. (Interview 2)

Identity

Identity refers to how a person understands his or her relationship to the world. Through the Learner Development Activities and interviews Mayu presented multiple constructs of herself. In Learner Development Activity 6, for example, Mayu chose an image of people dressed as sheep as one metaphor to represent herself as a language learner.

> I think it means that now I am in New Zealand, sometime I have to do the same thing … same study with Kiwi students. Like, not exactly, but I have to be like a New Zealander. Like this. (Interview 2)

Asked whether she felt she was successful in becoming a New Zealander, Mayu responded:

> Not sure. But I think my English is kind of Kiwi English now. But not so sure. My English was kind of very special. Not Japanese, not American English. I think now it is more Kiwi. (Interview 2)

In the same activity Mayu also conceptualized herself as a robot and as a relaxed person, reclining in a hammock because 'I think sometime we need a rest. And … or study by myself. At a quiet place' (Interview 2). Mayu presented a conceptualization of her future, imagined self, first as a member of a Kiwi family and as a global citizen, as we saw earlier, and also in terms of her working self.

> Hopefully, I want to work in many countries. To go and report their countries' issues to Japan. (Interview 3)

These images form part of Mayu's future, imagined identity. Visions of oneself in the future may provide the motivational basis for behaviour, in this case language learning behaviour (Dörnyei 2009). Norton (2000) refers to the learner's future imagined self as being situated in 'imagined communities', that is, a bond with or identification as a member of a community or group which we have not met yet, but hope to one day. Mayu's image of her future self is often contested or constrained by herself and others. As we saw above, Mayu's vision of her future self as a member of a Kiwi family was challenged by naughty children and lack of opportunities to communicate with her homestay parents, which led her to declare: 'I want a new family' (Interview 1). When individuals view their identities as less than satisfactory they may attempt to negotiate them by modifying their self-images or changing their group membership in order to view themselves more positively (Pavlenko 2001).

Mayu's vision of her future self as a global citizen and journalist is characterized by conflict with her ought-to self (Dörnyei 2009). Mayu knows what she ought to do in order to fulfil her own expectations of her future self; however, she seems to struggle at times.

> And also, in IR class there are lots of other Asian nationality students, their English is very good. And sometimes I can't follow them, so I thought, oh, I really need to improve. (Interview 3)

> I think still, I go to class, but opinion … I don't say much opinion in the class. Um, yes. So recently, I feel like I should say something, but always I think, oh, I am going to say this one, I am going to say this one. But other students say the same thing and it's gone on too long and, oh, no time. Just I am thinking that I should say something. (Interview 3)

In the final interview Mayu brought along two images to represent herself as a learner at the beginning of Semester 1 and at the conclusion of Semester 2. Her first image was that of a baby monkey, looking very nervous and vulnerable. The second image was also of a monkey, but one which is more upright in stance and equipped with tools, fire and shelter. In discussing the changes that these two images represent, Mayu explained:

> This one is like a baby monkey. I was a little unsure. I had already decided my major and I want to study something, I want to be something. I want to be a journalist or something ... So, now it is more clear. Just IR. My goal of ... my future goal is journalist, so I have already decide the company ... I want to be a news company that has news all over Japan. (Interview 3)

When asked about the meaning of the tools, fire and shelter, Mayu explained that she felt 'like I could come out from a little bit dark place. Um, but still a little bit nervous' (Interview 3). The tool she uses as a learner is 'just my will ... And I just start walking' (Interview 3).

Discussion

Through the snippets presented here of Mayu's experiences as a language learner we can see the socially mediated construction of her beliefs and identity as a language learner, and the intrinsic connection between her participation and interaction in the social world and the development of her ability to self-regulate and have agency over her learning. Mayu's imagined future self (as a global citizen, as a member of a New Zealand family and as a journalist) was the impetus for her to place herself within particular learning communities or contexts (study abroad in Denmark and New Zealand, homestay versus on-campus accommodation and choosing to study about the environment and international relations). These contexts are a site of struggle, uncertainty and nervousness, as she moves from other-regulated towards becoming self-regulated, which can be seen particularly in the last image created by Mayu. Mayu is simultaneously excited and nervous, she wants to study international relations, but finds it difficult and often loses her confidence; she wants to belong to a family, but is unable to spend meaningful time with them. As Yashima in Chapter 4 notes, it can be difficult for second language learners to gain access to communities and gain a voice for themselves in those communities. Yet, Mayu's sense of future self acts as a guide with which to navigate through and control her learning.

The role of others also features heavily in the construction of Mayu's beliefs about the nature of language and the nature of language learning. During her early experiences in the Japanese EFL context English was a 'dead language'. Her encounter with a native speaker of English altered her conceptualization of language and had some influence on her desire to study abroad. Mayu's metaphoric conceptualization of a language learner (a diamond in the rough) and the role of the learner (to polish the gem) are also mediated by others: her classmates and her teachers. Through her participation in social and learning contexts Mayu seems to be gaining an increasing understanding of who she is as a learner and a clearer identification of her goals, her future self, leading to greater control or self-regulation of her learning behaviour.

Conclusion

The original intent of the research project presented in this chapter was to foster learner autonomy through learners' self-exploration of their beliefs about language learning. Whether this objective was achieved or not is not the focus of this chapter. Rather, it is the investigative lens, presented in Figure 7.1, through which the learner, Mayu, was examined, which has featured. Without abandoning the individual as the unit of analysis, this lens proved to be a useful mechanism with which to examine the concepts of autonomy, beliefs and identity (as they relate to Mayu) not simply as individual differences or 'componentized subpersonal parts' (Bandura 2001, as cited in Ushioda 2009: 216). This allowed us to view Mayu more holistically as a 'person-in-context' Ushioda (2009: 215).

The lens, as it is represented diagrammatically in Figure 7.1, though, does not truly reflect the tensions and conflicts at the interface between context and the elements of autonomy, beliefs and identity, which we saw through Mayu's experience. On reflection, visually, Figure 7.1 seems to show a seemingly fluid or straightforward relationship between these elements. However, as we have seen through Mayu, the development of the learner can also be constrained within social contexts, which may require the learner to negotiate or reposition him/herself within these contexts. Further: the importance of 'possible selves' emerged quite strongly out of the data and does not seem to be adequately accounted for in Figure 7.1. Possible selves act as 'future self-guides', reflecting a more dynamic conceptualization of individual motivation that can explain how someone is moved from the present towards the future within sociocultural contexts (Markus and Nurius 1986, cited in Dörnyei 2009: 11). This forward motion can be expressed as the 'trajectory of the self' (Hanson 2009: 553) that the individual gives voice to through a coherent narrative about themselves. For any one individual a 'trajectory of self' could be conceptualized as an array of paths that move through multiple social contexts, and that over time, might lengthen and widen, branch out, criss-cross or peter out (Miller and Blackman, n.d.). The posters created during the Learner Development Activities and subsequent interviews represent Mayu's own conceptualization of her learning 'trajectory of the self' from past to future: from a junior high school student studying English in Japan to studying International Relations in a tertiary context in New Zealand to one day becoming a journalist. Mayu creates a coherent narrative about herself in the posters and in comments such as: 'I wanted to learn international relations', 'I want to work in many countries', 'I want to have a family in New Zealand' and 'I can have many cultures ... And if I graduate [from university] and it is all finished, but if I have a family, I can visit New Zealand again.' It is this clear sense of imagined future selves which places Mayu on particular learning pathways and provides the motivational basis for her learning behaviour which propels her along her individual learning trajectory.

In conclusion, Benson and Cooker (Chapter 1, this volume) speak of a dialectic (or what van Lier 2002 terms 'ecology') between the individual and the social and pose the question of 'how the individual is to be conceptualized within this relationship'. It may seem overly simplistic, yet when we look at Mayu and her learning trajectory, we might respond by saying, let us conceptualize the learner as she is: a complex individual who exists in complex, multiple contexts over time and space, which can be at times sites of struggle and which she must navigate her way through.

Appendix 7.1: Learner Development Activities

Activity 1	Language learning history On the poster paper, draw a timeline to show your language learning history. Include on the timeline significant events in your learning history by drawing a picture representing these events and/or by writing a few sentences describing each of the events.
Activity 2	Goals and motivations What are your dreams, your goals and your aspirations? What do you want to do? What do you want be? What DON'T you want to do? What DON'T you want to be? On the poster paper, create a collage of images to answer these questions.
Activity 3	The language learning process Draw a diagram or flowchart (or any image you like) that shows the process of learning a second language.

Activity 4	Influences Step 1: On the poster paper, draw a picture of yourself as a language learner (that is, how do you see yourself as a language learner). Step 2: Think of the people, things or events which have influenced you in becoming the person you described in the picture. These influences can be positive or negative. You can draw a picture, attach a photo or write a few sentences to represent these influences.
Activity 5	SWOT Analysis On the poster paper, describe yourself in terms of your: Strengths – things you feel you do well Weaknesses – things you feel you don't do well Opportunities – things (including events and people) that are available to you and that will help you to achieve your goals Threats – things (including events and people) that might hinder you in achieving your goals.
Activity 6	Language students are like … Think of a metaphor to describe language students. Draw a picture or use a picture from a magazine that represents this metaphor.
Activity 7	Language teachers are like … Think of a metaphor to describe language teachers. Draw a picture or use a picture from a magazine that represents this metaphor.

8 Teenagers making sense of their foreign language practices: individual accounts indexing social discourses

Anne Pitkänen-Huhta and Tarja Nikula

Introduction

This chapter reports on an ethnographically oriented study on the ways in which Finnish teenagers make sense of their everyday practices with English: where and when they encounter it and use it, what values and meanings they attach to it, and how they see themselves as learners of it. The study looks at language learning through the individual experiences of a small number of teenagers, focusing on the diversity and sharedness of these experiences (see Benson 2005). The picture of learning that emerges in these accounts is not one of cognitive processes or of conscious attempts to reach a certain level of proficiency; instead, teenagers' accounts point towards active engagement and participation in activities in which English is one meaningful and necessary linguistic resource among others.

Our stance on the individual in the process of language learning draws on sociocultural approaches to language learning and on discursive views of language practices. In line with these views, the individual is essentially a social being, 'whose individuality ... is derived from social relationships and participation in culturally organized activities' (Lantolf, Chapter 2, this volume; see also Lantolf and Pavlenko 2001). There is thus a strong connection between the individual and the social: the micro-level practices of the individual index the macro-level of social structures, values and practices, that is, there are 'connections between language form and social and cultural patterns' and indexical meanings are 'verbal and nonverbal, behavioural "cues" that suggest a fit between utterances and contextual spaces' (Blommaert 2005: 41). Accordingly, individual agency is also socially oriented. This means that the methodologies used to examine language learning also need to take this into account. We consequently chose an ethnographic approach, because it enables us to approach larger social constructs through the experiences and perceptions of individuals, and thus make connections between them. In Heller's words (2008: 250), ethnographies 'allow us … to discover how and why language matters to people in their own terms'. Such an emic approach is particularly useful in exploring today's increasingly multilingual, technologically mediated and complex societies and the effects of this complexity on individuals and how and why they learn and use languages.

Language learning and individuality: a discursive and sociocultural approach

As mentioned above, the theoretical basis of this study is twofold: we subscribe to a social and discursive view of language and literacy (Blommaert 2005; Scollon and Scollon 2004) and adopt a sociocultural approach to learning (e.g. Norton 2000; Block 2003; Lantolf and Thorne 2006). This background has strong implications for our view of individuality and agency. First, the constant interplay between the individual and the social is apparent in sociocultural approaches to language learning, which place strong emphasis on the need to conceptualize language learning not only in terms of acquisition but also as participation (see Sfard 1998; Pavlenko and Lantolf 2000; Block 2003). In other words, unlike cognitive orientations, for which language is a formal system best studied by focusing on 'the individual mind and the internalization of knowledge' (Pavlenko and Lantolf 2000: 156), sociocultural approaches view learning as an inherently social process. Social processes and participation, in turn, are brought into being by individuals and their agency, that is, their active engagement through language in personally meaningful activities and practices which, moreover, take place in 'specific social, historical and cultural contexts' (Norton and Toohey 2001a: 310; Lantolf, Chapter 2, this volume), as well as their earlier learning experiences. In short, the sociocultural approach to learning tries to explicate the relationship between the individual language learners/users and the broader social world in which the individuals function and of which they attempt to become members, and how they construct their identities within various communities of practice (Block 2003; Norton 2000). Significantly from the perspective of this chapter, an important means of exploring this relationship is to direct attention towards individuals' own understandings and perceptions of their language learning and use, to how they make sense of their social and discursive realities and how their identities as language learners and users are constructed. This is why in this chapter we approach the dialogue between the social and the individual by focusing on individual teenagers' understanding and perceptions of their using and learning English.

Second, our view of individuality as something that entails connections with larger social patterns and structures is influenced by the adoption of a discursive approach to language and literacies. We follow Blommaert (2005: 3) in seeing discourse as consisting of 'all forms of meaningful semiotic human activity seen in connection with social, cultural and historical patterns of development and use'. The discursive approach to language thus always entails attention not only to language per se but to the use of language (and other semiotic means) as a way of making sense of and constructing social realities. Thus, being engaged in discursive and literacy practices is a matter of performing social actions, and these practices always involve ways of behaving, thinking, interacting, feeling and valuing (see e.g. Street 1984; Barton 1994; Barton and Hamilton 1998). In Scollon and Scollon's (2004) terms, discourse *is* social action and social action is always related to social, cultural and historical patterns, both reproducing and recreating them. As regards the role of the individual, micro-level analyses of language use and language practices open up opportunities to study individuals, but these individual practices are also inherently connected to larger macro-practices and processes, both reflecting and constituting them. In other words, there is a reflexive relationship between micro- and macro-levels: they are indexically linked to each other (see Blommaert 2005). In our research this means that the way individual teenagers represent their relationship with English both in discussions and through visual means (i.e. photographs, see 'Data and methodology' below) may also index more general social structures, processes and ideologies relating to the role of English in Finland. In other words, we are interested in teenagers' individuality and agency as regards their experiences with English, but this individuality, rather than existing in a vacuum, is also shaped by and shapes broader social realities and structures. In Blommaert's (2007) words, it is important to bear in mind that all social events are always situated, 'lodged in various layers of context', the same applying to young Finns' personal accounts of English. Our ethnographic approach makes it possible to focus both on the individual and the individual in relation to larger social processes and practices, and thus to move from one scale (the individual) to another (the collective), and see how these two scales index broader social values and expectations (Blommaert 2010).

Data and methodology

The case studies reported in this chapter are part of a larger ethnographically oriented project examining how Finnish adolescents perceive and make sense of their English-related language and literacy practices (Nikula and Pitkänen-Huhta 2008). Our participants were three groups of 14–16-year-old Finns (three boys, four girls and three girls). The teenagers in each group were in the same class and were also friends outside school. Our decision to work with groups of friends was motivated by our wish to focus on their out-of-school activities and to reduce issues of stress and power imbalance often present in researcher-researched relationships (see e.g. Hodge and Jones 2000). In accordance with our emic approach, we did not systematically collect background information, but we let the participants decide which aspects of their background they wished to share with us. However, their socio-economic backgrounds were fairly similar to each other with no clear extremes. They were all students in a state-owned comprehensive school and their domestic situations were varied: some of them came from nuclear families, some had single-parent or blended families.

Following the principles of ethnography, we maintained steady contact with the participants for several months to discuss issues related to their language and literacy practices. During the research process we used different methods to gain access into these teenagers' worlds. These included group discussions with girls and boys separately both at the beginning and end of the project, group discussion based on the photographs the participants took of their contacts with English, discussions on their literacy diaries concerning encounters with texts in English and Finnish, the participants' discussions in pairs about specific contexts where they had used English (conducted and recorded without the researchers being present), and individual discussions based on a visual task depicting the participants' relationship with both English and Finnish.

All ten participants had many features in common regarding their practices of using and learning English, but there was also evidence of highly personalized encounters with and relationships to English. We have therefore selected three cases that are representative in that they help to illustrate both the shared understanding among the participants and the types of individual differences that emerged during the analysis. In our discussion of the cases our aim is both to illustrate how the participants' practices with English are shaped by their individual interests and aspirations, and also to demonstrate that certain common features and patterns emerge. This interplay between individuality and sharedness sketches a complex picture of what using and learning English means for these young people.

Three individual takes on English in Finnish teenagers' lives

In this section, we will examine more closely the teenagers' experiences with English in their everyday lives. As mentioned above, our focus will be on three cases: one boy, Eerik, and two girls, Eeva and Alisa. Table 8.1 summarizes the background information of these three adolescents.

Table 8.1 The cases

	Age (at the start of the project)	Years of learning English at school	Hobbies and other interests
Eerik	15	7	skate- and snowboarding football ice-hockey
Eeva	14	6	ballroom dancing fashion, beauty, and women's magazines
Alisa	14	6	track and field athletics scouting reading

Before going into details of the cases, it is worth briefly describing the sociolinguistic context in which these young people live. Finland, a small European country with about five million inhabitants, is officially bilingual, with Finnish and Swedish as the two national languages. However, the Swedish-speaking population only comprises approximately 6 per cent of the whole population; that is, the great majority of Finns are speakers of Finnish. Sámi, Romany and Finnish sign language are officially acknowledged minority languages. With increasing immigration during recent years, the number of other languages spoken in Finland has been on the increase (Latomaa and Nuolijärvi 2005). English has no official status in Finland, but it is the most widely studied foreign language at school and due to technological developments and globalization, English enters people's lives for example through the media, such as TV, films, music and the Internet (Leppänen and Nikula 2007; Taavitsainen and Pahta 2008). The young especially are active and sophisticated users of the new media, with English so closely intertwined in their media consumption that encounters with English are lived, daily reality for many young people in Finland (Leppänen *et al.* 2009). Moreover, English is clearly visible in Finnish society, widely embraced in different social domains, by different age groups and in different geographical locations, as a recent survey on the uses and functions of English in Finland shows (Leppänen *et al.* 2011). As one of the young people in our study aptly puts it: 'it's [English] really a daily business and it's basically everywhere all the time'.

When analysing the cases, three recurrent themes relating to the teenagers' experiences with English emerged from the data: their uses of and contacts with English, their attitudes to English revealed through their discursive choices, and their perceptions of themselves as learners of English. The discussion of the three cases below is organized around these themes.

Eerik

Our first case is Eerik, who at the time of the data collection was 15 years old and was in the final year of compulsory education at comprehensive school. As a personality, Eerik seemed very mature for his age: he was calm and good at expressing his thoughts and feelings verbally. English as a school subject was not among the favourites he listed: PE, biology and civics. His main hobby was sports, especially team sports such as football and ice-hockey. He had played football for years in the local team, but he had just stopped that because it had become, to his taste, too professional. But he still played with his friends: football in the summer and ice-hockey in the winter. He was also a keen skateboarder. His sports activities formed an important space for different types of encounters with English. For example, his use of English was to a large extent connected to sports terminology, as the terminology related to his hobbies was very often in English or derived from English. Eerik said that 'in skateboarding [...] all the tricks are in English'. This seems understandable in sports which have reached Finland fairly recently, such as skateboarding and snowboarding, and which have created a community of practice around them, but English terminology was used even in sports considered almost national sports in Finland, such as ice-hockey. According to Eerik, the terms 'stick' or 'rocket' were often used instead of the corresponding Finnish word: 'maila is usually stick or rocket'. Moreover, to follow his interests, Eerik also visited various web sites regularly where the use of English was again necessary: 'but then there's the web site of this football team which is in English [...] and there you had to cope in English and I did cope quite well'. In addition to these receptive or fragmented uses of English, Eerik also occasionally had contact with people with whom English is the only means of communication, a common lingua franca, as their teams sometimes travelled to tournaments abroad or the team might have a visiting coach from abroad.

Another type of engagement with English which was present daily and which Eerik (and the other boys) mentioned was making use of elements from English as an insider language or generally when talking with friends. This kind of language use is thus typically hybrid, in the sense that it involves extensive code-switching and use of originally English forms adapted to Finnish morphology and/or pronunciation. Insider language was often related to specific interest groups. Eerik, for example, mentioned that some of his school mates who play a specific computer game speak a language that is completely incomprehensible to an outsider: 'in the school corridor when you sit close [to a group] and start listening, you're completely clueless'. He also wonders to what extent the language he uses with his friends when talking about skateboarding – full of trick names in English – is understandable to others. Another example of English being a commonplace resource in the language use of the young is expressing feelings, anger in particular, for example by swearing in English. These examples are instances of youth language which are created around specific interest groups and communities of practice and which function as a means of creating group identity (Androusopoulos and Georgakopoulou 2003).

As far as Eerik's attitudes towards English are concerned, his relation to English could be characterized as practical. He deems knowledge of English essential in international communication, in following his hobby in magazines and on the internet, and in coping with new technology. This practical attitude is enforced by Eerik assigning different roles to Finnish and English: 'you do everything possible in Finnish and then in English those things that you kind of have to do in English'. On the other hand, certain values related to English also came up in his accounts. First of all, he connected English to information that is more up-to-date and advanced and pointed out that, especially concerning skateboarding, Finns are somewhat 'behind' while the Americans are more developed and advanced in these matters: 'skateboarding magazines are generally, or the best ones are of course from abroad, they're in English … it's a lot more advanced there [in America] and then of course you'd rather read something that is more advanced … in Finland we're a bit behind in this'. Another value-loaded attitude surfaced when he talked about the language used among friends: 'even if you're with your Finnish friends, even then it's more natural to say some things in English and it's cooler, of course it's always a little cooler to be English-speaking'. It seems that by using English with friends you can create new identities; you can pretend to be someone you are not or play a role you might have picked up from TV or movies. Eerik's point that it is somehow self-evidently cooler to be English-speaking is telling in this respect. The English-speaking world thus appears to be glamorous to young people and this is most likely due to popular culture, TV series and movie characters they want to identify with (see Murray 2008). Here the use of English is related to an imagined community (Anderson 1983; Norton 2001; Yashima, Chapter 4, this volume), something beyond the here and now, beyond the immediate communities of practice (see discussion on Eeva below).

As a user of English, Eerik seemed to be fairly competent and confident, and he said that some things can even be expressed better in English: 'then some things you can just somehow, it feels that you can express some things a lot better in English than in Finnish, or some funny thing can be a lot better in English than in Finnish'. Here Eerik's language ideological stance becomes evident as well: some things are just better in English and the humour may be lost in translation. Eerik's confidence as a user of English is probably derived from his regular contacts with English through the media, and he was indeed well aware of learning English through his daily contacts with it. He even said that most of his learning has come from the media: 'at least some eighty or seventy per cent of my learning is from the media'. By listening to music and watching TV (there is no dubbing of foreign TV programmes in Finland; instead, subtitles are used) and films in English, he has developed an ear for languages and he feels that he does not have to learn grammar and vocabulary the hard way. Instead, he maintains that 'if grammar is taught in class I don't cram rules or anything [...] you somehow develop an ear for the language when you listen to music and movies and all that'. Learning English is somehow automatic and, as Eerik said, you might hear good jokes on TV and 'you mull them over in your head and they just stick in your head'. Thus the everyday learning of English seems to involve little effort: the language is acquired automatically and somehow incidentally and unconsciously when there is enough exposure and, importantly, when the language is related to personal interests and is tied to meaningful and purposeful real-life activities.

Eeva

Our second case, Eeva, was a 14-year-old, outgoing, talkative girl whose favourite hobby was ballroom dancing. English as a school subject seemed to be only mildly interesting ('well I like English quite a lot'), but outside school she had frequent contacts with English and had a very positive attitude towards it. She was interested in following the fashion and beauty world and was an avid reader of glossy magazines such as *Cosmopolitan*, *Vogue*, *Teen Vogue* and *Elle*. Instead of merely pointing this out in discussions, she also attached strong positive value judgements to this activity: 'Cosmo is like a million times better in English' [than in Finnish] (see Eerik's comment about skateboarding magazines above). As with Eerik, Eeva's hobby also provided her with opportunities to use English outside the school context: some of her ballroom dancing team members were from abroad which was why, according to Eeva, the training sessions were mostly conducted in English. Furthermore, occasional competitions abroad and visiting trainers from abroad provided opportunities to use English as a common lingua franca.

What is noteworthy in Eeva's relationship with English is that she discursively constructed English as an important asset for her future aspirations. She mentioned several times her wish to work abroad and English as something that will make this possible: 'it [knowing English] will probably be quite useful 'cos most likely I won't stay here in Finland, this place is a bit too small for me'. The value of English as a gateway for the 'good life' is thus obvious. Furthermore, in Eeva's case it is clear that for her English was valuable in allowing participation in what could be called imagined communities in the sense of Anderson (1983), Norton (2001) and Yashima (Chapter 4, this volume), that is, communities which 'project into the future and imagine a more distant community to which they hope someday to belong' (Murphey *et al.* 2005: 88). For Eeva, these imagined communities seemed to consist of people who are 'international' and 'cool': 'I just feel that I'll want something more international; my friends and I spoke in English [during an international dancing competition] because it was cooler than using Finnish'. In other words, she saw English as a valuable investment for her future and, perhaps for this reason, also had a very positive attitude towards it. English thus played an important role in Eeva's identity work, functioning as an important means of segregating the 'hip and modern' from the others. The following extract, where Eeva equated those with no skills in English as hicks-from-the-sticks, is a clear indication of her wish to dissociate herself from them: 'it feels good to be able to speak English, you know I feel like I'm kind of more international and you know have a grasp of things and I'm not some kind of hicks-from-the-sticks you know like some outsider because you know I just do understand it [English]'. Eeva's favourable attitude to English also shows in that of all the participants, she most often contrasted Finnish and English, usually strongly favouring the latter: 'I just like English a lot more 'cos Finnish, well it just feels like such an irritating language at times'.

As regards Eeva's self-perception as a learner of English, the impression gained is that she put more focus on her use of English than the act of learning it. Like Eerik, she depicted her learning in the everyday as something happening rather automatically, for example idioms and phrases 'just sticking in my head' when watching films in English. She also mentioned that when the dancing practice is in English she 'learns quite well', but overall, her focus in the everyday was more on what English enables her to do and be, rather than on learning it.

Alisa

Like Eeva, Alisa was a 14-year-old girl at the beginning of the project. She was less talkative and shyer than Eeva but she was also very friendly and quite willing to reflect upon her experiences with English. Alisa's main hobby was athletics and she was also an active scout. Reading was another of her pastimes. Alisa's overall attitude to studying English was quite positive, even if it was not her main interest at school: after having listed PE, home economics, arts and Swedish as her favourite subjects at school she added 'but I do like English too'. Alisa's main hobby, athletics, brings her into regular contact with English as she uses English with her coach, who is Italian. But where Eeva depicted using English as something 'cool', Alisa seemed to have a more down-to-earth attitude: using English is a necessity because the Italian coach 'only can say in Finnish hyva hyva [well done]'. Apart from speaking English with her coach, Alisa's contacts with English seemed mainly to take the form of hearing English when she either watched TV or listened to music. Although watching TV was the first thing she thought of when asked about her contacts with English: 'I watch TV not anything else really [in English]'. The role of music also became very clear as she pointed out that she practically always has music on: 'I always have music on, whenever I go to my room I always switch on the music, it's like always on in the background, it doesn't interfere with doing homework or anything'. Moreover, the music she listened to was almost always in English, something that applied to all the other participants in the study as well. Alisa thus captured a sentiment probably shared by the others as well when she said that 'at least for me music in Finnish would simply not be enough'.

The area where Alisa differed most clearly from Eerik and Eeva was that she more often talked about her encounters and activities with English in terms of consciously making an effort to study or learn English. Although the others also, for example, talked about looking up words in dictionaries, for Alisa this seemed to be a more common practice: 'for example with song lyrics, I quite often look for words in a dictionary or on the internet'. Moreover, she also explicitly made reference to 'memory' and 'remembering' and 'learning' in these connections, thus drawing on discourses of education, which quite often construct the process of language learning in ways that emphasize the importance of individuals' mental processes over the role of language use in social interaction. In a way, then, Alisa described her everyday activities with English as a means to accumulate her repository of words and phrases: 'but then individual words for example in songs if I don't know them I look them up in a dictionary, that way they'll stick in my memory so that it'll be possible to remember them later on'.

The way Alisa displayed her attitudes to English was in line with her quieter and calmer disposition: she did not show the same enthusiasm for English as Eeva, yet her accounts clearly indicated that English had more value to her than simply being a subject studied at school. On the one hand, English clearly had instrumental value; for example Alisa saw it as an essential asset in working life: 'nowadays you can't manage any more if you don't know English, I mean in many jobs you need language skills, in that sense it's really useful'. On the other hand, the way Alisa talked about English also suggests that it has various social functions. First, it provides a means of demarcation from those who do not know it as well: younger siblings and parents in particular. Alisa's accounts included references both to speaking English to her younger sister to show off ('and then sometimes I spoke to Maria [her sister] only in English and she didn't understand a thing [...] boy was I stupid') and to the use of English expressions, especially the more colloquial forms, as a shared code among teenagers ('maybe you don't speak the same way with parents, maybe it's used more with friends').

As already shown, Alisa talked about her experiences with English more often than others in terms of consciously making an effort to learn the language, for example when encountering new words in lyrics or texts that she read. In terms of her self-perception as a learner of English, she thus constructed an image of a diligent person who approached many everyday practices from the perspective of language learning. Although her everyday encounters with English were also a matter of learning, she seemed to be very clear about the different roles of language teaching at school and using English outside the school: the former is important especially in learning grammar and standard language ('grammar has to be in there; it's probably good that at school you learn the standard language'). She was also very clear about the difference between activities in and outside school in that while free time activities are driven by one's own interests, the rationale behind school practices is completely different. For example, when talking about texts in textbooks, she said that 'their contents don't really matter that much [...] 'cos it's mainly the learning that's at issue, grammar and words and such, whereas at home, in your spare time you really don't feel like reading anything that doesn't really interest you one bit'. There is thus no doubt that texts in and out of school have different value for Alisa, personal interest and individualized choice playing a far greater role in out-of-school activities.

Discussion

The analysis above has sketched a complex picture of teenagers' perceptions of English in their lives and their orientations to language learning. The cases show that English has a strong presence in teenagers' lives. In certain respects their accounts resemble each other, but there are also differences, especially as to how necessary they consider English to be for them. Thus both individual and shared factors emerged, each indexing values and attitudes prevalent more broadly in society, such as English being a necessity in a modern way of life. In other words, the analysis revealed interconnections between the individual and the social. To begin with features that the teenagers in our study have in common, English has almost constant presence in their lives as they encounter it daily, particularly through forms of popular culture, music and films. While these often entail receptive uses, there are also situations where English gets used, to varying degrees, alongside and mixed with Finnish, be it in interactions with non-Finnish coaches or in appropriations of English-origin expressions in hobby-related terminology or in-group language use among peers, that is, as a 'we-code', as described by Gumperz (1982). Another shared feature is that, unlike in formal contexts of learning, using English in everyday contexts does not seem to presuppose fully developed language skills for these teenagers. They do recognize their role as language learners also in the everyday, but seem to be less concerned about language as a formal system with a set of rules than in school contexts of learning, and less inclined to wait until their skills are advanced enough (by school standards) before using English in a real-life context. Their *language user* identities thus seem to be mainly the result of informal (out-of-school) contexts of learning and use (e.g. Tusting 2003). In contrast, in their accounts schooling gets constructed as the site where *language learner* identity prevails and where the aim is to learn about grammar and standard language rather than to use English for communication. It is worth emphasizing here that the teenagers' everyday uses of English could perhaps best be described in terms of truncated repertoires (Blommaert 2010) rather than treating language in essentialist terms as an entity. That is, their uses of English mainly occur in certain specified areas and related to their personal interests and shared communities, what Gee (2004) calls affinity groups, that is, in connection with language use linked to individual and purposeful activities and personally meaningful social practices.

Finally, what the teenagers also share is a positive overall attitude to English: it is described as necessary and useful, almost as a commodity that can be taken up when needed. This arguably indexes the more general attitudes towards English in Finland. After all, a recent survey of English in Finland (Leppänen *et al.* 2011) suggests that Finns' overall attitudes to English are often down-to-earth and practical: its everyday presence and importance in today's Finland is acknowledged, yet the majority of Finns do not see this as a threat to the national culture and languages. Perhaps typically of the young, these teenagers' accounts also reveal overly positive language ideologies: English represents internationalization, 'cool' lifestyles and modernity. This also has its counterparts in the more general ideologies prevalent in society, which often associate English with globalization. Rather than being unique to Finland, the situation where English has specific functions in contexts where it does not have an official status, is common to many other countries and cultures (cf. Dörnyei *et al.* 2006; Pennycook 2007).

As regards individuality, the overall theme of this volume, our findings also suggest that despite certain commonalities, at a more nuanced level English is not perceived and experienced in the same way by different Finnish teenagers. That is, they all have their specific unique orientations to English and their reasons for investing in English differ, which gives rise to individual user and learner 'profiles' – also social in nature. This finding is in line with Benson and Cooker's (Chapter 1, this volume) argument that socialization processes of young people in modern societies are about 'seeking out individualized spaces'. Individuality shows, first, in the participants' attitudes to English which, underneath the unanimously positive opinions, range from celebratory views of its 'coolness' and importance to a more practical orientation to it as a useful but not necessarily personally meaningful resource. In other words, while for some English is important in order to be up-to-date about the latest developments related to their hobbies, or closely connected to their personal future aspirations of becoming people of the world (see also Yashima, Chapter 4, this volume), others see it merely as a useful tool needed, for example, in modern working life or when encountering foreigners.

Another area where individuality is evident is the way in which the participants orient to language learning as part of their everyday practices: some put more emphasis on language learning happening automatically and unconsciously, without much effort. These teenagers are also likely to emphasize the role of informal learning contexts in their English skills.

Others seem to approach their learning of English in the everyday through discourses of education, highlighting their conscious efforts to learn more English, for example by looking up unfamiliar words in the dictionary and trying to memorize them. There thus seems to be a connection between the type and intensity of teenagers' engagement with English and their way of perceiving themselves as learners. Thus the learner profiles could be placed on a continuum ranging from practically and locally oriented language users, who value the practices of formal conscious learning, to future-oriented savvy language users, who pick up the language automatically in their everyday activities – many, in fact, sharing features of both but with different emphases. In other words, the teenagers orient to wider social and discursive spaces in different ways when describing their personal experiences with English, some drawing more on discourses of education and others on discourses of internationalization. In both cases, however, their individualized accounts are linked with, or index, larger social realities (cf. Blommaert 2005).

There are thus complex and multilayered connections between individuality and broader social values and ideologies, the bridges from 'the unique to the common', in Blommaert's (2010) words. Hence we have argued that rather than operating in a social and cultural vacuum the teenagers draw on prevalent and emerging discourses in society when talking about their uses of and learning of English. When looking at teenagers as a group, their shared practices, values and attitudes are clearly connected to broader societal discourses. However, connections to the social are also evident when zooming in on individuals: their perceptions and personal orientations are also often related to how English is portrayed in prevalent discourses. Individuality and uniqueness arise from the fact that the teenagers' views, attitudes and values are often closely related to their personal interests (e.g. hobbies) and serve their personal aspirations (e.g. future orientations). In a sense, then, processes of socialization and individualization are concurrent by the teenagers turning prevalent societal discourses into their own by 'filtering' them through their personal interests and aspirations.

Conclusion

The study reported in this chapter has combined an ethnographic research orientation with a social and discursive view of language and literacy that emphasizes the indexical relationships between language and larger societal structures and processes (Blommaert 2005). The advantage of this combination is that while ethnography provides a rich and nuanced picture of how individual participants make sense of their encounters with English, a discursive approach offers possibilities to account for similarities and differences between individuals that go beyond mere description towards explanation by highlighting the inherent connectedness of the individual and social. Hence, we were able to explore not only shared and individualized features of teenagers' perceptions of English but also their connections to more general discourses on English prevalent in society, in particular discourses of education and internationalization.

As regards learning English in out-of-school contexts, our study has suggested that it takes on very different qualities in these teenagers' minds than learning in school contexts, so much so that these seem to constitute two different realities for them. Often the quite extensive individual engagement with English outside school is not perceived in terms of learning at all, but rather as English finding its way to teenagers' repertoires as if automatically and without conscious effort. There is clearly need for more research in this area to understand better whether there are meaningful ways to bridge the gap between learning in in-school and out-of-school contexts.

As our focus has been on teenagers' own understandings and perceptions of the role of English in their lives, we have used here discussions as data, which offer access to participants' personal views. We have not been able to investigate the relationship between their views and their own practices of language use, however, but have used information provided by earlier studies of uses of English by young Finns (e.g. Leppänen *et al.* 2009) when discussing practices of language use. A fruitful avenue for future research, then, would be to make use of data sets that would make it possible to explore the same participants' perceptions as well as language use to see the extent to which they correspond to one another.

9 Individuality in L2 identity construction: the stories of two Chinese learners of English

Mingyue (Michelle) Gu

Introduction

There is now a growing body of research adopting post-structuralist approaches to relationships between second language acquisition and identity development (e.g. Norton 2000; Norton and Toohey 2001b; Block 2007a; Chik and Benson 2008; Gu 2009a, 2009b, 2010). These studies reveal that the identities of L2 users and learning tend to be multiple, shifting and often contradictory, and are crucially related to sociocultural and political contexts and to agency and structure.

In view of the concerns of this volume with tensions between the social and the individual in Applied Linguistics research, the role of individuality in L2 identity construction deserves more attention. L2 identities are socioculturally conditioned, yet one could always find different learners with distinct learning histories who, in similar sociocultural settings, would experience different learning processes. Some researchers (e.g. Norton 2001) are also concerned about the historical dimension in identity construction, that is to say, its linking of the past, present and future. One way of building individuality and history into work on L2 identity is through the framework of Communities of Practice (CoP) (Lave and Wenger 1991; Wenger 1998), an approach which is adopted in this study to explore the situated, historical and social aspects of L2 identity for two Chinese learners of English.

The CoP model, discussed in more detail by Lamb (Chapter 3, this volume), allows us to view individuality in L2 identity in multiple dimensions through three modes of 'belonging': 'engagement', 'imagination' and 'alignment' (Wenger 1998: 173–4). In the dimension of engagement, we can explore how individual learners participate in activities in different ways and how their identities are shaped in relation to the different interpersonal relationships they enter into. In the dimension of imagination, we can consider identity in realms beyond the limitations of current time and space and locate the engagement in relation to past, future and 'elsewhere'. In the dimension of alignment, we can examine how individuals align their learning behaviours with the requirements and structures beyond their community of practice, in order to find a particular position for themselves in the broader social setting. Individual differences among learners can also be represented through investigating their learning experiences in the three modes of belonging, which link up situated activities, historical backgrounds and social practices.

In this chapter, I discuss a study in which I attempted to apply this framework to trace the processes of L2 identity formation of two college English L2 learners in China. The study aimed to capture the changes they experienced in their L2 identities over a prolonged period in similar learning contexts. The study asked how these two learners, as individual social agents, constructed their L2 identities in the face of both the spread of English that accompanies globalization, and also the rapid changes in Chinese society.

The study

Research context

To locate the participants in the broader social and historical practices of China, and to better understand the CoPs they are participating in, the English learning context of China is introduced. China's Open Door Policy has brought about an era of widespread English language learning and teaching (Adamson 2004; Lam 2005). The country's successful hosting of the 2008 Olympic Games, and its entry into the World Trade Organization (WTO) have fuelled the English learning fever even further. China has the largest population of English language learners – 200 to 350 million – in the world (Yang 2006), and is thus a vital element in understanding English language learning today. At the same time, the pace of international interaction has increased through the establishment of international schools and multi-national enterprises, and through the consequent formation of numerous English-speaking communities in China. Chinese culture, heavily influenced by more than 5,000 years of philosophical and historical traditions, is undergoing major changes due to the powerful influence of the sociocultural shifts surrounding English language learning. Chinese people are faced with a potential conflict between Chinese culture and those cultures associated with the English language.

English, as a vehicle of western culture, tends to be seen as the language of 'modernity, science and technology, success, national "unity", democracy, and other such positive features' (Skutnabb-Kangas 2000: xi). To Chinese learners, it is also more than just another foreign language, since the learning of English inevitably throws up some complex questions. What does English mean to Chinese people? How will learning English affect these learners, with respect not only to linguistic improvement, but also their identities, values and ideologies?

Participants

The participants in my study were both students in their third year of study in the English Department of a key university in China when I approached them about participating in this study. I focused on English majors in order to examine how different learners with varied learning histories develop different motivations in similar learning situations. Jocelyn's and Pauline's (pseudonyms) stories were of interest because they illustrated sharply contrasting processes of identity formation developing within essentially similar learning experiences and learning contexts. This chapter investigates how the two individual learners enacted their agency within the process of 'becoming' while they interacted with the immediate learning community, their historical backgrounds and future imaginations and the broader social context. To anchor the following comparative analysis of the two participants' stories, their profiles are provided in Table 9.1.

Table 9.1 Participants' profiles.

Name	Major	Origin	Learning history
Jocelyn	English	small-size city	A high-achieving language learner in middle school and college; wide interests in politics and Chinese culture; English is her first choice of major in college entrance exam
Pauline	English	countryside	A high-achieving language learner in middle school and college; pragmatics values; strongly goal-oriented; English was her second choice of major in college entrance exam

Methods

A variety of techniques were adopted to collect data, including interviews, diary studies, and online chatting and email correspondence. The different sources of data provided different perspectives on the two learners' identity development. I also continuously checked 'data, analytic categories, interpretations, and conclusions' with the informants, both formally and informally, to ascertain their assessment of their 'overall adequacy' (Lincoln and Guba 1985: 314). The data collected during this project are summarized in Table 9.2.

Table 9.2 Dataset summary.

Data	Method of collection	Quantity	Language
Interviews (over two years)	Interviews were conducted in Chinese with the participants every four months over a period of two years.	Jocelyn (6) Pauline (6)	Chinese
Diaries (over two years)	The informants wrote the diaries on a three to four week basis and sent the diary to me through email.	Jocelyn (30) Pauline (16)	English (75%) Chinese (25%)
Email correspondences (over two years)	All the emails were in English at the request of the participants.	Jocelyn (9) Pauline (9)	English

This investigation was conducted over two years during the students' third and fourth years of college study. The students were interviewed (in Chinese) every four months about their college language learning experiences. The interviews were semi-structured, with open questions. The participants also made diary entries tri-weekly, noting their reflections on English language learning, and allowing them to introspectively and/or retrospectively observe their language learning experiences (Allwright and Bailey 1991). Seventy-five per cent of the diary entries were written in English, although the participants were allowed to use the language with which they felt most comfortable; this prevalence of English did not undermine the quality of the data, as the written mode in a second language can secure a confident representation of language learners' identity (Kramsch and Lam 1999). Email correspondence and online chat topics were not limited to English learning, but also touched on such areas as their experiences of growing up, interpersonal relationships, future concerns and so on, which to a great extent compensated for the physical distance between the participants and me during most of the study and helped to establish a rapport.

Data analysis

The process of data analysis was ongoing, recursive and iterative, and operated in tandem with the data collection. As soon as an interview was conducted or a diary entry was received, data would be analysed; this preliminary analysis often generated new questions, which were then posed in subsequent interviews or email correspondence. Data from different sources were treated together for cross-referencing.

A 'selected reading approach' (van Manen 1990: 93) was adopted to uncover themes related to the focus of this inquiry, meaning that as I was reading and re-reading the data, I examined what statements, phrases and words used by the participants seemed to reveal about the interaction between the individual and the social in L2 identity construction (e.g. interaction with the learning community at the departmental level, the influence of the previous English-learning experiences, the social influence on learning English and future aspirations). After the relations between themes were identified and considered, more theoretical categories were constructed, informed by the data, and the CoP theoretical framework, including: (a) engagement with the immediate learning community; (b) imagination; and (c) alignment with social discourses. After the data analysis was done, I discussed the findings with the participants, who confirmed that they accurately represented what they wanted to express. Unless otherwise indicated, all excerpts in this paper are translated versions from the original Chinese.

Engagement with the immediate learning community

Engagement involves participation in, and negotiation of meanings around, a shared practice. In this study, 'the immediate learning community' refers to the departmental community in which the students operate. In the process of learning as engagement, the participants interact with other participants including teachers and students, and participate in activities through negotiating meanings and developing shared practices. Both Jocelyn and Pauline were top students in their year. According to some research findings, students in China with high academic achievement tend to be favoured by teachers and fellow classmates (Zhao and Guo 2002). However, Jocelyn and Pauline recounted different experiences in the department.

The following exchange between Jocelyn and me suggests a sharp contrast between her own values and ideals and those of many students in the department:

MG:	Do you think you belong to the mainstream community in your department?
Jocelyn:	No, I think I am at the margin.
MG:	Why? They didn't accept you or you didn't want to join?
Jocelyn:	Both. Most students don't have high life objectives and don't study English hard although it is their major. Making more money is what they are most concerned with. I have little in common with most classmates and I cannot win respect from others. I dream of being successful but I hope my dream will benefit not only myself, but (the) others … I think young people should not be selfish, but should try to play a role in advancing the nation. So I work hard on English not merely for myself.

(Interview 3, month 12)

In addition to her disappointment with peer relationships, Jocelyn indicated that the institutional power wielded by some teachers excluded her from such learning opportunities as on-site interpretation and entry into English contests:

Jocelyn:	I have never been given any opportunities by teachers.
MG:	Why?
Jocelyn:	Maybe because I don't know how to develop a close relationship with the teachers … Information about chances such as internships and English contests has never been made public. Everything seems to be carried out unjustly and unfairly.

(Interview 4, month 16)

Instead of passively waiting for chances to practise, Jocelyn sought out private companies that needed temporary interpreters, inviting her classmates to accompany her. She documented her feelings in a diary entry from her senior year:

> What I want to do now, is just to work hard on English, and to create opportunities by myself. I would not expect anything from my professors. Whenever this idea came into my mind, I have summoned up my strength and my morale has been lightened. I think I can earn respect from others through my own efforts.
> (Diary 26, original English, month 22)

While Jocelyn failed to gain legitimate membership in the learning community, Pauline had a totally different story. The urban discourse in the community of the English Department was new to Pauline. Asked about her feelings as a newcomer in the first year, she recalled:

> Everything was new to me when I first came here, the communication style, the standard for 'being cool and stylish', the course design and so on. But I learnt new things quickly and soon got along with others well. (Interview 2, month 4)

Compared to Jocelyn, who was not content with the overall atmosphere in the English Department, Pauline adapted herself to the community well and successfully gained recognition by proving her value to those popular in the department. She said,

> People in my circle don't like the persons who isolated themselves only in the classroom and study English all day. We call them bookworms. We compete not only in academic scores, but also in communication skills, dressing and so on.` (Interview 3, month 8)

Unlike Jocelyn, Pauline didn't think she was ever marginalized, because she was 'quite sociable and fashionable' and 'knew how to play hard and enjoy life' (Interview 3, month 8). Paradoxically perhaps, Pauline also said that, although she was a legitimate member of the community, she had different pursuits from most classmates in that 'they only desired to have a good job and a steady life; while I have a lot of dreams to realize, and I would not be satisfied if I only lead a quiet life' (Interview 5, month 20). Nonetheless, Pauline adjusted her own behaviours in order to establish close relationships with her fellow classmates and to avoid being marginalized:

> Actually I am not always interested in what they are doing, but sometimes I must pretend to be very interested in doing things together with others, since otherwise they will marginalize me.
> (Interview 3, month 8)

Despite her overall enthusiasm for 'playing hard', Pauline was a dedicated English learner:

> Many classmates are surprised that I spent little time studying but could always get high grades in examinations. Actually I work very very hard, but they don't know. I was very concentrated when I was studying English. (Interview 4, month 12)

Asked about her relationship with her teachers, Pauline indicated that she was a favoured student because she knew how to behave in ways that would appeal to them (Interview 4).

While Jocelyn and Pauline both had initial difficulty adapting to university life, they appear to have constructed different patterns of interpersonal relationships in the same learning community. Jocelyn's statements portray a tension between her own beliefs and values and those held by the mainstream discourse in the English Department, which inhibited her from gaining greater access to opportunities to practise English, but she also found some impetus in these contradictions, in that she wanted to get herself and her beliefs recognized. In contrast to Jocelyn, Pauline quickly established a harmonious relationship with teachers and classmates in the learner community. She then claimed there was a good match between her beliefs and the community's. However, underlying the apparent coherence there were also contradictions in that Pauline was keen to develop her English, which distinguished her from others. She strategically concealed the inherent differences and gained a position in the mainstream group. Jocelyn and Pauline were both highly motivated English learners. However, Jocelyn remained in a marginal position, while Pauline strategically positioned herself within the community, with whose discourse she was not familiar and for which she felt a lack of resonance, and gained a legitimate membership.

Imagination

The idea of 'imagination', as one of the three modes of belonging in the CoP model, enables us to examine the participants' identity construction in the ongoing learning process or trajectory, through incorporating past experiences and future imagination into present activities. The notion allows us to overcome the dichotomy between agency and structure evident in certain more extreme versions of constructivism, which overemphasize the role of the social in shaping the individual, while leaving the agency of the individual somewhat unaccounted for. Imagination is one of the three modes of belonging to a community of practice, and provides space for the learners to enact their agency within social structures. Through imagination in particular, I can examine the ongoing process of identity formation of the participants that bridges the past, the future and the present. As reflected in the data, the participants' imagined identities are constructed in the interaction between individual learners, historical process and social practice.

Jocelyn was born and grew up in a medium-sized city in northern China, as the only child in her family, with both of her parents having received tertiary education. The most common topics of conversation in her family were history, economics and politics. Inspired by this, Jocelyn dreamed of a wonderful and successful life that would be meaningful in terms of both personal development and social value. She had many different ideas about her future, including being an educator, an astronomer, a scientist, an entrepreneur, a politician and a scholar. From childhood, Jocelyn's parents encouraged her to be the best she could be. Due to the extreme emphasis put on academic achievement in the Chinese social system, especially in Jocelyn's hometown, hard work and striving to be the top student was one way, if not the only way, for Jocelyn to demonstrate her worth. Jocelyn's strong sense of being Chinese was deeply rooted in her family education and values and she struggled to have her identity as an English user and her cultural identity as a Chinese co-exist in harmony. As an English major, Jocelyn relied to a large extent on her English proficiency for career advancement. On the one hand, she had positive feelings about western cultures, especially in the first two years in college. On the other hand, she used to regard a strong identification with English language cultures as a 'betrayal' of her mother culture (Interview 2, month 4). Asked how she outgrew the uneasy struggle, Jocelyn described her experience of being interviewed by an American journalist in an international exchange event at the university in her senior year:

> An American journalist interviewed my friends and me during a social event to welcome some exchange students from America ... Though I was very tired at that time, when it was my turn, I became very excited. It is a good opportunity to show Americans how Chinese students behave. My ideal image is a Chinese girl, learned, gentle and nice, polite, speaking English fluently, but also very proud of her own culture. I want to change many American's attitudes toward China. China is not backward, poor, over populated but energetic, cultured and enthusiastic ... I wanted to show that I have interests in western cultures, but I was rooted in Chinese cultures. (Diary 20, month 15, original in English)

In this situation, Jocelyn drew on her English proficiency to establish her imagined identities as a competent English user and as a person rooted in her mother cultures, before English speakers. Here it seems that Jocelyn's L2 identity and cultural identity were no longer placed in opposition but mutually constituted.

While Jocelyn aspired to live a meaningful life, Pauline held a more utilitarian worldview. Pauline was born and grew up in rural central China, the oldest of the three children in her family. Since her parents did not have any steady employment, the family's financial situation was not good. Determined not to repeat her parents' lifestyle, she dreamed of a comfortable (or 'luxurious' in her words) childhood. She thus had high demands for rather material things. She knew clearly that she could not rely on anyone but herself, and that she had to strive to get what she wanted on her own:

> I was a very aggressive girl, and even so am I now. In my childhood, I knew that if I wanted to live a kind of life different from my parents, I had to work hard and change it on my own.
> (Journal 3, month 3, original English)

Pauline held a pragmatic worldview, only exerting energy and time on 'useful' things. In this regard, she was quite different from Jocelyn, who dealt with all tasks carefully in the hopes of both proving and improving her ability in the process. For example, Pauline gave priority to those subjects that would be used to calculate academic rankings, and didn't 'waste' time on other subjects; she remained the top student in the English Department throughout her university period. Besides performing well in her studies, she took several part-time jobs such as tutor and translator and was almost financially independent in university, which is not common among undergraduates in China. Pauline seemed to have multi-faceted characteristics. She was a quick learner with wide interests. Her attention was often diverted to opportunities which she would try to grasp. She was always energetic but had no enthusiasm before things with no utilitarian value. The complexity of Pauline's experience is discussed in greater depth below.

Pauline asserted that her knowledge of English language and cultures was simply a tool for her to achieve her dreams:

> I worked very hard on English and became a proficient English user to gain respect and admire from others, to live a better life than my parents, to obtain what I could not have in my whole childhood. (Telephone interview, month 18)

Pauline employed her identity as 'a proficient English user' to seek working and learning opportunities. Asked how she could find employment while still a student, Pauline credited her confidence in, and her continual efforts to improve her English ability:

> I believed that I was qualified to do this job because I had been practising speaking and reading so hard. Actually I am linguistically and academically stronger than most of my classmates.
>
> (Interview 3, month 8)

Later, in her fourth year in college, Pauline thought her English ability was sufficiently advanced and that she should try some more challenging part-time jobs. As such, she applied for and got a teaching position at a well-known English training school offering services to those needing to take GRE and TOEFL exams that would allow them to study in North America. Pauline said this was a very competitive position, with applicants going through three rounds of interviews. Pauline found the teaching job full of challenges; she had to learn more and work harder to deal with the complex and difficult tasks. It seems that Pauline used her L2 identity to position herself in a competitive society:

> MG: What does English mean to you?
>
> Pauline: English ability is the most important equipment for me to survive and to make a good living. I have to work hard and strive to be better than others.
>
> (Interview 5, month 20)

Pauline asserted that she wanted to be herself, rather than be changed by English-related cultures. She said English was a tool for her to live well, but that she would never be restricted by the language and its culture; she would like to become a person open to the diverse cultures, opportunities and challenges the world has to offer (Interview 5, month 20). Interestingly, this somewhat resonates with the experience of Japanese gay men in Moore (Chapter 10, this volume), who saw English-related cultures as their way to escape from Japan.

Jocelyn experienced a struggle in recognizing that her L2 identity and cultural identity were not necessarily in opposition. She finally found that her proficiency in English could help present her cultural identity and that her L2 identity could even constitute her cultural identity. On the other hand, Pauline had no trouble reconciling her L2 identity with her cultural identity. L2 identity was utilized by Pauline as a symbolic resource in work and life. Not holding such a strong sense of national identity as Jocelyn, Pauline would rather not be restricted by any particular language or culture.

Alignment with social discourses

Through the notion of alignment, I explore how the participants constructed their identities in the broader social community by examining how they undertook various actions to coordinate with historical, social and cultural discourses, towards which they express contrasting views. Jocelyn took pride in the profundity of Chinese traditional culture and wanted her achievements to benefit the nation (Interview 2, month 4). However, in an interview in her fourth year in college, when she was asked if there were reasons other than benefiting society for working hard on English, Jocelyn admitted, perhaps reluctantly, that she hoped that her identity as a high-achieving English learner could help her gain recognition and respect in society:

> Fame and reputation are extremely emphasized in society. Whether one is rich has become a very important standard for success. I think this is wrong, but cannot resist enjoying being recognized by others when they know that I can continue the postgraduate study with exemption of exam because of my high GPA.
>
> (Interview 4, month 12)

It seems that Jocelyn developed an ambivalent attitude towards 'fame and reputation' that is valued in the current Chinese society. On the one hand, she disliked materialism; while on the other hand, she enjoyed being recognized for her L2 identity. In Pauline's view, however, the rapidly changing Chinese society was a stage for her to realize dreams. Asked whether societal changes had influenced her English study, Pauline had no reservations about the high value placed on 'fame and reputation' in social discourses. Instead, these were her goals:

> There are so many opportunities waiting for me to explore in China today. My hard work on learning English has started to get rewarded. I took part in a lot of social activities that used English as the media and knew a lot of new things. I believe my dreams can come true as long as I try in such a swiftly developing society. Actually I don't care much about the social problems, and I am concerned more about things that have immediate relationship with me. (Interview 4, month 12)

The apparent tension in the expression of Jocelyn's views represents the dialogic relationship between the individual and the social. It seems that, although Jocelyn states that she dislikes the frantic pursuit of wealth common to many people in China, its social values have nevertheless influenced her learning behaviours. She oscillates on a continuum with the pursuit of material wealth at one end and the conduct of a highly meaningful life at the other, and is influenced by each in turn. Unlike Jocelyn who always wanted to explore the essence of Chinese traditional cultures and somewhat oscillated between her personal preferences and the social trend, Pauline was quite adaptable to social discourses and focused on her self-realization with the help of her L2 identity.

Discussion

This study has attempted to investigate individuality in the L2 identity construction of two Chinese learners of English within a CoP framework. It is found that L2 learning is uniquely experienced by individual learners who have different historical backgrounds and material resources and who, as active agents, continue to establish new relationships with their surroundings and create new layers of social structure, thus shaping and altering the learning context. At the methodological level, the participants' experiences, feelings, attitudes and emotions were documented over a prolonged period with multiple research methods, to a great extent ensuring a full presentation and explanation of the richness and complexity of individuals' behaviours and experiences. Therefore, the research methods used in this study have to a large extent helped retain the degree to which the participants appear as individuals.

The CoP model, which allows for a more specific consideration of the social, spatial and historical dimensions of identity construction, has proved useful in investigating individuality in L2 identity formation in this study. The three modes of belonging, engagement, imagination and alignment, proposed by Wenger (1998: 173–4) allow us to explore learners' formation of identity in communities at different levels, that is, the immediate learning community, the learning trajectory linking up the past, present and future and the broader social context. By means of engagement and alignment, we explore how individual learners legitimate their own positions in the learning community and how they negotiate and establish their L2 identity and cultural identity within social enterprises. By means of imagination, learners' historical and social backgrounds are considered together with their current practices and future expectations. This enables us to see to what extent individual learners' present and future are shaped by their past experiences. Using this model, this study found that the formation of individual learners' identities emerged as a complex process of contingency over time. It appeared that the two learners' conceptions on the contextual factors were historically and socially constructed, and that the constant interaction they had with the social context, provided an ongoing shaping effect on identity formation.

Despite the fact that they were studying in the same immediate learning community, Jocelyn and Pauline showed their individual differences. While Jocelyn remained true to her own values even at the cost of being marginalized from mainstream students in the learning community, Pauline quickly adapted her self-image to measure up to the new standard. While Jocelyn enthusiastically pursued new things in the hope of enriching her English knowledge, Pauline chose to do only what was 'useful' to her at the moment. While Jocelyn loved the challenges of studying and practising English, and gained satisfaction from overcoming problems, Pauline took on challenges to gain more opportunities for actual benefits. Moreover, while Jocelyn had very strong national identity that helped her balance her power relations with English cultures and speakers, Pauline was more concerned with establishing self-images that were 'popular' in the immediate and the social context. Whereas Jocelyn experienced a personal struggle in reconciling her Chinese cultural identity and her L2 identity, Pauline strategically used her L2 identity as a resource to achieve goals. Furthermore, Jocelyn sensed the contradiction between her values and prevailing societal values and thus had contradictory feelings about working hard on English. On one hand, the life objective of benefiting others and society had long been embedded into her L2 identity; on the other hand, she gradually realized that a higher social status was a prerequisite for being respected and recognized, and thus had to admit that pursuing individual success and wealth was a component of her English learning. However, unlike Jocelyn, Pauline thought China's changing society had plenty of opportunities for her self-realization; she claimed that larger societal problems did not immediately affect her, and concentrated instead on what she was doing.

The above findings indicate that the informants' individuality is historically and socially constructed. It seems that their different social backgrounds make the CoP a different context for Jocelyn and Pauline. This may explain why Pauline and Jocelyn had different conceptions of and responses to contextual factors in the English Department and in the broader society, which shaped their relationships with English. This may also explain why Jocelyn, whose parents have been encouraging her to lead a meaningful life since childhood, experienced struggle when faced with values and practices that were found contradictory to her own; and why Pauline, who developed a pragmatic worldview from the hard life when she was young, appeared to be very adaptable to outer surroundings. In addition to their historical backgrounds, the findings suggest that the situational and social contexts have been also exerting influences on learners' future goals, values and concerns.

In this sense, their different values, perceptions and behaviours are socially constructed, rather than individually enacted.

Through the lens of the CoP framework, the two learners' experiences are explored in terms of the relationships between identity, interpersonal relationships, situated learning activities, the learning trajectories, and negotiation and coordination with social enterprises. Both learners demonstrated considerable agency in the language learning process. It seems that agency is constructed and developed in the interplay between the individual and the social. For instance, Jocelyn exercised agency to create learning opportunities for herself and some classmates against her marginal status in the department; Pauline concealed the fact that she was a dedicated English learner from her fellow classmates so as to gain legitimacy. It also appears that language learners are individually different and that individuality is not a fixed quantity that can be determined beforehand, but a variable that can be mutually produced in the interactions between individual learners and their participation in the communities of practice. For example, that is why, although Jocelyn could not initially identify with some prevalent social values, she found herself gradually influenced by them; that is also why Pauline can shift her identity from a person 'who knows how to play' in the immediate learning community to a person 'who works hard to meet the social requirement' and 'has high English proficiency' in the broader social setting.

It is important to note that although the CoP framework, emphasizing individuals' participation in social activities, has helped us to account for L2 identity construction in practice in this study, Wenger's (1998) theory had been criticized for lacking an adequate theory of the role of language in constituting identity (Creese 2005) and failing to adequately account for conflict and resistance (Clarke 2008). As Weedon (1997) points out, 'language is the place where actual and possible forms of social organization and their likely social and political consequences are defined and contested. Yet it is also the place where our sense of ourselves, our subjectivity, is constructed' (p. 21). Therefore, it is important to have an account of the mutual effect between language and identity. It is also important to explore the resistance or conflict when individuals respond to marginalism, because, for example, these phenomena can represent the attempt of the students to legitimate their own position and project their own identities within the learning and the social communities. In the future research, a comprehensive understanding of the identity construction of L2 learners may be achieved by incorporating discourse theory (e.g. Torfing 1999; Fairclough 2003) to explore how identity is constructed both in practice and discourse and examine the potential for resistance and conflict involved in L2 learners' identity formation.

Conclusion

This study has specifically explored the processes of L2 identity formation of two college English L2 learners in China. From Jocelyn's and Pauline's cases, we can see that homogeneity in gender, age and English proficiency among language learners does not mean that they will tread identical learning paths. Learners' historical backgrounds, their future expectations and their own value systems all play parts in shaping their L2 identities. This indicates that we need not only to recognize the role the society plays in shaping the individual learner, but also the agency of the individual learner in identity research. It is therefore important to recognize learners as active and purposeful individuals with different personalities, learning histories, orientations and values. While working on the study, I deepened my understanding of individuality and observed that individual differences, such as the conceptions on contextual factors and the learning orientations, are deeply rooted in individual learners' family backgrounds and learning histories, rather than exist statically and unchangeably as individual traits. This finding thus raises the question of how individuality is constructed as the learners constantly interact with the social, cultural and historical contexts. In sum, this suggests that in-depth longitudinal case study approaches that emphasize the changing and social nature of learners' individuality should play a more important role in L2 learning research.

10 The ideal sexual self: the motivational investments of Japanese gay male learners of English

Ashley R. Moore

Introduction

This study explores how five Japanese individuals experienced one facet of their identity, their sexual identity as self-identifying gay men, across differing sociolinguistic contexts. It then attempts to establish emerging commonalities across these individual accounts that illuminate the ways in which these experiences influenced their motivational investments and agency in learning English as an international language. As Benson and Cooker (Chapter 1, this volume) discuss, Applied Linguists seeking to understand language learners as individuals from a sociocultural perspective are compelled to delineate what they understand to be the relationship that exists between the social world and the individual. This study utilizes a social realist approach (Sealey and Carter 2004) in understanding the concepts of the individual, identity, agency and the relationships that they have with the social world.

Following Layder (1997), Sealey and Carter describe the social world as consisting of a number of embedded, interlinked domains. The domains range from psychobiography (an individual's unique biography) to, at the level furthest removed from the individual, contextual resources which refer to the 'anterior distributions of material and cultural capital which social actors inherit as a consequence of being born in a particular place at a particular time' (2004: 140). Within this stratified social world there exist various entities that form a complex system. Social structure and individual agency, two of these entities, are considered both real and distinct from one another, each possessing its own specific properties and powers. Realist social theory upholds the agency of the individual to 'maintain or modify the world' (*ibid.* 11) whilst also maintaining that social structure possesses the power to both constrain and enable individual agency. Sealey and Carter (*ibid*: 12) state that, as social structure and individual agency interact, certain properties, such as language and other social practices, emerge through the interaction. These properties are not reducible to their constituent elements, which is to say that it is extremely difficult (if not impossible) for us to establish exactly where an emergent property, such as language, 'comes from' as it is both creatively produced by individuals and normatively maintained through elements of social structure such as the educational system. These emergent cultural properties possess powers of their own that can affect both structure and agency.

Social realism and identity

Identity can also be seen as an emergent property, experienced at the point of intersection between individual agency and social structure, something Jenkins (2008) (who, though not an avowed social realist, shares a great deal with social realist theory in terms of his explanation of the social world and how identity works) terms the 'internal-external dialectic of identification' (p. 40). Realist social theory resists the post-structural view that identity is something that is performed by individuals and 'unstable, fragmented, ongoing [and] discursively constructed' (Block 2006: 35). In post-structuralist theory, an individual's agency and resultant speech acts are afforded primacy in the 'performance' of identity (Nelson 1999: 375). However, as Saunston and Kyratzis (2007) argue, the speech acts employed in an individual's performance of identity are actually unstable and must be understood in terms of the sociocultural context in which they are produced and received. Moreover, as Jenkins (2008) maintains, any identity work performed by an individual must be 'accepted by significant others before an identity can be said to be "taken on"' (p. 44). 'Significant others' here can be read as other individuals or even those individuals that might be collectively represented as components of social structure such as 'the legal system' or 'the government'. Here, identity is conceptualized as an interactional process that one participates in and experiences rather than an individual performance or construction.

Social realist theory, then, accounts for how the relationships between the social, the individual and identity are understood in this study. However, as Sealey and Carter have noted, there are very few studies or models within Applied Linguistics that utilize an identified social realist framework (2004: 183). As such, in seeking to understand the experiences and behaviours of individuals engaged in language learning, I found it necessary to draw upon models and studies from within the field that were not grounded in a social realist understanding of the individual and the social world but still helped to inform my understanding of the emergent trends in the data. I will now discuss this literature, with particular reference to Dörnyei's (2005; 2009) model of the L2 Motivational Self System whilst also illustrating how a social realist perspective may diverge from other social approaches prevalent in Applied Linguistics.

Border crossing and possible selves

As individuals cross borders and move between contexts, the social structure with which they interact changes, as do the culturally emergent properties such as language and identity. It should be noted that the contexts and resultant borders that I refer to here need not necessarily be geographically separate countries; they may be smaller social groups or, in today's increasingly virtual world, online communities. Yashima (Chapter 4, this volume) has discussed the potential for these new spaces and communities to afford individuals the 'capacity to create new ways of being'. Although a social realist perspective would also seek to examine the ways in which new contexts and communities might impose new constraints and subjectivities on individual agency, it is clear that for people wishing to move to another context in which a language other than their L1 is dominant, the possibility of increasing one's cultural capital (Bourdieu 1977) could also influence their motivational investment in learning an L2.

The links between the possibilities of a second language context, the desires of the individual language learner and the learner's motivation are captured in the 'L2 Motivational Self System' model developed by Dörnyei (2009). His model consists of three components, one of which is the ideal L2 self, a possible L2-speaking self that the learner would like to become. Drawing on Higgins's (1987) theory of self-discrepancy, Dörnyei posits that the ideal L2 self is a powerful motivator to learn the L2 due to the desire to reduce the discrepancy between our actual and ideal possible selves. The ideal L2 self is linked to the imagined L2 communities of the learner in that these communities (and the cultural capital that they are perceived to possess) provide salient models through which the ideal L2 self is developed and reinforced. That is to say, as a learner moves from the periphery of an L2 community towards becoming a fully participatory member, those who are already participatory members provide the best models to the learner. By gradually aligning oneself to the constituent practices of the community, the goal of a realized ideal L2 self that belongs to a desired community moves closer (see Lamb, Chapter 3, this volume). A social realist perspective seeks to explicitly account for the fact that communities of practice are embedded within social structure and as such, the extent to which an individual can make the transition from the periphery towards becoming a fully participatory member will be subject to certain constraints of the kind that Lamb discusses in reference to agency.

The Japanese context: international posture and the L1 'push'

A number of scholars have argued that the most relevant L2 community for Japanese learners of English is not that of a geographically specific country but an international community of English speakers (Nakata 1995; McClelland 2000; Yashima 2000, 2009; Ryan 2009). Yashima (2009) uses the term 'international posture' to refer to this tendency and has isolated a number of attitudes that are indicative of this motivated stance such as an individual's willingness to communicate with L2 speakers, desire to participate in international activity, and adoption of a non-ethnocentric approach to different cultures. However, as Sealey (2007) notes, it is important to explicitly acknowledge that investing in another language as a linguistic resource and crossing borders may carry with them objective consequences, such as a decrease in earnings or restricted access to resources, that may or may not be apparent to the learner. Nevertheless, the notion of learners investing into the cultural capital associated with a second language provides us with some idea about how such border crossings might be linked to the motivations of some people.

Realist social theory, as noted above, explicitly acknowledges the power of social structure to both make affordances for and impose constraints upon individual agency and the experience of identity. Given this, it can be used to understand what might be termed the motivational 'push' from L1 contexts experienced by some learners attempting to cross borders, whether this crossing is an actual physical relocation or a more abstract crossing such as individuals participating in second language mediated online communities. Current models of motivation in SLA that incorporate an understanding of how identity can influence a learner's motivational investment (including the L2 Motivational Self System) tend to focus on the positive effects of learners identifying with a target sociocultural context, whether this is a specific nationality or simply a broadly defined international space. That said, it seems logical that people's motivational investments in learning a second language stem not only from their experiences and attitudes towards the L2 but also from their subjective experiences of their relationship to their L1 context and its social structure. That is to say, if the external expectations or the sense of social responsibility that an individual feels is inherent in his or her L1 culture stand at odds with his or her desires or wishes for the future, this could also engender development of a salient ideal L2 self.

Several studies focusing on the Japanese context seem to suggest that the process through which ideal L2 selves are engendered and developed may also be attributed to the learner's sense of conflict with their L1 sociocultural context. Kelsky (1999, 2001) explored how a small group of internationalized professional women in Japan undertook the learning of English or other western languages in order to (symbolically at least) emancipate themselves from what they saw as the gender-stratified corporate and family structures prevalent in Japan. The women felt that their first language context and the gender-specific social expectation it symbolized were at odds with their sense of who they were and what they wanted to become. Thus the women wished to make a defection to their imagined international community which they felt could make a more positive contribution to their gender identity. McMahill (2001), too, has noted how the students of a Japanese feminist English class were motivationally driven by their desires to compete in the international job market and provide opportunities for themselves as women which they felt were unavailable in their L1 context. Similarly, McLelland (2000), in his exploration of male homosexuality in modern Japan, notes that many of the individuals he interviewed drew a sharp distinction between the possibilities of gay life in Japan and in the west (the social and legal situations facing gay men in Japan have been discussed relatively recently by Sunagawa (2006) and Taniguchi (2006) respectively). From the participants' perspectives, living a 'gay lifestyle' was possible only outside of Japan and this often fostered a desire to live abroad. To this end, one of McLelland's participants chose to study foreign languages at university in order to 'facilitate his escape from Japan' (2000: 229).

As the above discussion suggests, for some individuals, conflict between their experiences of their L1 sociocultural context and their own selfhood (including who they would like to be in the future) contributes to their development of an ideal L2 self. Their desire to reduce the discrepancy between their actual selves and their ideal L2 selves can motivate a number of attitudes and behaviours that engage them in the language learning process in order to participate in L2 sociocultural contexts. Participation is seen as a pathway to availing themselves of the symbolic and material resources of the L2 context but it also necessitates negotiation with the constraints and modes of understanding prevalent in another sociocultural context.

The study, then, explores the gay men's individual accounts of their experiences of sexual identity across varying sociolinguistic contexts (and thus, differing social structures). It seeks to explore both the emerging affordances and constraints that they experienced and their reported emotional responses and resultant agency, in order to better understand the ongoing language learning processes in which they are engaged.

The study

Informed by the substantive ideas and findings discussed above, this study set out to answer the following general question: In what ways does the sexual identity of Japanese, gay, male learners of English interact with the second language acquisition process? To this end several sub-questions were asked:

1. Do the Japanese gay men who participated in this study perceive a difference in the possibilities and limitations of sexual identity between Japanese and English-speaking contexts?
2. To what extent, if at all, do these differences affect how they feel about Japanese and English-speaking contexts in general?
3. Do such feelings, whether positive or negative, have an effect on their motivational investment in learning English?

The participants all self-identified as gay men although 'gay' was not seen as a monolithic term and participants were asked to discuss which terms they would use to describe their sexual identity, in which situations, and what they understood those terms to mean. All names are pseudonyms (Table 10.1).

In order to elicit what are essentially the participants' subjective accounts of their experiences of sexual identity in differing sociocultural contexts, a methodological framework was needed that was flexible enough to reflect the variation that exists between individual experiences. Given this need, semi-structured, in-depth interviews were used in order to both direct the conversation and to allow each participant the time and conversational 'space' to relate their experiences. The interview was piloted and four broad topic areas were developed:

- factual biographical information;
- experiences of learning English;
- experiences of sexual identity in Japan; and
- experiences of sexual identity in English-speaking contexts.

Table 10.1 Biographical profiles of participants

Name	Age	Residence during formative years in Japan	Current place of residence	Educational background	Current occupation
Kenta	29	Born and raised in Tokyo	Small city, United Kingdom	Graduated from senior high school that specialized in EFL. Studied French and German at a Japanese university Currently PhD candidate at a British university	Post-graduate student
Hiro	33	Born and raised in small town in southern Kyushu	London, United Kingdom	Graduated from senior high school Attended several ESL schools in United Kingdom	Student, chef in Japanese restaurant (part-time)
Masa	30	Born in Hiroshima	Tokyo, Japan	Studied English at a Japanese university, obtained an MA in Applied Linguistics from a British university	EFL teacher
Shiro	24	Born and raised in large city in Kyushu	London, United Kingdom	Studied English with a focus on British literature at a Japanese university Also spent one year studying linguistics at a British university Qualified Japanese language teacher	Waiter in Japanese restaurant
Yoshi	25	Born in small town in southern Kyushu	London, United Kingdom	Graduated senior high school in Japan Majored in Geography and Theatre Arts at an American university	Sales assistant in sandwich shop (part-time)

Four of the five Japanese men participated in onsite interviews in the United Kingdom. The remaining individual, Masa, participated in an asynchronous email interview as he was living in Japan at the time of the study. Common emerging topics that pertained to the research questions were delineated, such as the participants' negative experiences of the gay scene in Japan. These topics were then consolidated under more general nodes such as 'Experiences of gay scenes in Japan and English-speaking contexts' and the data was then coded. After the coding was complete I organized the data into the thematic subsections that also serve as the structure for the following presentation of the findings. This act of organization is something that I will return to in the conclusion, reflecting on the way in which the act of analysis may obfuscate the individual in studies of this kind.

Findings

It seems prudent to reiterate the fact that the data presented here represent the reported accounts of the participants' subjective experiences and interpretations of an objective reality that may be viewed in different ways. Indeed, the findings, such as the opinion held by some of the participants that English-speaking contexts were more 'gay-friendly' than Japan, may be at odds with certain critical cultural perspectives such as McLelland's (2000) counsel that those researching sexual minorities in Japan resist dichotomous presentations of a '"permissive" west and a "repressive" Japan' (p. 231). Their presentation and discussion are justified in terms of the bearing that they have on the participants' own self-understandings and behaviours.

Images of homosexuality: attitudes, resistance and change

All of the interviewees identified themselves as gay and noted that they would use *gei*, a Japanese term taken from English, if describing themselves in Japanese. In general, most felt that other Japanese people would understand the same-sex desiring identity that this refers to. However, the value judgements that they felt Japanese people associated with the term were often negative. Kenta and Hiro felt that most Japanese people thought of gays as 'crazy' or 'freaks'. Masa expressed mixed feelings upon first feeling attracted to another boy at high school as, whilst he enjoyed the feeling of attraction, he felt afraid that others would treat him 'unkindly as someone strange or weird'. Such negative attitudes were often attributed to a general lack of understanding on the part of Japanese people, as Shiro expressed when he said that people who 'are not used to gay people will be confused … when gay people come out'.

As one might expect when exploring the experiences of five individuals with disparate personal histories and feelings, there was a great deal of variation in terms of the extent to which the participants had come out to others as being gay. Interestingly however, both Yoshi and Hiro talked about feeling more comfortable coming out to Japanese people who had also lived abroad as they used this as an indicator of whether or not the other person would understand such a speech act as they intended. For example, Yoshi stated that he had come out to the Japanese friends he met in San Francisco because 'they know what the gay people are'. Yoshi and Hiro's opinions illustrate how vital the recognition and acceptance of identity work by significant others is to understanding the construction of identification.

Markedly, all of the interviewees discussed the prevalence of an effeminate stereotype of gay men prevalent in both the popular imagination of Japanese society of gay identities and the Japanese gay scene itself. A visibly effeminate identity was resisted by Shiro and Masa as 'disgusting' or 'sissy' and put forward as one of the primary reasons for their negative attitudes towards the Japanese gay scene. Similarly, when talking about the gay scene in Tokyo, Kenta described how he felt uncomfortable: 'the people there er looks weird for me and some of them are so girly it's like a trave-travestile and so, so some of them looks like a queen and I don't like that kind of stuff …'.

Images of gay men in the Japanese media were also generally negatively evaluated as participants expressed dissatisfaction with what they saw as the persistent portrayal of gay men as entertainers or comedians. This image of the 'gay entertainer' was also felt to contribute to the lack of understanding of more masculine and politicized possibilities of gay identity on the part of Japanese people in general. Yoshi felt that images in the media of drag queens and Hard Gay (a Japanese comedian, popular at the time of the interview, who dressed in leather hot pants and cap) were prevalent at the expense of gay political issues such as gay marriage and gay pride. Both Masa and Hiro felt that such images engendered the general notion in society that gay people and the topics pertaining to them were 'just TV things' or specific only to the world of entertainment rather than real everyday experience. Having said this, Yoshi felt that Hard Gay and his image of an overtly masculine gay man is a positive influence as it offered a 'totally different stereotype' to mainstream Japanese society and, as he put it, 'that's the beginning … to know gay people in Japanese society'.

More positively, all of the participants noted that both tolerance and understanding of gay people and lifestyles were increasing. However, Shiro, Hiro and Yoshi geographically associated this change with large cities such as Tokyo which are perhaps more progressive. It should also be noted that Yoshi, Hiro and Kenta all reported that this change in attitudes and understanding was proceeding slowly and that the situation remained 'frustrating'. As Kenta reflected, 'it's more tolerant but … still it's hard to be a gay'.

Whilst all of the participants felt that the sociocultural context surrounding gay men in Japan was changing for the better, most expressed some negative feelings concerning both the pace and extent of this change. Furthermore, one of the most salient commonalities was a resistance to what they saw as the gay identities (the gay 'entertainer', the camp gay man and the gay man living in large cities) that dominate both the Japanese gay community and Japanese society's understanding of gay people in general. This resistance illustrates the importance that the participants placed on having their identities accepted and validated by significant others, in this case, the mainstream media, their families and the gay community itself.

Conflict between the Japanese sociocultural context and living as a gay man

All of the participants professed to feeling that living as a gay man in Japan often brought them into conflict with both the corporate and family structures that are prevalent in Japanese society. Masa talked about why he felt that many Japanese gay people find it difficult to come out. As he explained:

> Japanese people basically place much value on 'uniformity' and tend to feel comfortable if they find that they have a lot in common with others. So if they recognize that they are different from others in some ways, they tend to feel uncomfortable.

More often than not, the pressure to conform to this notion of uniformity presents itself to the participants in the expectations of others such as bosses at work, other family members or Japanese people as a whole. Although not all of the participants considered being unmarried to be a handicap in terms of career progression, when I asked Yoshi if it was helpful to be married in order to progress in your career in Japan he replied:

> Japanese culture … they have standards that – what you need to be in a certain age. Like my age twenty five I should have a nice job and … not part-time and have a girlfriend or have married

> already ... If you don't follow the standard people ... just don't think you're normal in that kind of way ... So I mean that affects your career for some reason people think you're not normal.

Hiro also stressed what he saw as the importance of conforming to the group in Japanese culture at the expense of the personality of the individual. In terms of living as a gay man in Japan, this pressure to conform manifested itself when Hiro was in his late twenties and people began to ask him when he was intending to find a girlfriend and marry. Tellingly, Hiro countered that he did not care about such expectations as he had 'itchy feet'. Indeed, the desire to join an international community and travel widely outside of Japan often featured in the participants' accounts of how they avoided the various pressures to conform to the perceived 'standards' of Japanese life.

International travel as a form of escape

Hiro further elaborated on how having 'itchy feet', or a strong desire to travel, helped him to circumvent the normative expectations of his family and other members of the small community in which he lived in Japan. He explained that as someone who frequently travels and lives abroad, people assume that he is 'busy' and that this was thought to be the reason why he has still not married. Similarly, Yoshi explained how the pressure he felt to be 'normal' in Japan drove his love of travel:

> That's why I always go abroad because I can be who I, you know, who I want to be. 'Cause it's really hard, it's not only like gay but anything that Japanese people expect me to be someone else I don't want to be.

Referring to the L2 Motivational Self System, it could be argued that one of Yoshi's ideal selves ('who I want to be') was inextricably linked with the contexts that he described broadly as 'abroad'. For Yoshi, as I will discuss later, this ideal self also spoke an L2 (English) in order to facilitate his desire to go 'abroad'. Shiro, too, stated that he felt more comfortable living in the United Kingdom as a gay man as he was geographically and metaphorically far away from his perceived expectations of his family. In response to what the participants felt to be an inherent conflict between the Japanese sociocultural context and living as a gay man, the participants had come to consider the international world (defined here as a sociocultural space existing independently from Japan) as a space in which they could 'escape' and live their lives more comfortably as gay men.

Sociocultural context, language and sexual identity

Given that language and culture relate to and influence each other in so many ways, it is perhaps not surprising that the 'push' away from the Japanese sociocultural context described by the participants should also manifest itself in their experiences of speaking in Japanese and their feelings towards the language itself (particularly when talking about gay subjects). For example, Masa attests that he feels more comfortable speaking English than speaking Japanese and his explanation of the cause of this feeling clearly and explicitly illustrates how he views the relationship between the Japanese sociocultural context and the language itself:

> That's mainly because speaking English means that I'm communicating with people from various countries, so I don't necessarily pay attention to the Japanese original cultural perspectives such as 'uniformity' ... In other words, I can make simpler, clearer and more direct what I would like to tell without considering such perspectives. On the other hand, speaking Japanese basically means that I'm talking to Japanese people who have such perspectives in their mind. So when speaking Japanese, I unconsciously happen to think about such perspectives at the same time in talking to people, which quite often makes me feel fed up with them.

Thus, for Masa the Japanese language is inextricably linked to the sociocultural context in which it primarily exists. A pattern emerges from the participants' discourse which suggests that, when talking about gay topics at least, they do not feel comfortable speaking in Japanese, as Yoshi explained:

> I think I wouldn't speak about my like sexual relationship, that I couldn't do it in Japanese. If I speak to you in Japanese, I don't know I would tell you or not ... I use Japanese in Japan ... Not in US and UK, that maybe it reminds me that I shouldn't be a gay or something kind of like I'm just- only one gay person in Japan. Some kind of feeling, maybe unconsciously I'm thinking about it when I speak it in Engli- I mean Japanese. Something kind of stop me.

Similarly Kenta explicitly asked whether the interview would be conducted in English or Japanese, later explaining that he was concerned because 'if I talk in Japanese probably I try to be not honest because spontaneously I try to- I try to protect me- not to be gay because in Japanese it's not very common to speak as, er gay stuff.'

Clearly, for both Yoshi and Kenta their experiences of living as gay men in the Japanese sociocultural context, mediated through the Japanese language, have resulted in a feeling of general unease when talking in Japanese about their experiences. This can be seen to reinforce any 'push' that they may feel from their native culture towards an imagined international context and community. It should be noted at this point that none of the participants explicitly identified English as a 'gay language' or the only option available to them. Indeed Kenta agreed that he would feel just as comfortable talking about his gay experiences in French or German. As he put it: 'Oh whatever … except Japanese'.

Investing in English as a global language

The 'push' away from the Japanese sociocultural context towards an imagined international context also contributed to the participants' motivational investments in learning English. They rarely associated their motivation to learn English with a desire to join a geographically specific language community. Instead, they often described their motivation in terms of a desire to experience life in other countries and communicate with foreign (non-Japanese) people in general. As Kenta noted, he enjoyed learning foreign languages in general, not solely English. Interestingly Kenta explicitly explained his motivation in terms of his desire to experience foreign cultures and because he perceived foreign cultures to be 'more liberal for gays'.

The participants viewed English as a linguistic tool that they could use to communicate with countries and people outside of Japan. Shiro, Masa and Yoshi viewed English as a 'common language' that could be used to communicate with people all over the world. As Yoshi further explains:

> English definitely is the most useful language in the world. You can, you go anywhere if you can speak English or like someone can speak it in a different country. And so communicating with other people that's the most part I want to study it.

It could be argued then that English represented the highest potential gain on the participants' motivational investments, as it was perceived to maximize their chances of escaping from Japan and reducing the discrepancy between their actual selves and their ideal selves. This also illustrates the complex ways in which the participants' ideal L2 selves were closely linked with what could be termed their ideal sexual selves.

Limitations of a global gay identity

As noted above, the participants expressed a strong desire to learn English and experience life as gay men outside of Japan in an international community that was both imagined and, in part, experienced. However, that is not to say that they accepted their experiences of 'being' gay in other contexts unproblematically. Although Kenta described England as a 'paradise' for gay men, he still did not feel comfortable enough to come out to his heterosexual friends or join the Lesbian/Gay/Bisexual/Transgender (LGBT) society at his university because, as he told me, 'if I go there [to an LGBT event] which means I come out right?' This seemed to indicate that Kenta was wary of claiming membership of the LGBT society and the level of 'out-ness' that he associated with it. In a similar vein, Hiro also indicated a slight feeling of annoyance when his foreign friends introduced him to new acquaintances first and foremost as a gay man, perhaps suggesting that he too was uncomfortable with the primacy afforded to sexual identity in many western contexts. Both Yoshi and Masa expressed similar feelings of discomfort or unease that were associated with very strong or highly visible gay identities they had observed. For example, Masa reported that he had not enjoyed visiting gay bars in the United Kingdom as he dislikes gay people 'who obviously behave as gay (e.g. the way they speak and wear …), and the places I visited were full of those guys'.

Both Hiro and Shiro acknowledged that, whilst gay men in England can sometimes hold hands in public, physically demonstrative acts of same-sex affection are usually geographically confined to 'safe' areas such as London's Soho district. Thus, at the same time as 'western', international sociocultural contexts were viewed more positively by the participants (in comparison to their experiences in Japan) they were also aware of some of the constraints that could affect them.

Discussion

Through its use of psychobiographical data, the study is rooted in subjective accounts of individual agency and experience. By utilizing a framework that explicitly acknowledged both the agency of the individual and the possible constraints of a given sociocultural context on that agency, this study was able to capture both the possibilities and the limits of the subjectivities available through the L2 contexts that the participants experienced. The various accounts of the choices they made and the paths that they took illustrated the power of the individual within both life and the learning process.

This agency, however, is not boundless but subject to the constraints of social structure. For example, although Hiro was able to stay in the United Kingdom on a student visa, his primary desire was not to study in the United Kingdom but simply to live there. His student visa restricted the number of hours he could work to 20 hours (during term time) and he stated that he found it difficult to live comfortably on the money that he could legally earn. Hiro's agency as an individual was constrained and directed by the macro-level social structure in which he was embedded.

All five participants expressed a sense of resistance towards what they saw as the prevalent modes of gay identity available to them in the Japanese sociocultural context. The participants were often dissatisfied with the disjuncture between their own self-images as gay men and the conception of gay men dominant in both the media and the understanding of the general Japanese populace. They also frequently perceived their lives as gay men as conflicting with various social structures in Japan such as family or corporate structures. Together, these affective responses to the Japanese sociocultural context seemed to work as a 'push' away from it and towards the sociocultural spaces outside of Japan. Based on their experiences and knowledge of foreign sociocultural contexts the participants had developed a generally positive (though not unproblematic) conception of an imagined international community in which they felt they could live more comfortably as gay men. Through envisaging their own participation within this community, it could be argued that they had also developed what might be termed ideal sexual selves. These possible selves, borne from their experiences of their sexual identity, were also linked to their ideal L2 selves as the participants tended to view English (in its capacity as a global language) as a linguistic resource that could be used to help them in their struggle for participation.

Although all five of the participants had, at some time, participated in geographically specific English-speaking contexts, they tended to frame their motivations and actions in terms of their participation in a broader international community and desire to communicate with people from around the world. These attitudes and behaviours would support the notion of Japanese EFL learners' international posture. For example, none of the participants described any strong desires to 'integrate' with a specific nation state, instead privileging participation within an international community. They also demonstrated, through their agency in choosing to cultivate relationships with foreign people, what Yashima refers to as an 'intergroup approach tendency' (2009: 146), or a willingness to engage with foreign people who do not share the same first language. I would go further, however, and suggest that for the five participants, their experiences of conflict with the social structure prevalent in Japan and the resultant desire to experience life outside of it seem to demonstrate a motivational drive somewhat stronger than that denoted by the international posture construct.

Returning to the central concerns of this volume, the extent to which the approaches adopted here can be said to illuminate the individual within Applied Linguistics requires discussion. The L2 Motivation Self System offered a framework within which the agency exhibited by the participants in their language learning endeavours could be understood in terms of them seeking to reduce a gap between their actual selves and their ideal L2 selves. In other words, the L2 Motivational Self System allowed me to take a closer look at the motivational 'pull' experienced by the participants towards learning English. It was, however, less useful when it came to understanding the motivational 'push' that many of the participants felt from Japan. Social realism offers an approach through which this motivational drive or 'L1 push' can be understood as emerging through the dialectic between the individual and the social structure in which he or she is embedded. The participants did not feel that the social structure prevalent in Japan would permit or recognize the sexual identities that they desired. This resulted in resistance towards this structure and a high motivation to seek out other social structures in which the identities they wished to claim might be better understood and accepted.

The study, grounded in social realist theory, raises questions as to the extent to which it is possible for studies of this kind to focus on and ultimately illuminate an individual. The post-structural approaches to identity that have been pervasive in the Applied Linguistics literature to date (Canagarajah 2006) tend to put forward the individual as both the source of identity and its controlling force. However, as noted above, the social realist framework maintains that identity is an emergent property of the dialectic between the individual and the social. Thus, in focusing on the participants' sexual identity, the findings must, to some extent, lose sight of the individual if we accept that identity 'happens' at some level of remove from the individual. For example, it is possible to discuss the participants' experience of identity as it emerges through the dialectic between the individual and social structure but it is extremely difficult to separate which parts of this experience can be solely attributed to the agency of the individual.

In addition, in this study I have attempted to identify potentially insightful commonalities that emerge through the participants' accounts, such as their resistance to what they considered to be the effeminate modes of gay identity available to them in Japan or their desires to learn English in order to participate within an international community. In doing so, the study inevitably cannot fully reflect the extent to which the participants differed on an individual level and space constraints prevent these instances of difference from being fully discussed here. Indeed, as soon as a researcher begins to analyse the data and establish these commonalities through coding, grouping and reorganization of the data, he or she is also moving away from the individuality of the participants. Whilst I hope that the participants would recognize themselves in the study and agree with the narrative logic of the findings, it would be interesting to find out whether this is the case.

Lastly, it should be acknowledged that an individual's psychobiography will be made up of a number of facets, much like an individual's identity. As the interview topics centred on the participants' experiences of their sexual identity as gay Japanese men, these other dimensions of their individual psychobiographies are not directly considered in this study. However, other accounts of the self and its experiences (for example, a person's professional psychobiography) are considered where they overlap with an individual's gay psychobiography. Nevertheless, in choosing to focus on one aspect of an individual's identity, the study necessarily offers what can only be a partial account of these individuals' language learning stories. Despite this limitation inherent in methodology adopted here, the study does provide evidence of the ways in which this particular group of participants who shared somewhat common experiences might differ from other learners such as heterosexual Japanese male learners of English.

Conclusion

In focusing on the experiences of just five Japanese gay men, this study necessarily limits itself in terms of generalizability. Furthermore, I do not wish to present the findings of the study as the common experiences of all Japanese gay men or even all Japanese gay men who invested in learning English. However, the themes that emerged through the pilot study (in which the participant was Taiwanese), anecdotal evidence from several colleagues and a growing body of studies that specifically focus on self-identified gay individuals involved in language learning (Nelson 2009, 2010; King 2008) suggest that the experiences and motivational investments of the participants in this study may be similar to those of other gay learners 'moving between' other linguistic sociocultural contexts. Future studies that explore the issues raised here in different contexts and with different kinds of queer identities would contribute to a more thorough understanding of how the sexual identity of second language learners interacts with the second language acquisition process.

11 Using Complexity Theory in linguistic data analysis: a language ecology approach to the study of individual and social process

Anne Whiteside

Introduction

In this chapter, I draw on two theoretical frameworks discussed by Menezes (Chapter 5, this volume) – Complexity Theory (Larsen-Freeman and Cameron 2008a, b) (sometimes called Dynamic Systems Theory: de Bot 2008) and Language Ecology (Kramsch 2002; van Lier 2004) – to analyse data on the language practices of transnational migrants to the United States. By recognizing individual behaviour as both idiosyncratic and constrained by social context, these two frameworks treat it as both socially and self-determined. Borrowing concepts from biology and ecology, they treat the relationship between individuals and their environment as open, dynamic and symbiotic. And although Complexity Theory is at this stage still a meta-theory, with some way to go in developing methods, protocols and procedures, and Language Ecology a more general approach to the study of language as a cross-disciplinary endeavour, I would argue both have the potential to resolve some of the tensions between the social and the individual in Applied Linguistics that Benson and Cooker (Chapter 1, this volume) refer to.

To show how these two strands of theory can potentially account for individual language choices, I will discuss data from my doctoral study of language practices of Mexican migrants to the United States (Whiteside 2006), using concepts from Complexity Theory and Language Ecology. These concepts allowed me to look at dynamic social tensions in the linguistic practices of transnational migrants who work in multicultural multilingual cities and who inhabit two worlds simultaneously, moving seamlessly between face-to-face conversations and those via cell phones made cheap by phone cards or Skype, to family back home. My study focused on recently arrived Yucatec Maya-speaking immigrants, who had left south-western Yucatan as competition from global markets and the tourist industry decimated their hometown economies (Yucatec Maya, which belongs to the Mayan language family, has close to a million speakers: *Censo General de Población y Vivienda* 2000).

These Spanish/Maya bilinguals, marginalized both by colonial discourses and the global economy that exploits undocumented, temporary labourers, were now picking up English. To understand practices and ideologies that confer dramatically different social statuses on these three languages, and strategic choices made by individuals, I looked at patterns of language use across a range of social contexts, interviewed people about their histories and linguistic choices, and recorded conversations between four individuals and people in the community as they went about their daily lives.

Before describing the study in more detail, I will briefly describe the two strands of theory, Complexity Theory and Language Ecology. Then I will outline some findings from my study, looking in detail at one case history and three conversations to see what kind of analysis these strands of theory can yield. Finally, I will discuss some advantages and limitations associated with these approaches.

Complexity Theory/Language Ecology

Drawing attention to parallels between language and non-linear, complex systems, Larsen Freeman (1997) posed a fundamental challenge to Second Language Acquisition (SLA) theory. Inspired by Chaos/Complexity Theory in the natural sciences, she urged researchers to reconceptualize the ends and means of second language research, arguing that the present positivist emphasis on simplicity, linearity and causality, and an avoidance of language 'use' inherited from Chomskian linguistics were getting in the way of looking at language in its natural habitat. By limiting themselves to the study of structured exchanges in classrooms, she and others later argued, researchers were missing some basic points: that language is a dynamic, complex system; that learning is a provisional unstable state, for which there is no endpoint. Rather than relying on mechanical models of change used in psycholinguistic research, she suggested researchers look to biological models of complex systems that encompass rather than seek to reduce or eliminate variability. Linguistic processes are heterogeneous and non-linear; languages are open, not closed systems. Research should focus on patterns of linguistic behaviour that emerge from dynamic interactions between various elements or levels of organization, and at different time scales, she argued. Chaos Theory had shown that small elements can have disproportionate effects on complex systems; effects are not always attributable to causes, and prediction not always feasible (see Menezes, Chapter 5, this volume). Therefore empirical language research should not limit itself to causal relations or predictability (Larsen-Freeman 1997; Larsen-Freeman and Cameron 2008b).

More recently, Larsen-Freeman and Cameron (2008a, b) have elaborated a research agenda, with a commitment to: broaden the scope of language development research; examine both context and individual as dynamically related; focus on processes, self-organization, emergence, changes in relationship and feedback; include equilibrium, stability and change; and emphasize reciprocal causality or co-adaptation rather than linear causality.

During the same period Kramsch (2002) and others were developing an approach they called Language Ecology, which included replacing conventional learning-as-mechanical-process metaphors with ecological concepts that view change as emergent and self-organizing, and individual/context distinctions as phenomena seen at various levels of organization or time scales (van Lier 2000, 2002, 2004; Kramsch 2002). According to Language Ecologists, learning a language entails being socialized into cultural ways of knowing and doing, or a 'habitus' (Bourdieu 1977). Identities are constituted through and by language, as interlocutors take stances *vis-à-vis* each other, aligning themselves positively or negatively with a previous turn of talk (Ochs 2002). Ochs uses a post-structuralist emphasis on 'subject positions', performance and stance to define social identity as something that emerges in the situated meaning of an utterance, 'an inferential outcome of linguistically coded acts and stances' (1993: 295).

According Bourdieu's (1977) practice theory, individual choice is neither entirely 'self-determined' nor entirely 'socially determined'. Related to his concept of 'habitus', 'dispositions', in Bourdieu's framework, are the socially and culturally durable ways of doing and thinking which individuals internalize as they become socialized to a particular social context. The concept of 'habitus' thus allows for individual strategic choice, or agency, which is nevertheless highly constrained by dispositions that have become internalized, naturalized and invisible to the individual. Through habitual practice, individuals become 'disposed' towards socially acceptable behaviours which reproduce the status quo. The habitus is the nexus of the social and individual, or as Bourdieu and Wacquant (1992: 126) put it: 'habitus is socialized subjectivity'. But although Bourdieu allows space for individual agency, his theory of symbolic domination represents individuals as being complicit in their own domination. Critics suggest that individuals can also use language strategically to resist domination. Pavlenko and Blackledge (2004: 13), for example, point to ways in which individuals use their linguistic resources to legitimize, challenge, and negotiate particular identities and to open up new identity options for oppressed and subjugated individuals and groups.

How do these concepts and meta-theories change the analysis of linguistic data? First, by turning the focus to processes like self-organization, co-adaptation and emergence rather than on stability, or variables and cause and effect, researchers can entertain contradictory findings and behaviour that varies over space and time. In this model individuals struggle with historical and contextual constraints, sometimes ignoring their dispositions, or, like Shakespearean characters, are full of conflict and self-doubt. To give an example of how this works, I now turn to the data analysis of my doctoral research.

Using Complexity Theory and Language Ecology to analyse my research data

To collect my thesis data, I made use of four of the methodologies considered by Larsen-Freeman and Cameron (2008a, b) to be consistent with underlying premises of their approach: ethnography, which provides data on the macro/micro-level data, and describes relationships between shared and individual practices; action research, which studies systems with a view to changing them, and includes researcher as actor; case study, which allows researchers to document change and variability over time; and Conversation Analysis, which uses empirical methods to study dynamics at the micro-level of discourse through turns at talk. Less clearly delineated in both theoretical approaches, as we shall see, is how to integrate the analyses resulting from these four methodologies. My goal was to generate data on language practices at three levels: the population, the individual and the conversation. At the population level, I looked at general practices, the linguistic habitus of community members. In the case studies, I was looking at how these practices played out over time. And in the conversations, I looked at 'reciprocal co-adaptation' in the turns-at-talk, and the identities that emerge over a stretch of discourse.

To study community language practices, I did two years of participant observation in a neighbourhood where Yucatecan immigrants were clustered. For action research, I designed a language survey in collaboration with members of a community-based organization and Maya-speaking members of student club at the Community College where I teach. For case studies, I interviewed and followed four people over a period of a year. And for conversational data, I recorded conversations between these four individuals and members of the community as they went about their daily lives. In retrospect, my mosaic-like methodology meets many of the commitments outlined by Larsen-Freeman and Cameron. Lacking space here to go into detail on all four, I will briefly describe some relevant findings based on the first three methods, then go into some detail on the fourth, Conversation Analysis.

Findings from an ethnographic study and action research

To study community language practices, I did two years of participant observation in a Yucatecan immigrant neighbourhood and interviewed policemen, teachers and community service providers. I found that linguistic environments vary tremendously across spaces and time, and that each context structures and constrains language differently. One overriding issue was whether legal status counted in a particular context: like other Mexican immigrants entering California (Passel *et al.* 2004), many Yucatecans come without legal papers, drawn by jobs in a post-industrial economy that relies increasingly on cheap immigrant labour. At work they tended to use lingua franca English with other immigrants. Among fellow Spanish speakers, their Yucatecan variety Spanish has low prestige (Lope Blanch 1987), leading some to adopt new accents or pretend to be from elsewhere. People also avoid using Maya in unknown spaces out of concern that it might mark them or draw the attention to their legal status; childcare workers or day labourers felt legal status was not an issue.

Maya has historically suffered from low prestige in Yucatan (Gabbert 2004; Güemez Pineda 2006), an attitude that persists among immigrants. This historically inherited habitus of prejudice against Maya leads to widespread linguistic insecurity and avoidance of using Maya in public 'because it makes you feel (bad, ashamed) (*da pena*)'. But in 'enclave' communities, their Maya helps establish networks and find jobs. Still, many informants expressed the notion that they do not speak 'the real, legitimate' Maya, which they say is spoken only in historically isolated areas free from Spanish influence (Pfeiler 1996).

This sense of linguistic insecurity was corroborated by findings from an action research project, a language and literacy survey designed by myself and a team of six Maya-speaking club members, in collaboration with a local community-based organization, using a Community Based Participatory Research (CBPR) approach. The team interviewed 170 adult Yucatecan immigrants of Maya heritage, in Spanish and Maya. Bilingualism is the norm in this sample, but over a third of these bilinguals question their own proficiency in either language. Although 97 per cent of those surveyed said they speak Maya and 81 per cent reported using Maya at home, only 61 per cent claimed to speak it 'very well'; among those who claim to speak Spanish, only 65 per cent consider that they speak it very well.

From a Complexity Theory/Language Ecology perspective: these parameters of historical context and 'habitus' would constrain but not determine individual attitudes towards the three languages, and language choices made in a given context. And as we see next, at the micro-level, these parameters set the stage, but ultimately do not determine the outcomes of an interaction.

Case studies: individual histories

My project included four case studies of individuals and their language histories, one of which I describe here. A man in his twenties, JS, as I will call him, expressed a range of attitudes toward his native Maya and his own linguistic competence. From a Complexity Theory standpoint, attitudes are not stable states, but rather characterized by emergence and influenced by environmental feedback. JS's attitudes varied across events and contexts, and changes were not unidirectional. Referring to himself and his fellow Yucatecans, he once said: 'We don't speak Maya, Spanish or English'. But he could also be quite confident in English and proud of his Maya.

Over the course of his childhood, JS's ideas about language changed repeatedly. Raised speaking Spanish by Maya-speaking parents, who believed it would give him more advantages, JS quickly learned Maya from schoolmates, but was schooled in Spanish. Following his father's death, he dropped out of school at 13, hiring Maya-speaking cousins to help him run the family farm. He spoke Maya with these cousins hoping to minimize what he perceived as their social distance. A stint as an interpreter with a Catholic evangelical group convinced him that Maya could get him a job, but he wanted to study at university, where Spanish was required.

Once in California JS progressed rapidly in English but disliked his accented English, describing it as 'all ruined'. Asked to pick a pseudonym for my research, he told me to use 'John Smith', '...so they'll think it's a *gringo* messing up English'. He avoids using English in front of his Maya-speaking co-workers 'because they would think I was arrogant, I use it only when I'm going to talk to the boss or the chef. And there they will realize how much I know or how much I don't' and again 'I'm not interested in in, putting myself ahead of them, the way they think, they're already jealous, and they started to treat me badly...'.

During my fieldwork, JS was living in a predominantly Latino and Asian neighbourhood, with Maya and English-speaking housemates, one of whom appears in the transcriptions below. JS switched jobs six times during that time, working in a Mexican restaurant, a Japanese-French restaurant with Mexican cooks, and a Turkish restaurant run by an Arab family. He had a number of jobs in Middle Eastern restaurants, working with Czech, British, Arabic, Japanese and, always, Maya-speaking co-workers. At the time of the interviews, he was working in an Italian/Greek restaurant with Russian, Greek, British and Maya staff (see conversations below). His Maya co-worker pretended at first not to speak Maya, which JS attributed to 'insecurity, more than anything'. Despite this dissembling, for JS this co-worker's Maya identity was non-negotiable: 'I don't care … I know how he is and who he is…'.

JS's story illustrates how the habitus people are raised within can vary through time and space. From a complexity point of view, these changes in attitudes and identities can be seen as self-organizing and emergent. JS negotiated around the particularities of each linguistic context in ways constrained by 'dispositions', but also as a function of ad hoc choices he was making. Maya is part of his core identity, the 'who and what he is'. But in this post-industrial urban context, where identity is not stable, we see JS constantly renegotiating his social status, with language choice part of a symbolic tool-kit that he uses strategically. English confers advantage in one context, but damages feelings of class solidarity in another. Maya speakers take their time deciding whether to disclose their Maya proficiency, a strategic choice but one which contributes to their 'symbolic domination'. Other case studies showed that, in restaurants where Chinese-speaking managers know Spanish, Maya-speaking kitchen staffers switch to Maya to complain, an example of 'resistance' to domination. These choices draw on the 'symbolic competence' of the interlocutors, their ability to use available semiotic resources strategically to individual advantage (Kramsch and Whiteside 2008).

Conversation Analysis and second language use

Next, we turn to a transcription from a 20-minute conversation JS taped himself at home with his Anglo-American male roommate (Rmt) from New York. During this conversation, JS successfully navigates around the negative stereotype land mines attributed to 'people like him' by his interlocutor, and manages to use his limited English to construct a noble identity that defies these stereotypes. In doing so, he creates a performance of himself as a multilingual, intelligent potential university student, which produces reactions of admiration from his roommate: 'You're pretty smart, huh' and 'You use big words, homo-sapiens, Bering Strait, that's crazy!!' and envy 'University's a hard school to get into, all MY friends cannot get in'. Using Conversation Analysis, we look at JS's decision-making at the micro-level, as the two interlocutors negotiate for control over topic and affective tone, and performing identities on a turn-by-turn basis.

In Excerpt 1, JS is explaining why he is part of a Maya club. In the course of the conversation, Rmt discovers that JS is Mayan, and a member of a group he thought was 'extinct', an assertion JS leaves unchallenged. It becomes apparent later in the conversation that Rmt does not know that both JS and the other roommate speak Maya.

Excerpt 1

1	Rmt:	So you wanna teach?/
2		or you wanna= just be a ^student\
3	JS:	I=first of all
4		I have to
5		To= to found,
6		to search many 'words uh… were ^lost,
7		because, Mayan,
8		Mayan 'language is= missing a ^lot,
9		a ^lot 'words.\
10	Rmt:	Right.\
11	JS:	A=nd all, all the Yucatecs here in ^San Francisco is…-- -- is from ^differents 'towns.\
12	Rmt:	Right\
13	JS:	And [that's..]
14	Rmt:	[So you're] descendents of ^Mayan people?
15	JS:	[[Yah]]
16	Rmt:	[[Mayan?]]
17		Really?
18	JS:	Yah.
19	Rmt:	^That's been extinct for like a%…. a a 'thousand ^years or somethin,\
20		right?/
21	JS:	Yah yah yah.
22	Rmt:	That's [a long] time,
23	JS:	[that's]
24	Rmt:	[[right?]]
25	JS:	[[Yah, a]] long time, and…we
26	Rmt:	Flat out 'crazy how ^Mayans like built the ^pyramids/
27		you know, at the same time as, like, ^Egypt,/ and stuff like that?
28	JS:	Yeah.
29		Yeah yeah yeah(0)
30	Rmt:	(0) Like acro=ss the [world.]
31	JS:	[Yeah.]
32		[[@@]]
33	Rmt:	[[That's]] cra::zy,
34	JS:	[yeah]

In #3–8, JS's topic is lost Maya vocabulary, to which Rmt responds 'right right', although he does not yet know that JS speaks Maya. JS continues building on the topic of Maya speakers (#11), but Rmt changes the topic (#14), incredulous that JS is of Mayan descent. In #25 JS uses Rmt's topic 'a long time' to go back to his topic, but Rmt interrupts with his 'flat out crazy' changing the topic to the parallel between Egyptians and Mayans. JS encourages this in #29 (yeah yeah yeah), and they seem to be in agreement.

Despite this apparent agreement, Rmt continues to make derogatory comments about Maya language and culture that JS either ignores or affirms, as in the exchange in Excerpt 2:

Excerpt 2

1	JS:	An= d..(2)
2		And the ^main thing is is to=
3		First of all to,
4		to learn the, the ^language,
5		to, to give tha=t,
6		to give it a, a, a grammar, /
7		and then…we can 'teach ^others.\
8	Rmt:	Right.\
9		Why do you want to ^learn it?/…(3)
10	JS:	The ^new words, but uh,
11		the ^main 'thing what <@ we can@> we have to do is, to=
to,		
12		to translate the /z/ieroglyphics.
13	Rmt:	It's like a /^dead \ language, right?
14		Nobody ^speaks it 'to[day,]
15	JS:	[yeah, right, yeah]

Despite some ambiguity in JS's turns in #6 (give it a grammar), Rmt aligns himself with them (#8). His question (#9) moves away from this messy topic, a kind of off record repair. Rmt then asks, 'Why do you want to learn it?' suggesting that JS does not yet speak Maya. JS attempts to clarify what it is he wants to learn (#10), 'the new words', then changes the topic again using 'the main thing'. By managing to negotiate away from these misunderstandings, he maintains the affective unity. When JS mispronounces hieroglyphics, adding a soft 'g' to the beginning of the word, Rmt avoids a request for repair by starting his own topic: 'It's like a dead language, right?' using tag question to ask for confirmation. Switching to the indicative in #14, JS responds affirmatively, 'yeah right yeah'. There is no indication that either of them have understood the previous turn, but they willingly override uncertainty in favour of maintaining their inter-subjectivity.

Later in the conversation, having established himself as the expert on Mayan, in Excerpt 3 JS introduces the topic of Maya writing:

Excerpt 3

Rmt: Were they ^symbols? /
Like they'd be ^symbols, /
like a symbol, [like?]
JS: [Yeah] because there is in, in ^Spa=n,
in ^Spain,
in ^Alemany,
in ^London,
a lot / / ai/ roglyphics there..and
Rmt: Hieroglyphics/,..yeah.\
JS: Yeah.
Rmt: That's what they ^used?
Hieroglyphics?
JS: Yeah.
Rmt: The ^Egyptians did that.
JS: Yeah…(2)
Rmt: That's crazy.
JS: @[@@]
Rmt: [I didn't know] you knew all that.
JS: @@ Yeah.
<LO That's crazy LO>..(2.5)
Rmt: THAT's pretty cool you're ^interested in all that… (4)
JS: <LO Yeah it's a interesting to…LO>

This time, in #9, Rmt repairs JS's mispronounced 'hieroglyphs', adding a backchannel 'yeah' to downplay the face threat, then nominates the topic 'Egyptians' over which he has more epistemic control. After JS agrees with this, Rmt expresses affective intensity with his ambiguous 'That's crazy', and JS laughs. Rmt then clarifies the ambiguity by expressing surprise to which JS responds with an also ambiguous 'crazy' but his low voice, followed by a pause, suggests that the affective unity may be breaking down. Rmt then adds to the positive evaluation with a compliment, shifting from surprise to admiration.

JS later characterized his roommate and his reticence to challenge Rmt's ideas this way:

> A person in that camp isn't capable of understanding … Because you have to leave him without any idea …There are people who still believe that by being white they are superior to any other person. Ah= … ideologies that people have. Well I believe that

> he's no exception, he still thinks that North America is the greatest in the world, no other idea exists.

But in their conversation JS uses his turns not to argue but to nominate topics he knows more about, using epistemic stance to enact the identity of a smart, competent English speaker with a bright future. This identity overrides the stereotypes and earns Rmt's respect. Rmt, who begins the conversations secure in his native speaker status, referring to 'Extinct' Mayans, their 'dead language', ends up expressing admiration that JS is multilingual. In the restaurants where they both work, multilingualism is the norm, and Rmt's 'centre' status is undermined by his inability to speak Spanish. Although JS's show of agency is a fleeting triumph in a system heavily stacked against him, a Complexity Theory analysis includes the possibility that such small changes emerging interactively may have long-term or sustaining consequences.

Conclusion

I hope these analyses have shown some advantages of casting a broad net in collecting data on language practices, and the utility of a model which enables researchers to consider contradictory data gathered at different levels of organization. Research at the population level brings insight into language ideologies that affect motivation and use, the constraints that structure opportunities to learn and practise language, the contradictions which lead Rmt, a member both of a dominant identity (Anglo-American) and also a minority (working in an industry dominated by immigrants) to feel both superior and inferior *vis-à-vis* JS. Action research adds member perspectives on motivations and tensions operative in speech communities; the fact that our survey was designed and administered by Maya-speaking community members allowed us to incorporate questions of interest to the community into the survey, and facilitated interviews with people highly resistant to outside researchers. Case studies supply a historical sense of how individual experiences and language socialization contribute over time to dispositions that constrain individual choice, and how these constraints and choices vary over time. Conversation Analysis gets beyond the propositional content of utterances into dynamic interaction, capturing patterns of affective and epistemic choices that show the rich use of symbolic resources by native and non-native speakers missing from conventional research on second language conversations. We can see how turn-by-turn decisions cumulatively establish identities and actions for the interlocutors. But while Conversation Analysis alone can show empirically how JS gains control over topics and affective tone, it can't account for JS's disposition to keep quiet in the face of derogatory comments about Maya.

By combining methodologies, Complexity Theory allows us to consider both social constraints and self-determination of individuals. Case histories show the complex interaction of historical and individual memory, and how they structure the behaviour of an idiosyncratic person. The same is true at the macro level: while a system's history might constrain its potential, it does not fully determine it (Larsen-Freeman and Cameron 2008 a, b). JS's conversations suggest that although constraints from macro and local forces operate at the micro level, he still finds room to resist them, drawing on symbolic competencies that go beyond linguistics and sociolinguistic competence (Kramsch 2007; Kramsch and Whiteside 2008). A model which allows for both, which sees events as dynamic, self-organizing and responsive to feedback, provides a three dimensional meta-framework that includes places for data that change across space and time, which may be inconsistent yet both empirically based.

But by the same token, if we are to use data from divergent levels of organization (e.g. policy, mainstream society, enclaves, worksite, interactional pairs, individuals) the intersection/interaction between levels need to be further theorized, and the epistemologies of these various methodologies need to be coordinated. This, I would argue, is where Language Ecology and Complexity Theory need to develop more tools. Perhaps we have more to learn from the biological sciences while a system's history might constrain its potential, it does not fully determine it.

Transcription conventions

@	Laugh
/	Rising tone
\	Falling tone
^	Low-high-low tone
%	Glottal stop

12 A tale of two teachers: teacher identity and care of the self in an era of accountability

Matthew Clarke

> There is always resentment in reaction ... to induce man [sic] to be actional, by maintaining in his circularity the respect of the fundamental values that make the world human, that is the task of the utmost urgency for him [sic] who, after careful reflection, prepares to act. (Fanon 1952/2008: 197)

Introduction

Maintaining a pro-active sense of professional and personal agency is a challenge for any new language teacher in the face of multiple competing demands; but in the current era, with its endless rounds of testing, evaluation and performance standards, reflecting the steady importation of neoliberal business and market ideologies into education generally (Marginson 1997; Luke 2006; Sleeter 2007), teachers have never been more accountable. Described by one recent commentator as 'external assaults' that aim to 'deprofessionalize teaching by devaluing the professional preparation of teachers' (Sleeter 2008: 1947), this global trend has been researched and reported in a range of contexts.

Criticisms levelled against the hegemonic influence of neoliberal ideologies in relation to the work of teachers in recent years include charges that they reduce diversity, undermine professionalism, and 'attempt to rebrand teachers as "servants of the state" merely carrying out public policy' rather than 'public intellectuals' (Grimmett *et al.* 2009: 5); and that they have led to 'increased bureaucratic scrutiny directed towards the work of schools and teachers ... contributing to significant work intensification' (Bloomfield 2009: 34). This bureaucratic scrutiny is facilitated by the articulation of performance indicators and standards which seek 'to specify, often in distressing detail, what students, teachers and future teachers should be able to know, say and do' (Apple 2001: 188). Of significance too in this discourse of distrust is the neoliberal 'accreditation squeeze', which is 'trivializing teacher education' in global contexts as diverse as the United States and the United Arab Emirates (Johnson *et al.* 2005). As Hill (2007: 212) bluntly and forcefully states, 'teachers are being controlled!'

Neoliberal reforms in education are not as entirely devoid of merit as the above picture implies; they were motivated by desire for, and have not been without benefits in relation to, greater openness, transparency, accountability and communication in relation to educational quality and standards. Yet, as a growing body of literature indicates, the drive for accountability has led to a narrowing of what it means to be a teacher and a diminishment of teachers' individuality, leading one recent commentator to talk of the 'rampant normalization associated with high stakes accountability' (Gunzenhauser 2008: 2237). Even more sinisterly, such approaches are fundamentally anti-democratic in that they are unlikely to foster critique of the neoliberal forms of governance that align with and produce such forms of subjectivity (Dean 1994).

In this chapter, I want to explore an approach to sustaining professional agency and self-empowerment in this context of neoliberal reform that builds on the recent focus on language teaching as a matter of the formation, development and deployment of a teacher identity (Morgan 2004; Richards 2006; Tsui 2007; Clarke 2008). Drawing as it does on teachers' personal and professional biographies, as well as institutional and cultural values and attitudes, identity offers a more complex way of thinking about teaching – and critically for this volume, one that provides space for individuality and agency – than do the 'identikit', standards-based models that have contemporary political valence. This approach draws on the later, 'ethical' works of Foucault (1985, 1986, 1997a) and their concern with ethical self-formation and 'care of the self'.

In particular, given the diminishment of conceptual and practical spaces for teachers' agency and autonomy in the current era of accountability, I want to explore the possibilities offered by Foucault's theorization of identity as a project to be worked on over time. By looking at two vignettes of novice teacher identities, I hope to suggest ways in which notions of ethical self-formation and care of the self could offer a resource that 'may provide promising directions for responding to the crisis of the self brought about by the constraints of high stakes accountability' (Gunzenhauser 2008: 2241). My argument is that Foucault's ethics can be drawn on by researchers and teachers in teacher education as a conceptual resource for resisting the sort of normalization practices represented by neoliberalism – or to put it more positively, as a set of techniques for shaping the self – through practices of critical reflection, and inter-subjective engagement, which Foucault refers to in his notion of 'care of the self'. As such, the paper builds on the work by teacher educators like Infinito (2003b), who has explored Foucault's concept of ethical self-formation as a tool for promoting commitments to social justice amongst preservice teachers in the US. Like Infinito, my concern is with the way neoliberal discourses of accountability to such unchallengeable, hegemonic (yet essentially empty, vacuous and hence manipulable) notions as 'quality', 'effectiveness' and 'standards' has squeezed out conceptual and practical spaces for engaged and open-ended critique in relation to the ultimate aims and purposes of education, and hence diminished the critical agency of teachers (see also Biesta 2010). In this context, Infinito has argued that:

> Of all his theoretical work, Foucault's consideration of ethics, which deals specifically with the process of self-creation, proves most valuable for use in education ... Foucault's notion of ethical self-formation is foundational to issues of individual freedom and identity, to issues of the proper response to 'the other', and to the maintenance of pluralistic and creative spaces in our society, all of which are rightly educational concerns. (2003a: 155)

Given the narrowing influence of discourses of accountability in education that commentators from a range of global contexts have remarked on, these concerns would seem to be particularly significant ones at the present time. Foucault's ideas offer conceptual tools with which to disrupt the taken-for-grantedness of contemporary discourses of accountability in education by highlighting their social and historical contingency and for me, this is a significant aspect of their appeal. But importantly, such 'unmasking' or 'unbracketing' of naturalized beliefs and assumptions also pertains to the relationship between researcher, research study and research text. In this sense, the writing up of this research is one of many possibilities, 'none of which has a sole purchase on truth' (Peters 2007: 188). Its shape and content reflects my subjectivity as a researcher, providing an example of what Phillips and Jørgensen (2002) refer to as a 'positioned opening for discussion' (p. 203). Nonetheless, the appeal of Foucault's notion of ethics is that, within the constraints suggested by these caveats, it allows me to put forward a substantive line of argument for others to engage with, something that is surely a key 'ethical' responsibility of researchers and research.

Ethical self-formation and the care of the self

In the context of the tension between the determined and self-determining individual (Benson and Cooker, Chapter 1, this volume), Foucault is often seen as a sort of prophet of doom, relentlessly laying bare our hapless imprisonment in oppressive regimes of disciplinary power, as we languish ensnared by totalizing discourses. In their chapter on Foucault's methods in the third edition of the Sage *Handbook of Qualitative Research*, for example, Scheurich and McKenzie (2005) are struck by 'how unrelenting Foucault is in his critique of the social forms in which we live' (p. 860). Yet Scheurich and McKenzie focus on Foucault's archaeological and genealogical works from his early and middle periods, rather than the later 'ethical' works, which a number of scholars have seen as offering a corrective balance to the grimly deterministic representations of human society portrayed in his work from the earlier periods, offering enhanced scope for thinking about issues of freedom and for theorizing resistance (O'Leary 2002; May 2006; Besley and Peters 2007; Wain 2007). As Infinito notes, 'Foucault's ethics is a direct political response to normalization's effect of blocking us from asserting an identity, a self, and a future of our own making' (2003a: 160).

In his later work, Foucault (1980: 119) views power as a productive, rather than a purely repressive force, that 'doesn't only weigh on us as a force that says no', but needs to be considered as a 'productive network which runs through the whole social body'. Schools, colleges and universities as state institutions, curricula as state policy documents, and teachers as state agents all exercise power in different ways; yet this power is not only a matter of domination. Ideally, educational institutions, curricula and teachers combine and interact to produce knowledge in students. Yet if this knowledge is to be critical and if students are to be more than passive dupes, there must be possibilities for resistance. Here again, Foucault views power as not only productive but as always existing in a relationship with freedom: 'in order for power relations to come into play, there must be at least a certain degree of freedom on both sides ... If there are relations of power in every social field, this is because there is freedom everywhere' (Foucault 1997a: 292). In particular, Foucault's ethical works (Foucault 1985, 1986, 1997a) provide a model for thinking about freedom and resistance in education – for theorizing the ways in which, as Olssen (2006: 153) puts it, individuals can 'learn how to pull the strings', rather than remaining passive puppets of power/knowledge systems. It is important to recognize, however, that the autonomy proffered here is relative rather than absolute and still entails interdependence and connectedness to others (Benson, Chapter 6, this volume).

In his ethical works, Foucault employs a four-part schema, first used to analyse dimensions of the genealogy of power in Foucault (1977), as a framework for thinking about the different ways in which ethics was conceived in the Greek, Roman and early Christian eras. His four axes of ethics were: (1) the ethical substance (the part of the self pertaining to ethics); (2) the mode of ethical subjection (the authority sources of ethics); (3) ethical self-practices; and (4) the *telos*, or endpoint, of ethics (May 2006; O'Leary 2002). When conceived in this way, the four dimensions of the genealogy of power become four axes for critical work focused on the genealogy of the subject; it is in this sense that Foucault talks of ethical self-formation when he writes about ethics. But what does Foucault's ethics have to say to us as Applied Linguists? Here I want to suggest that we can usefully translate these four axes into 'axes of teacher identity' and think specifically about language teachers' identities in terms of: (1) the substance of teacher identity; (2) its sources of authority; (3) the self-practices of teacher identity; and (4) the endpoint of teacher identity (Figure 12.1).

Ethical self-formation and language teacher identity

The first axis in Figure 12.1, referring to the substance of teacher identity, addresses the forms of subjectivity that constitute – or that I use to constitute – my teaching self and the part of myself that pertains to teaching. For example, does my teaching self only relate to my intellect or does it involve cognitive and affective aspects of my being? The second axis concerns what sources of authority I recognize as a teacher and why I should cultivate certain attitudes, beliefs and behaviours. For example, I might feel that 'practical' experience in the classroom is the only relevant source of potential insights into my teaching, considering language teaching and learning 'theory' to be a waste of time. Or, conversely, I might recognize the authority of constructivist theories of learning and be reluctant to base decisions about classroom practice on experience alone without considering it in light of my favoured theories. The third axis relates to the techniques and

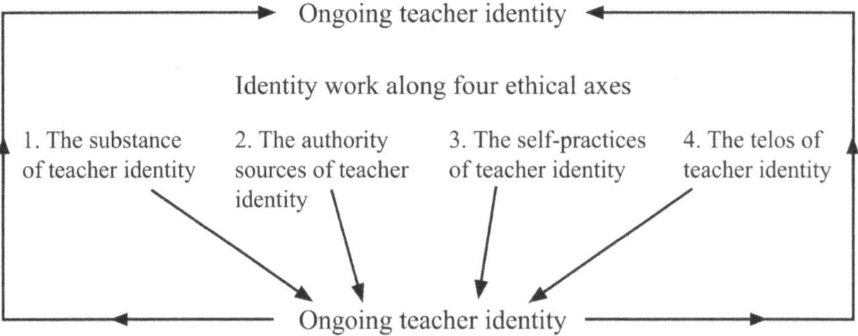

Figure 12.1 A diagram for doing ethical 'identity work' in teacher education (Clarke 2009b)

practices I use to fashion and shape my teaching self. For instance, I might keep an individual reflective journal, or I might make a point of regularly engaging in collaborative forms of ongoing professional development. The fourth axis concerns what I see as my ultimate endpoint, goal or purpose as a teacher. This might be a matter of striving to 'make a difference' to the lives of my students or it may involve ambitions to maximize my professional growth, or any of a myriad of other possible purposes.

With each of these axes, if a teacher becomes conscious of her history and strives 'to pull the strings' (to quote Olssen 2006 again) by engaging in critical reflection and reaching out to others, she may open up possibilities for change that she would otherwise never have considered. Engaging in critical reflection and inter-subjective engagement within the framework provided by these four axes of teacher identity is a form of 'care of the self', which is neither entirely self-regarding nor wholly other-regarding but represents a challenge to this dichotomy. The practice of care of the self as advocated by Foucault is in essence the practice of intellectual freedom by way of a process of problematizing and questioning the social, historical and political forces shaping our subjectivity. The pursuit of these questions manifests an assumption of ethical responsibility. Moreover, this process is inherently social insofar as it involves engaging in ongoing critical dialogue and consultation with others, who are also subject to the same forces that are shaping us; it is 'not an exercise in solitude, but a true social practice … The care of the self – or the attention that one devotes to the care that others should take of themselves – appears then as an intensification of social relations' (Foucault 1986: 51, 53). As Gore (1993: 129) notes, 'care of the self' is not about self-absorption but rather, 'suggests an ethic of self-disengagement and self-invention', a process of standing back from who we are in order to find out who we might become.

The research

So what might care of the self within teacher education and development look like in practice? In order to explore this question in this chapter I discuss two preservice language teachers, examining their ongoing reflections on themselves as teachers, in relation to Foucault's four axes of ethics. The two teachers are both in their final year of a four-year Bachelor of Education degree though they are becoming English language teachers in two quite different contexts: the United Arab Emirates (UAE) in the case of Alya and Hong Kong in the case of Henry. The data were derived from an initial study with preservice teachers in the UAE and a later follow-up comparative study in Hong Kong, both involving (non-assessed) online discussion forums, in which the preservice teachers shared their beliefs about teaching and discussed critical classroom incidents by posting and responding to messages. Two vignettes of these novice language teachers are offered below,[1] the data in one case coming from a number of postings, in the other case deriving from one extended posting. In each case, the discussion is illustrative and exploratory rather than definitive, providing an initial consideration of the potential of Foucault's ethics for thinking about the possibilities for doing identity work in teacher education. My hope is that examining the different ways in which these preservice teachers do or do not engage in ethical self-formation – in self-disengagement and self-invention, to cite Gore (1993) again – offers potential insights into the applicability of Foucault's ethical theory for teacher identity and suggests ways it could be taken further in research and practice within this era of accountability.

Henry: 'I can do nothing to change my character'

My analysis of Henry's emerging teacher identity draws on several messages Henry posted on the online discussion forum in the Hong Kong teacher education programme in order to share his ongoing concerns with his peers. A highly committed, if not particularly confident, preservice teacher, Henry is particularly concerned about gaining the respect of his students and a great deal of his energy is directed towards improving his image (as he sees it) in the classroom. In terms of the first ethical axis, Henry sees teaching as being primarily concerned, not with the cognitive or affective domains, but with character:

> Sometimes I feel I am not a suitable person to teach because I am not the type of person who can scold people. Sometimes I feel very sad because I know my students are taking advantage of my kind and gentle character while I can do nothing to change my character ... some of my students misbehave in the lessons because they know me very well and they know that I am a kind person.

Henry is clearly concerned about improving his relationships with his students and gaining their affection and respect, though the two things may well be in tension. Yet he limits his potential options for working on this aspect of his practice by basing his view of his teaching capacity on his 'character', which he sees as unchanging and unchangeable. As a possible alternative, Henry could explore how he can establish a more professional relationship with his students by focusing on his teacher identity – something which is not fixed and static but rather something that is shaped through ongoing interaction with his students and engaging in classroom practice, as well as through critical reflection on each of these. As part of his identity work, he might also reach out to his students and share his aspirations and concerns with them, seeking to establish a classroom ethos of joint responsibility. The point is not that there is any right or wrong basis upon which to constitute the teaching self but that how we construct this self – upon what basis it rests and what is excluded – will critically constrain and/or enable other possibilities.

For the second axis, involving the sources of authority we recognize in our teaching, Henry embraces notions of lifelong learning and professional responsibility.

> Teachers nowadays need to keep on learning new teaching strategies and reflecting on the effectiveness of their lessons in order to improve the quality of their teaching. Teachers should know that teaching can affect a person's life. If teachers know that their acts might have lasting impacts on students' developments, they are willing to put more effort into teaching.

Indicators of the sources of authority Henry recognizes can be seen in the values he assumes to be shared. Here these include ongoing self-improvement in which teachers 'keep on learning new teaching strategies'. We can also recognize Henry's authority sources in the way he frames these requirements that he stipulates for teachers, through the use of explicit modal markers such as 'teachers nowadays need to' and 'teachers should'. He also employs rationalization, explaining the requirement of putting effort into teaching in terms of its consequences in the form of 'lasting impacts on students' developments'.

For the third axis, focused on the self-practices we use to shape our ongoing teaching identities, the practices Henry focuses on mainly involve experimenting with techniques in the classroom:

> I have learned techniques on controlling classroom discipline because I am rather weak in this aspect and I have difficulties in dealing with off-task behaviours. Also, I have learnt some tasks that are exploratory in nature because these tasks can motivate students to think, explore, and solve problems, which are very effective in their learning.

Given his concern about his relationships in the classroom with students, Henry's favoured self-practice is not surprising. Yet beyond this, what is striking is the lack of a sense of inter-subjective engagement with others. Inter-subjectively oriented practices could involve reaching out to and seeking guidance from 'critical friends', who could be more experienced teachers working in the practicum school, his university supervisor, or peers, any of whom could potentially offer valuable assistance to Henry as he strives to shape and develop his teaching identity. It is also important to note that the very act of writing email messages to peers on forums such as the one from which this data derives, in which he shares his experiences and thoughts about teaching and describes and reflects on critical incidents in the classroom, are examples of practices of self-formation. Were Henry to explicitly recognize the potential of such practices he might be in a position to benefit from them more fully, for engaging in such practice

> is a not matter of pursuing the unsayable, nor of revealing the hidden, nor of saying the unsaid, but on the contrary of capturing the already-said, of reassembling what one could hear or read, and this for an end that is nothing less than the constitution of the self. (Foucault 1997b: 237)

In relation to the fourth axis, connected to our ultimate goal or purpose in teaching, Henry comments: 'I think teaching is a very meaningful and rewarding job. If you can help a rude, irresponsible student who has limited motivation to study to become a well-behaved person, you will have a great sense of achievement.' Henry construes the purpose of teaching here in moralizing, almost missionary, terms, whereby the meaning of teaching derives from achieving redemption for pathologized ('rude', 'irresponsible') students, who have strayed from assumed social values, thus reflecting a fairly conservative model where schooling endorses and reproduces dominant values. Henry's uncritical use of terms like 'irresponsible' and 'well-behaved' to label students demonstrates little awareness that the education system, the school, or indeed teachers such as himself, might be at issue and at least partially play a central role in producing the students' 'rudeness'.

What are we to make, then, of Henry's current potential for engaging in ethical self-formation of his teacher identity? We might note that, despite his desire to improve his teaching, his wish to improve relations with his students, and his belief in continual improvement and professional development, his scope for achieving these aims is limited by a number of factors. These include the significance he attaches to a fixed notion of character, his reluctance to reach out to others for assistance, and his uncritical, unreflecting and pathologizing characterization of his students. Each of these limitations combine to reduce Henry's capacity for seeing how 'the effort to think one's own history can free thought from what it silently thinks, and so enable it to think differently' (Foucault 1985: 9).

Alya: 'I feel that reflection, somehow, makes me a better person'

My consideration of the second preservice teacher, from the UAE, involves mainly analysing just one extended excerpt from an online posting. In discussing Alya's teacher identity formation in relation to this posting, I will again use the four axes of teacher identity as a matrix for analysis. Alya, like Henry, is highly committed to teaching; but unlike Henry, she exudes a sense of confidence, linked to the way she believes that her experiences in teaching have facilitated positive development in her personality and her skills in a range of ways.

> Teaching has changed my life in so many ways. It made me more professional in the way I deal with different people and different personalities and contributed to developing my communication skills. Five years ago, I would have avoided working or interacting with people whose opinions and ideas were different to mine. However … I have begun to discuss different issues and ideas with my principals, teachers and sometimes my peers. I am more willing now to share my ideas and point of view with them even if they do not agree with me (which is the case most of the time). In fact, having a good understanding of educational theories and putting them into practice encourages me to negotiate things with different people from different backgrounds and with different perspectives. I try to let them understand that my beliefs about teaching and teaching strategies might be different from theirs but that does not mean that they are meaningless or not as effective as theirs. I have also learned that the way we discuss subjects plays a role in persuading others of our point of view. Moreover, I believe that teaching reinforced my sense of responsibility … I feel responsible for each child in the classroom and I try as much as I can to respond to the students' individual differences. I like the fact that I make the children my main concern and think of their learning as a priority … Teaching helped me work on fostering my creativity. I am not a very creative person but teaching motivated me to surf the net, read books or even ask for other peers' support so I can use good teaching strategies and resources that get the students interested and motivated. Teaching enhanced my critical thinking skills. It made me a reflective person who reflects constantly on everything, not only on the incidents that take place in school but also on every article I read or programme I watch. I just feel that reflection deepens my understanding of certain things and strengthens my beliefs about teaching. I know that what I am going to say might seem odd to some of you, but I feel that reflection, somehow, makes me a better person!

In terms of the first ethical axis, the substance of our teacher identities, and in contrast to Henry, Alya foregrounds aspects of her identity that are dynamic and dialogic, in the sense that they are changeable and inter-subjectively connected to others. Thus she describes what she sees as her growing professionalism and relates this to her developing interpersonal communication skills in handling differences of opinion and belief with other educators in a constructive manner. She also refers to a growing sense of responsibility, which encourages her to focus on the learning of her students. In both cases her inward focus on herself is linked to an outward focus on others. Additionally, and in contrast to Henry whose teaching identity was anchored in a static notion of 'character' ('I can do nothing to change my character'), Alya emphasizes growth and change in terms of her developing creative skills and her critical thinking and reflective skills, which, she says, 'deepens my understanding of certain things and strengthens my beliefs about teaching'. Overall, Alya's view of her teaching self – the substance of her teaching identity, which is the focus of axis one – is both broader and more amenable to change than we saw Henry's to be.

In relation to the second axis, involving the sources of authority we draw on in shaping our teacher identities, Alya highlights the influence of her experiences of learning, both in college and in schools. She also places significant value on the educational theories that she has been able to put into practice in the classroom and which she says have increased her confidence in discussing educational issues with other educators. Again, we see dynamism and inter-subjective engagement at work here as she interweaves theory and practice in a way that 'encourages me to negotiate things with different people from different backgrounds and with different perspectives'. In contrast to Henry, who drew authority mainly from experimentation in the classroom, Alya has established a wider set of resources that she is able to draw on in shaping her emerging teaching self.

In relation to the third axis, connected to the self-practices of our teacher identities, Alya's practice of discussing different issues with a range of other people, including her mentor teachers, other teachers and school principals, as well as her peers, is clearly a self-practice that is focused on inter-subjective engagement. Her admission that 'I have also learned that *the way* we discuss subjects plays a role in persuading others of our point of view', whilst emphasizing changing others than on being open to change, also illustrates the dynamic, ongoing nature of her learning, while her self-practice of 'fostering my creativity' is other-directed in that its purpose is to provide a more effective learning environment for her students. Perhaps most striking though are her self-practices of critical thinking and reflection – she describes herself as 'a reflective person who reflects constantly on everything' and believes that 'reflection, somehow, makes me a better person'. The strength of these statements clearly reveals that critique and reflection have been significant and powerful self-shaping practices in terms of Alya's developing teacher identity and, like many of her other comments, seem indicative of considerably greater levels of self-awareness than was the case for Henry.

In relation to the fourth axis, the *telos*, or ultimate goal, of our teaching identities, Alya states that 'I like the fact that I make the children my main concern and think of their learning as a priority' and student learning is clearly one guiding purpose for her as a teacher. An emphasis on student engagement and learning is also reflected in her comments about the value of fostering her creativity to assist her in developing 'good teaching strategies and resources that get the students interested and motivated'. However, she also links her practices of critical thinking and reflection as sources of deepening understanding, strengthened beliefs, and ultimately becoming 'a better person'. Overall, it seems that the value she places on her own ongoing self-development as a teacher, both personally and professionally, is inseparable from the value she places on her effectiveness as a teacher and on her students' learning in the classroom.

When we consider Alya's posting in terms of all four axes of teacher identity, the difference in relation to Henry is striking. Not only do we get a strong sense of 'care of the self' in her explicit concern for and nurturing of her evolving teacher identity, but at the same time, this care of the self is closely connected with a sense of care of others, including her students and the other professional educators working around her. Moreover, she seems to be aware that her engagement in practices of 'care of the self' is itself contributing to nurturing a critical, engaged and ethical responsiveness to others – 'having a good understanding of educational theories and putting them into practice encourages me to negotiate things with different people from different backgrounds and with different perspectives' – and vice versa in relation to the contribution that her inter-subjective engagement is having on the shaping of her own identity as a teacher, in what we might describe as a virtuous circle of ethical self-formation.

In relation to Alya's engagement with others, it is worth briefly noting one of the criticisms made of Foucault's ethics, namely that it is too private an affair, involving a disengagement with public issues in order to focus on the self (Best and Kellner 1991). Whilst a number of Foucault scholars have challenged such an interpretation as understating the extent to which the ethical self is socially and politically situated (Infinito 2003a; Olssen 2006), Alya seems to provide a living instance of this insofar as her concern for her own development, rather than reflecting some sort of solipsistic self-absorption, is intimately connected to, and provides a source of, her responsiveness to others. As Olssen notes: 'The care of the self, then, is always at the same time concerned with care for others' (2006: 166).

Conclusion: towards an ethics of teacher identity through care of the self

Given the global entrenchment of neoliberal accountability regimes – as Braidotti (2006: 1) comments, 'times are definitely no longer a-changing' – and the prevalence of discourses promoting a view of teaching as a matter of meeting centrally prescribed performance criteria, and given the narrowing effect that this, along with the overwhelming torrent of educational reform, is having on teacher professionalism, it seems clear that researchers in Applied Linguistics need to explore alternative models that offer scope for foregrounding and investigating the professional formation and development of teachers as individuals and communities. I have argued here that Foucault's work on ethical self-formation, and in particular, his notion of 'care of the self', which is inseparably linked to care for others, offer significant potential for addressing these concerns by highlighting the ways in which individuals and communities are shaped by contingent social, historical and political factors, as well as foregrounding the ways in which they question and resist, or unquestioningly comply with, these influences. Certainly, whilst recognizing the exploratory nature of this analysis, the case of Alya would seem to suggest that such ethical work is possible and that it may promote both self-creation and critical responsiveness to others, while Henry (particularly in comments like 'Sometimes I feel very sad because I know my students are taking advantage of my kind and gentle character while I can do nothing to change my character') seems to reflect the risks of resentment flowing from reactiveness highlighted by Fanon in the epigraph to this chapter.

However, the contrast between Henry's focus on himself as a somewhat isolated individual and Alya's more connected sense of herself can also be linked more broadly to the changing status of the notion of the 'individual' in Applied Linguistics and second language learning, where, in a game of catch-up with developments in other social sciences (Block 2007a: 2), atomistic, psychologistic models are being increasingly challenged by ideas from post-structuralist and Sociocultural Theory, which foreground the social and linguistic origins of the individual. Ironically, this 'decentring' of the individual empowers us to recognize and attempt to get to grips with the significance and impact of social, historical and political forces on all of us as individuals. Indeed, as ethically and politically engaged applied linguistic researchers in a political and educational age that promotes unquestioning compliance through ever more sophisticated techniques of accountability and that, moreover, discourages any questioning of the fundamental aims and purposes of education through the repeated performance and hegemonic acceptance of essentially empty terms like 'quality', 'effectiveness' and 'standards' (Biesta 2010); in such times, I would argue, it behoves us to seek models that highlight the social, historical and political situating of language teachers and teaching, and that have the potential to reinsert individual agency and autonomy into the language teaching endeavour.

Foucault's ethical work, as outlined in the above discussion and exemplified through two vignettes of novice language teachers, offers one such approach. In its emphasis on the social origins of the individual, it shares a good deal of common ground with other approaches, such as Sociocultural Theory (Lantolf, Chapter 2, this volume), Situated Learning Theory (Lamb, Chapter 3) and other social approaches. However, despite the increasing attention to issues of ethics and politics in the latter (Thorne 2006), I would argue that the central recognition of relations of power, and explicit attention to their manifestation in discursive regimes of knowledge and truth, provide Foucauldian approaches with a greater critical edge. Certainly, the argument of this chapter is that powerful, transformative critique of self and other is needed more than ever in the current era of accountability, performativity and compliance; that such critique may be fostered by the ethos of self-creation and inter-subjective engagement inhering in Foucauldian notions of ethical self-formation and care of the self; and that as Applied Linguistics researchers, we should be actively interested in such possibilities in relation to the sort of interpretive research described here, as well as in relation to interventionist research that may – and I would add here, should – flow from such interpretations. For ultimately, the blurring between ethics and politics inherent in the Foucauldian orientation to ethics may enable researchers (as well as teachers) to see links between their work and wider social and political issues, thus encouraging them to actively engage with breathing new life into democracy as they work with teachers, students and communities. There can surely be no higher accountability for researchers in Applied Linguistics.

Note

1. I have discussed these preservice teachers individually elsewhere (Clarke 2009a and 2009b), but here I bring them together for comparative purposes.

13 The Applied Linguistic individual: gaining perspective

Phil Benson and Lucy Cooker

Introduction

The main aim of this book has been to explore what we chose in Chapter 1 to call a 'paradox' in social approaches to Applied Linguistics research. To recap, these social approaches have carved out their territory largely by defining themselves as alternatives to their 'individualistic' others (see, for example, Zuengler and Miller 2006). From a social perspective, SLA research is individualistic because it locates language acquisition in the individual mind. Learner-centred educational practices that focus on autonomy and individual language development are also judged to be individualistic, because they fail to recognize the roles of interaction, socialization and community in language learning and the ways in which they constrain access to resources and freedom in learning. Learner-centred practices are said to isolate the individual from the social context of learning, in much the same way as SLA research isolates the individual mind from the social contexts in which human beings live and learn. The paradox that we are concerned with is that, despite these objections to the individualism of other approaches, social approaches to Applied Linguistics are often intensely engaged with the notions of individual identity and agency, through research that is often strongly focused on individuals.

As editors, our interest in this paradox stems from a sense that our own involvement in research on autonomy in language learning has placed us on the wrong side of the divide between 'social' and 'individualistic' approaches, despite having been engaged in more than two decades of debate on the social character of autonomy. From our perspective, however, the legitimacy of this divide hinges upon a stronger articulation of the interest in individuals and individuality that we find in social approaches. We felt, therefore, that a book that explored how the idea of individuality fits into social approaches to Applied Linguistics research would make an important contribution to the field, by establishing common ground and highlighting differences among the different approaches to socially oriented research.

We believe that the book has succeeded in this goal, but we should also state from the outset that we do not believe that it has *resolved* the questions that it has raised. In particular, the diversity of approaches discussed means that we cannot really identify a single social approach to Applied Linguistics or specify how it should deal with issues of individuality. Instead, we have a range of approaches that attach different values to individuality and use different terminologies to talk about it. Individuality also creeps in at another level, in that the approaches that we have identified by name – Sociocultural Theory, Situated Learning Theory, Complexity Theory and so on – are interpreted differently by individual researchers, who are often willing to combine them or look beyond established theories when framing empirical work. The question that arises is whether or not this tendency towards diversity and eclecticism is a good thing. Is it desirable, or even feasible, to work towards a single accepted view of the relationship between the social and the individual in Applied Linguistics? In order to think about this question, we need to take a step backwards to look at the origins of current social approaches in Applied Linguistics in the crisis of academic Marxism of the 1970s.

From the 1970s onwards, Marxist approaches to the social sciences were subjected to sustained critique, based on the possibly erroneous assumption that Marxism held that all ideological and cultural phenomena (which would include language and educational practices) were determined by the economic, or material, 'base' of the prevailing relations of production. Deterministic accounts of 'base' and 'superstructure' were most radically challenged by post-modern thinkers, who asserted the autonomy of ideology and culture, but also by post-structuralist thinkers, such as Althusser (1969), Bourdieu (1977) and Hall (1981), who explored how ideology and culture might be autonomous without being disconnected from the economic base. Within the terms of the 'structure vs. agency' debate, discussed in Chapter 1, traditional Marxism offers a strong structuralist account, in which relations of material production are the primary determining structure. Post-structuralist accounts were so called because they remained within the orbit of Marxist structuralism but sought out spaces in which ideological and cultural phenomena could be seen as relatively autonomous and, perhaps, determinative in their own right.

The point of this excursion into the history of the modern social sciences is that the social approaches that entered Applied Linguistics in the 1990s have largely built upon this body of post-Marxist theories. Sociocultural Theory is, for example, as Lantolf explains in Chapter 2 of this volume, an explicitly Marxist theory, but it appears to be Marxist more in its view of learning as socialization than in any insistence on the primacy of relations of material production. More generally, the desire to reconnect language learning and use to social context ties in with a post-structuralist shift from models of economic determinism to somewhat looser models of sociocultural determinism, in which individual thought and action (rather than ideology and culture) are determined by social circumstances. Though Lantolf and Thorne (2006) begin their book on Sociocultural Theory by identifying earlier work on post-Marxist linguistics, critiques of traditional Marxism in social theory have had little impact on mainstream Applied Linguistics. Social theory entered Applied Linguistics in the 1990s, therefore, not in response to deterministic accounts of language learning and use, but as part of a socially inspired critique of 'scientific' approaches that appeared to have placed cognitive-linguistic SLA processes beyond the reach of social structure altogether. What we see in social approaches to Applied Linguistics, in other words, is an essentially Marxist objection to the autonomy of the cognitive-linguistic system and the abstraction of language learning and use from their social contexts, which is, at the same time, informed by a post-Marxist concern to avoid economic determinism. As we have seen in this book, these concerns constitute the common ground on which different social approaches stand; this ground is also shared by much research on autonomy in language learning, which has, in a sense, arrived at a social perspective from the opposite direction.

The core principle in social approaches to Applied Linguistics is, therefore, that language learning and use always take place in a social context that must be accounted for in research. This in turn implies that social context somehow 'determines', 'constrains', 'shapes' or 'conditions' language learning and use, or in some accounts that they are 'mutually constitutive'. The differing terminologies, here, also hint at the differences among these approaches, which tend to boil down to differences over the power that social context exercises over language learning and use. Returning to the question of whether the common ground can be narrowed down further, however, it seems important to note that the approaches that are current in Applied Linguistics represent the tip of an iceberg of a vast body of social theory that has tended to diverge rather than converge on this issue. This is understandable, moreover, when we consider how post-structuralist theory has moved from a relatively straightforward assumption of economic determinism to a position where every aspect of social and cultural life potentially determines (or does not determine) every other aspect. It is also worth noting that in introducing social theory to Applied Linguistics, researchers first argued for a broadening of the scope of the theories that were admissible in Applied Linguistics at a time when some SLA researchers were arguing that it should be narrowed down (Block 1996; Lantolf 1996). At that time, the argument was not simply for the adoption of social approaches, but for a greater tolerance of interdisciplinarity, expressed in Lantolf's (1996) subtitle as a spirit of 'letting all the flowers bloom'. Within the domain of social approaches to Applied Linguistics, we should, perhaps, maintain the same spirit of open-mindedness, recognizing that we are still in a phase where exploration of differences and new areas of social theory is likely to be more productive than a solidification of positions and stances. In this spirit, we want look at some of the differences – concerned with identity, agency and autonomy – that have emerged in the course of this book, not with the intention of resolving them, but with a view to identifying directions for future research.

Identity

If we track the history of the concept of identity in Applied Linguistics, we see that it has been understood in two very different ways. In one understanding, language follows identity; we can, in effect, 'read off' a person's social identity from their language and speech. Identity, here, involves aspects such as ethnicity, nationality, social status, gender and sexual orientation, and language repertoires and affiliations; these identities are expressed, in part, through features of language such as pronunciation, vocabulary, grammar and idiomatic usage. In the second understanding, it is identity that follows language, in the sense that identities are constantly being negotiated and renegotiated in the course of communicative interaction. These different understandings of the relationship between language and identity are also connected to debates over structure and agency; the first implies that language use is determined by social identity, which is in turn determined by how we are positioned in relation to social structures of various kinds, whereas the second implies that language users play an active part in the negotiation of their own identities through language use.

This second understanding of the relationship between identity and language use is, moreover, one of the distinctive contributions of social approaches to Applied Linguistics, which have often addressed questions of agency and autonomy through the concept of identity. As van Lier (2007: 58) argues, 'we do not merely look for the learners' identities in their past histories (important though these are), but we also promote agency in the present through activity that is both thoughtful and mindful ... The learner thus does not only learn to communicate, "This is where I come from", but also "This is what I am doing right now" and "This is where I want to go".' According to this view, individual identities are, in part, socially or historically determined, but they are also open to negotiation in the here and now. It is also in the here and now that language education has the potential to help students renegotiate their histories and build new identities. This kind of thinking, however, only makes sense if we begin, as social approaches to Applied Linguistics do, by looking at and working with learners in the social contexts of their learning. From this perspective, identities are not fixed but mutable, and their mutability is conditioned by communicative interactions with what Menezes (Chapter 5) would call 'affordances' in the environment. This is part of the common ground on which the various social approaches stand, but we have also seen that there are variations in the ways in which they deal with the construct of identity.

Among the approaches discussed in this book, Situated Learning Theory (Lamb, Chapter 3) evidently has the most to say about identity, because it views learning, almost by definition, as a matter of acquiring and developing new identities in communities of practice. As Wenger (1998: 75–6) puts it, each participant in a community of practice also has a 'unique place' and a 'unique identity', which is further defined in the course of engagement. Assuming that individuals are participants in multiple communities of practice, identities can be understood as being both dynamic and complex, and highly individual; language identities can also be understood as being highly individual products of the use of different languages in different communities of practice. Sociocultural Theory, on the other hand, addresses issues of identity mainly through the idea that the individual emerges from socialization processes, involving socialization into language use, that are mediated by cultural artefacts and social relationships (Lantolf, Chapter 2). From this perspective, individual identities appear to emerge from the fact that we are socialized in different ways, although the cultural settings in which we are socialized also loom large. In comparison to the complex and dynamic identities of Situated Learning Theory, there is also a sense in Sociocultural Theory that identity formation is a more linear process and that identity outcomes are more stable, and tied to the growth of a coherent and stable self within a particular cultural setting. It is interesting, in this context, that Lantolf mentions Hoffman's (1989) account of her struggle to reconstruct her identity through a different semiotic system after her migration from Poland to the United States. Her case is mentioned as an example of how difficult it is to arrive at a position where one is able to 'think in' a second language to the point where it becomes a medium for 'inner speech', which would be one indicator of a person having developed an identity that is mediated through the second language (cf. Block 2007a). This, in turn, suggests that for Sociocultural Theory the identities that emerge from language socialization are much less susceptible to negotiation and development than they are in other social approaches. Also, while Sociocultural Theory evidently views identities as outcomes of early socialization, it is much less clear whether they would be viewed as outcomes of learning involving higher mental processes.

These are, moreover, not the only ways in which the construct of identity is construed in this book. Identity is central to Yashima's (Chapter 4) discussion of language learning and imagination in a somewhat different way; imagined communities and ideal selves furnish identities that learners 'try on', as it were, in order to bridge the gap between second language use in first and second language communities. Menezes's (Chapter 5) discussion of identity in the context of Complexity and Social-Ecological Theory focuses on the ways in which learners mobilize different 'fractals' of their multiple identities in response to the affordances offered in different environments; her concern is more with the interaction of various aspects of social identity with language learning as a social process. Lastly, Benson's (Chapter 6), discussion of identity in the context of Autonomy Theory focuses on the ways in which language and social identities become more individualized as learners gain knowledge, experience and autonomy in second language learning and use.

What we see here then is a diversity of perspectives on identity that, perhaps, reflect the authors' individual interpretations of theoretical frameworks as much as they reflect the frameworks themselves. Identity is, perhaps, the most pervasive and least well understood construct in the social sciences at the present time and, when we read Applied Linguistics work on the topic, we often have to work hard to understand the precise senses in which the term is being used. From a 'letting all the flowers bloom' perspective, this may be no bad thing. Yet there might also be profit in a more rigorous interrogation of how different approaches view the ways in which the construct of identity is deployed by the others. Areas where more clarity is needed include the question of the stability and depth of identities (when Situated Learning Theory and Sociocultural Theory talk about identity, are they actually talking about the same thing?), the difference between social and individual identity (if such a difference exists), and the sense in which we can isolate 'language' or 'second language identity' within the broader constructs of social or individual identity.

Agency and autonomy

One point that emerges clearly from the discussion of identity in this book is that most contributors see identity as the medium through which we move from the social to the individual. Identities are evidently both social and individual. Attributes such as gender, ethnicity and so on merge our individualities into larger identity categories; the name, photograph and number on an identity document identify us individually. On the social side, therefore, we have various ways of thinking about the socialization of identities, while on the individual side we have various ways of thinking about what individuals themselves bring to negotiation of their own identities. In social approaches to Applied Linguistics, the individual side of identity is mainly addressed through the constructs of agency and autonomy.

One major difficulty in discussing this area lies in the fact that we are no longer dealing with different ways of conceptualizing a single construct, as we were with identity, but with different ways of conceptualizing two very closely related constructs and the differences between them. From the outset, therefore, we need to take account of the two different trajectories along which the two terms have arrived in this book. Autonomy has its own distinct history in the field of Applied Linguistics, dating back to the 1970s; beyond this field it is primarily a liberal-humanist philosophical construct (Benson, Chapter 6). The origins of the term agency are more obscure, partly because there is no philosophy of agency in the same sense that there is a philosophy of autonomy. However, the term was used at least as early as the eighteenth century in the context of discussions of free will and has become a core concept in the social sciences through numerous repetitions of the structure vs. agency debate. In post-Marxist theory, agency tends to account for whatever cannot be directly explained by social structure; it is essentially an allowance for the unpredictability of socially-determined human behaviour. Lantolf (Chapter 2) also makes the argument that individual agency is itself a product of socialization; it is effectively a higher function that develops through acculturation and mediated learning. In liberal-humanist philosophy, on the other hand, autonomy accounts for social structure itself, insofar as there is an assumption that a society of autonomous individuals is a 'good' society; the social constraints on autonomy derive from social interactions among autonomous individuals themselves. Rather than dig further into the issues of this kind, however, the point that we want to stress is that there is essentially no 'philosophy of agency' just as there is 'no sociology of autonomy'. In this sense, agency and autonomy are, perhaps, incommensurable terms, or at least terms that belong to two very different worlds. This may also explain why they are used in several ways in this book, and in some cases not at all.

Reading back through the chapters, we see that many of the contributors pay more attention to agency than to autonomy (e.g. Yashima, Chapter 4, and Gu, Chapter 9, who do not deal with autonomy at all), because the theory they draw on is more concerned with identity and agency. In some chapters, however, there is an attempt to cross the gap. In this respect, we find Lantolf's critique of autonomy an especially valuable contribution to the field, because it moves beyond the assumption that autonomy is an individualistic concept, by directly tackling accounts of autonomy that adopt a Vygotskyan perspective. Lamb (Chapter 3) also addresses both agency and autonomy in his chapter on Communities of Practice, where he treats them as distinct constructs, autonomy being aligned more to the development of learning and agency to the development of the individual. Clarke (Chapter 12), on the other hand, appears to use them as synonymous terms, which has some similarity to usage in social psychology where 'autonomous agency' is understood as one concept rather than two (e.g. Nahmias 2007). Both Menezes (Chapter 5) and Kehrwald (Chapter 7) treat agency as a sub-component of autonomy. Menezes describes agency as one of the ways in which autonomy is manifested, along with interdependence and control of the learning process, while for Kehrwald, autonomy is a complex combination of self-regulation and investment, with the notion of investment focusing on both identity and socially oriented agency.

There is, then, no general agreement on how the terms agency and autonomy should be used or differentiated. What we draw from this book, however, is a possibly 'mature' view that the difference is not defined by the social character of one or the individual character of the other. Looking forward, we also observe that by allowing these two constructs to rub up against each other in this book, we have in a sense redefined the problem from one of understanding the difference between agency and autonomy to one of examining in greater depth an area in which Applied Linguistic individuals 'escape', however temporarily, their socially and historically determined selves.

Conclusion

In conclusion, we hope that readers will share our view that the 13 chapters in this book have raised questions about, if not revealed a deeper awareness of, the intrinsically social nature of the individual language learner as the subject of Applied Linguistics research. Increasingly, it seems that we have moved away from the Individual Differences approach that dominated views of individuality in language learning, while simultaneously hiding it beneath a weight of social and psychological categorizations, for many years, and moved towards richer and more particular views of what it means to be a learner and user of languages in an increasingly globalized and networked world. The contributions to this book suggest that we are now focused on a more personal view of the learner, but that the personal is constrained, or perhaps liberated, by the social. They illustrate a variety of ways of exploring how the personal, individual learner is shaped to a greater or lesser degree by social forces which contribute to the negotiation of identities and the development of agency and autonomy. In doing so, they also show us how, paradoxically, one of the best ways to understand these social processes is through research that is intensely focused on experiences of language learning and use as they are embedded in individual lives. There is still a great deal to be learned, however, about the constraints or affordances of social systems for individual identity, agency and autonomy, and about the theoretical frameworks and research methodologies that will best elucidate the dialectic between the social and the individual in Applied Linguistics. In putting together this collection, we hope that we have begun a necessary conversation on this dialectic and that other researchers will be inspired to pursue the challenge of understanding the Applied Linguistic individual.

References

Adamson, B. (2004) *China's English: A History of English in Chinese Education.* Hong Kong: Hong Kong University Press.

Ahearn, L. M. (2001) Language and agency. *Annual Review of Anthropology* 30: 109–37.

Allwright, D. and Bailey, K. M. (1991) *Focus on the Language Classroom.* Cambridge: Cambridge University Press.

Althusser, L. (1969) *For Marx*. London: Allen Lane.

Amarante, R. (2009, February 18) Um hermano internacional. *Revista Veja* 42 (7): 125. Retrieved from http://veja.abril.com.br/180209/p_125.shtml

Anderson, B. (1983) *Imagined Communities: Reflections on the Origin and Spread of Nationalism*. London: Verso.

Androusopoulos, J. and Georgakopoulou, A. (2003) Discourse constructions of youth identities: Introduction. In J. K. Androusopoulos and A. Georgakopoulou (eds) *Discourse Construction of Youth Identities*, 1–25. Amsterdam: John Benjamins.

Aoki, N. (1999) Affect and the role of teacher in the development of learner autonomy. In J. Arnold (ed.) *Affect in Language Learning*, 142–54. Cambridge: Cambridge University Press.

Appadurai, A. (1996) *Modernity at Large: Cultural Dimension of Globalization.* Minneapolis, MN: University of Minnesota Press.

Apple, M. (2001) Markets, standards, teaching, and teacher education. *Journal of Teacher Education* 52 (2): 182–96.

Archer, M. S. (2000) *Being Human: The Problem of Agency.* Cambridge: Cambridge University Press.

Armstrong, K. (2005) *A Short History of Myth*. Edinburgh: Canongate Books.

Atkinson, D. (2002) Toward a sociocognitive approach to second language acquisition. *Modern Language Journal* 86 (4): 525–45.

Atkinson, D., Churchill, E., Nishino, T. and Okada, H. (2007) Alignment and interaction in a sociocognitive approach to second language acquisition. *Modern Language Journal* 91 (2): 169–88.

Auerbach, E. (2007) Necessary contradictions … and beyond. In A. Barfield and S. Brown (eds) *Reconstructing Autonomy in Language Education: Inquiry and Innovation*, 84–92. Basingstoke: Palgrave Macmillan.

Ausubel, D. P. (1970) Reception learning and the rote-meaningful dimension. In E. Stones (ed.) *Readings in Educational Psychology: Learning and Teaching*, 193–205. London: Methuen.

Aviram, A. (1995) Autonomy and commitment: Compatible ideals. *Journal of Philosophy of Education* 29 (1): 61–73.

Aviram, R. and Yonah, Y. (2004) 'Flexible control': Towards a conception of personal autonomy for postmodern education. *Educational Philosophy and Theory* 36 (1): 3–17.

Bakhurst, D. (2007) Vygotsky's demons. In H. Daniels, M. Cole and J. V. Wertsch (eds) *The Cambridge Companion to Vygotsky*, 50–76. New York, NY: Cambridge University Press.

Bandura, A. (2001) Social cognitive theory: An agentic perspective. *Annual Review of Psychology* 52, 1–26.

Barab, S. A. and Plucker, J. A. (2002) Smart people or smart contexts? Cognition, ability, and talent development in an age of situated approaches to knowing and learning. *Educational Psychologist* 37 (3): 165–82.

Barcelos, A. M. F. (2003) Researching beliefs about SLA: A critical review. In P. Kalaja and A. M. F. Barcelos (eds) *Beliefs about SLA: New Research Approaches*, 7–33. Netherlands: Kluwer Academic Publishers.

Barkhuizen, G. (ed.) (2011) Narrative research in TESOL. Special Issue of *TESOL Quarterly* 45 (3).

Barret, T. (n.d.) *Tom Barrett Quotes*. Retrieved from http://thinkexist.com/quotation/chaos_in_the_world_brings_uneasiness-but_it_also/225874.html

Barton, D. (1994) *Literacy: An Introduction to the Ecology of Written Language*. Oxford: Blackwell.

Barton, D. and M. Hamilton (1998) *Local Literacies. Reading and Writing in One Community*. London: Routledge.

Barton, D. and Tusting, K. (eds) (2005a) *Beyond Communities of Practice: Language, Power and Social Context*. Cambridge: University of Cambridge.

Barton, D. and Tusting, K. (2005b) Introduction. In D. Barton and K. Tusting (eds), *Beyond Communities of Practice: Language, Power, and Social Context*, 105–38. Cambridge: Cambridge University Press.

Bauman, Z. (2001) *The Individualized Society*. Cambridge: Polity.

Beck, U. and Beck-Gersheim, E. (2002) *Individualization: Institutionalized Individualism and its Social and Political Consequences*. London: Sage.

Bempechat, J. and Boulay, B. A. (2001) Beyond dichotomous characterizations of student learning: New directions in achievement motivation research. In D. McInerney and S. Van Etten (eds) *Research on Sociocultural Influences on Motivation and Learning Vol. I*, 17–36. Greenwich, CT: Information Age Publishing.

Benson, P. (2005) (Auto)biography and learner diversity. In P. Benson and D. Nunan (eds), *Learners' Stories: Difference and Diversity in Language Learning*, 4–21. Cambridge: Cambridge University Press.

Benson, P. (2008) Teachers' and learners' perspectives on autonomy. In T. Lamb and H. Reinders (eds) *Learner and Teacher Autonomy: Concepts, Realities and Responses*, 15–32. Amsterdam: John Benjamins.

Benson, P. (2011a) *Teaching and Researching Autonomy in Language Learning*. Second edition. London: Longman.

Benson, P. (2011). Language learning and teaching beyond the classroom: An introduction to the field. In P. Benson and H. Reinders (eds), *Beyond the Language Classroom*, 7–16. Basingstoke: Palgrave Macmillan.

Benson, P. and Chik, A. (2010) New literacies and autonomy in foreign language learning. In J. Luzon, N. Ruiz and L. Villanueva (eds) *Genre Theory and New Literacies: Applications to Autonomous Language Learning*, 63–80. New York, NY: Springer.

Benson, P. and Huang, J. (2008) Autonomy in the transition from foreign language learning to foreign language teaching. *DELTA: Documentação de Estudos em Linguística Teórica e Aplicada.* 24/Especial: 421–39.

Benson, P. and Nunan, D. (eds) (2002) The experience of language learning. Special issue of *The Hong Kong Journal of Applied Linguistics* 7 (2).

Benson, P. and Nunan, D. (eds) (2005) *Learners' Stories: Difference and Diversity in Language Learning.* Cambridge: Cambridge University Press.

Benson, P., Barkhuizen, G., Bodycott, P. and Brown, J. (2012) Second language identity and study abroad. *Applied Linguistics Review* 3 (1): 173–93.

Benson, P., Chik, A. and Lim, H. Y. (2003) Becoming autonomous in an Asian context: Autonomy as a sociocultural process. In D. Palfreyman and R. C. Smith (eds) *Learner Autonomy Across Cultures: Language Education Perspectives*, 23–40. Basingstoke: Palgrave Macmillan.

Berk, L. E. and Winsler A. (1995) *Scaffolding Children's Learning: Vygotsky and Early Childhood Education.* Washington, DC: National Association of the Education of Young Children.

Besley, T. and Peters, M. (2007) *Subjectivity and Truth: Foucault, Education and the Culture of Self.* New York, NY: Peter Lang.

Best, S. and Kellner, D. (1991) *Postmodern Theory: Critical Interrogations.* New York, NY: The Guilford Press.

Biesta, G. (2010) *Good Education in Age of Measurement: Ethics, Politics, Democracy.* Boulder, CO: Paradigm Publishers.

Block, D. (1996) Not so fast: Some thoughts on theory culling, relativism, accepted findings and the heart and soul of SLA. *Applied Linguistics* 17 (1): 63–83.

Block, D. (2003) *The Social Turn in Second Language Acquisition.* Edinburgh: Edinburgh University Press.

Block, D. (2006) Identity in applied linguistics. In T. Omoniyi and G. White (eds) *The Sociolinguistics of Identity*, 34–49. London: Continuum.

Block, D. (2007a) *Second Language Identities.* London: Continuum.

Block, D. (2007b) The rise of identity in SLA research, post Firth and Wagner (1997). *Modern Language Journal* 91 (Supplement S1): 863–76.

Blommaert, J. (2005) *Discourse: A Critical Introduction.* Cambridge: Cambridge University Press.

Blommaert, J. (2007) A course on ethnography 1–4. University of Jyväskylä.

Blommaert, J. (2010) *A Sociolinguistics of Globalization.* Cambridge: Cambridge University Press.

Bloom, S. L. (2000, August) Chaos, complexity, self-organization and us. *Email from America. Psychotherapy Review* 2 (8). Retrieved from http://www.freeinfosociety.com/pdfs/mathematics/chaos.pdf

Bloomfield, D. (2009) Working within and against neoliberal accreditation agendas: Opportunities for Professional Experience. *Asia-Pacific Journal of Teacher Education* 37 (1): 27–44.

Bonnett, M. and Cuypers, S. (2003) Autonomy and authenticity in education. In N. Blake, P. Smeyers, R. Smith and P. Standish (eds) *The Blackwell Guide to the Philosophy of Education*, 326–40. London: Blackwell.

Bourdieu, P. (1977) *Outline of a Theory of Practice.* Translated by R. Nice. Cambridge: Cambridge University Press.

Bourdieu, P. and Wacquant, L. (1992) *An Invitation to Reflexive Sociology.* Chicago, IL: University of Chicago Press.

Boylan, M. (2010) Ecologies of participation in school classrooms. *Teaching and Teacher Education* 26 (1): 61–70.

Braidotti, R. (2006) *Transpositions: On Nomadic Ethics.* Cambridge: Polity Press.

Breen, M. P. (1986) The social context of language learning: a neglected situation. *Studies in Second Language Acquisition* 7 (2): 135–58.

Breen, M. P. and Candlin, C. N. (1980) The essentials of a communicative curriculum in language teaching. *Applied Linguistics* 1 (2): 89–112.

Brookes, A. and Grundy, P. (eds) (1988) *Individualization and Autonomy in Language Learning.* ELT Documents 131. Modern English Publications in association with the British Council/Macmillan.

Brooks, M. (2007, May) Climate myths: chaotic systems are not predictable. *New Scientist* 16. Retrieved from http://www.newscientist.com/article/dn11641

Bruner, J. (1966) Some elements of discovery. In L. S. Shulman and E. R. Keislar (eds) *Learning by Discovery: A Critical Appraisal*, 101–13. Chicago, IL: Rand McNally.

Canagarajah, A. S. (1999) *Resisting Linguistic Imperialism in English Teaching.* Oxford: Oxford University Press.

Canagarajah, A. S. (2006) TESOL at forty: What are the issues? *TESOL Quarterly* 40 (1): 9–34.

Canale, M. and Swain, M. (1980) Theoretical bases of communicative approaches to second language teaching and testing. *Applied Linguistics* 1 (1): 1–47.

Candlin, C. N. and Candlin, S. (2007) Nursing through time and space: Some challenges to the construct of community of practice. In R. Iedema (ed.) *The Discourse of Hospital Communication: Tracing Complexities in Contemporary Health Care Organizations*, 244–67. Basingstoke: Palgrave Macmillan.

Cazden, C. B. (2008) It's time to bring together our theories about inter- and intramental processes: A response to Evensen. *Journal of Applied Linguistics* 5 (2): 205–13.

Cekaite, A. (2007) A child's development of interactional competence in a Swedish L2 classroom. *Modern Language Journal* 91 (1): 45–62.

Censo General de Población y Vivienda. (2000) Retrieved 6 October 2006 from http://www.inegi.gob.mx/inegi/default.asp

Centeno-Cortés, B. and Jiménez-Jiménez, A. (2004) Problem-solving tasks in a foreign language: The importance of the L1 in private verbal thinking. *International Journal of Applied Linguistics* 14 (1): 7–35.

Chik, A. and Benson, P. (2008) Frequent flyer: A narrative of overseas study in English. In P. Kalaja, V. Menezes and A. M. F. Barcelos (eds) *Narratives of Learning and Teaching EFL*, 155–68. London: Palgrave Macmillan.

Christman, J. (2004) Relational autonomy, liberal individualism, and the social constitution of selves. *Philosophical Studies* 117 (1/2): 143–64.

Clarke, M. (2008) *Language Teacher Identities: Co-constructing Discourse and Community.* Clevedon: Multilingual Matters.

Clarke, M. (2009a) Doing 'identity work' in teacher education: The case of a UAE teacher. In R. Sultana and A. Mazawi (eds) *World Yearbook of Education 2010: Education and the Arab World: Political Projects, Struggles and Geometries of Power*, 145–62. New York, NY: Routledge.

Clarke, M. (2009b) The ethico-politics of teacher identity. *Educational Philosophy and Theory* 41 (2): 185–200.

Coffey, S. and Street, B. (2008) Narrative and identity in the language learning project. *Modern Language Journal* 92 (3): 452–64.

Cole, M. (1995) The supra-individual envelope of development: Activity and practice, situation and context. *New Directions for Child Development* 67: 45–65.

Cook, G. and Kasper, G. (eds) (2006) Language emergence: Implications for Applied Linguistics. Special issue of *Applied Linguistics* 27 (4).

Coupland, N., Sarangi, S. and Candlin, C. N. (eds) (2001) *Sociolinguistics and Social Theory*. London: Longman.

Creese, A. (2005) Mediating allegations of racism in a multiethnic London school: What speech communities and communities of practice can tell us about discourse and power. In D. Barton and M. Hamilton (eds) *Beyond Communities of Practice*, 55–76. Cambridge: Cambridge University Press.

Cuypers, S. E. (1992) Is personal autonomy the first principle of education? *Journal of Philosophy of Education* 26 (1): 5–17.

Dam, L. (1995) *Learner Autonomy 3: From Theory to Classroom Practice*. Dublin: Authentik.

Davis, B. and Sumara, D. (2006) *Complexity and Education: Inquiries into Learning, Teaching, and Research*. Mahwah, NJ: Lawrence Erlbaum.

Davydov, V. V. (2004) *Problems of Developmental Instruction: A Theoretical and Experimental Psychological Study*. Translated by P. Moxhay. Moscow: Akadimiya.

de Bot, K. (ed.) (2008) Second language development as a dynamic process. Special issue of *Modern Language Journal* 92 (2).

Dean, M. (1994) *Critical and Effective Histories: Foucault's Methods and Historical Sociology*. London: Routledge.

Deguchi, T. and Yashima, T. (2008) Jissenkyodotaitoshiteno daigakuryoniokeru ryugakuseito nihonjingakuseino taijinkankei [Interpersonal relationships between international students and Japanese college students in a Japanese college dormitory as a Community of Practice]. *Multicultural Relations* 5: 33–47.

DePalma, R. (2008) When success makes me fail: (De)constructing failure and success in a conventional American classroom. *Mind, Culture, and Activity* 15 (2): 141–64.

Dewey, J. (1938/1997) *Experience and Education*. New York, NY: Touchstone.

Dickinson, L. (1987) *Self-instruction in Language Learning*. Cambridge: Cambridge University Press.

Dörnyei, Z. (2005) *The Psychology of the Language Learner: Individual Differences in Second Language Acquisition*. Mahwah, NJ: Lawrence Erlbaum Associates.

Dörnyei, Z. (2009) The L2 motivational self system. In Z. Dörnyei and E. Ushioda (eds) *Motivation, Language Identity and the L2 Self*, 9–43. Bristol: Multilingual Matters.

Dörnyei, Z. and Ushioda, E. (eds) (2009) *Motivation, Language Identity and the L2 Self*. Bristol: Multilingual Matters.

Dörnyei, Z., Csizér, K. and Németh, N. (2006) *Motivation, Language Attitudes and Globalisation: A Hungarian Perspective*. Bristol: Multilingual Matters.

Dufva, H. (2003) Beliefs in dialogue: A Bakhtinian view. In P. Kalaja and A. M. F. Barcelos (eds) *Beliefs about SLA: New Research Approaches*, 131–51. Netherlands: Kluwer Academic Publishers.

Edwards, A. (2005) Let's get beyond community and practice: The many meanings of learning by participating. *Curriculum Journal* 16 (1): 49–65.

Ellis, N. (2007) The associative-cognitive CREED. In B. VanPatten and J. Williams (eds) *Theories in Second Language Acquisition: An Introduction*, 77–96. Mahwah, NJ: Erlbaum.

Ellis, R. (1994) *The Study of Second Language Acquisition*. Oxford: Oxford University Press.

Ellis, R. (2004) Individual differences in second language learning. In A. Davies and C. Elder (eds) *The Handbook of Applied Linguistics*, 525–51. Oxford: Blackwell.

Engeström, Y. (2007) Putting Vygotsky to work: The change laboratory as an application of double stimulation. In H. Daniels, M. Cole and J. V. Wertsch (eds) *The Cambridge Companion to Vygotsky*, 363–82. Cambridge: Cambridge University Press.

Evensen, L. S. (2007) 'With a little help from my friends'? Theory of learning in applied linguistics and SLA. *Journal of Applied Linguistics* 4 (3): 333–53.

Evensen, L. S. (2008) The need for a *tertium comparationis* in Applied Linguistics and SLA: A reply to Lantolf and Cazden. *Journal of Applied Linguistics* 5 (2): 221–7.

Fairclough, N. (2003) *Analyzing Discourse: Textual Analysis for Social Research*. London: Routledge.

Fanon, F. (1952/2008) *Black Skins, White Masks*. New York, NY: Grove Weidenfeld.

Feigenbaum, P. (2009) Development of communicative competence through private and inner speech. In A. Winsler, C. Fernyhough and I. Montero (eds) *Private Speech, Executive Functioning, and the Development of Verbal Self-Regulation*, 105–20. New York, NY: Cambridge University Press.

Firth, A. and Wagner, J. (1997) On discourse, communication and (some) fundamental concepts in SLA research. *Modern Language Journal* 81 (3): 285–300.

Foucault, M. (1977) *Discipline and Punish: The Birth of the Prison*. London: Penguin.

Foucault, M. (1980) *Power/Knowledge: Selected Interviews and Other Writings 1972–1977*. Brighton: Harvester.

Foucault, M. (1985) *The Use of Pleasure: The History of Sexuality Vol. 2*. Translated by R. Hurley. New York, NY: Pantheon Books.

Foucault, M. (1986) *The Care of the Self: The History of Sexuality Vol. 3*. Translated by R. Hurley. London: Penguin.

Foucault, M. (1997a) The ethics of the concern for self as a practice of freedom. In P. Rabinow (ed.) *Ethics, Subjectivity and Truth: Essential Works of Foucault 1954–1984 Vol. 1*, 281–302. New York, NY: The New Press.

Foucault, M. (1997b) Writing the self. In A. Davidson (ed.) *Foucault and His Interlocutors*, 234–48. Chicago, IL: University of Chicago Press.

Frankfurt, H. G. (1999) *Necessity, Volition and Love*. Cambridge: Cambridge University Press.

Gabbert, W. (2004) *Becoming Maya: Ethnicity and Social Inequality in Yucatan since 1500*. Tucson, AZ: University of Arizona Press.

Gardner, R. C. and Lambert, W. E. (1972) *Attitudes and Motivation in Second Language Learning*. Rowley, MS: Newbury House.

Gee, J. P. (1992) *The Social Mind: Language, Ideology, and Social Practice*. New York, NY: Bergin and Garvey.

Gee, J. P. (2004) *Situated Language and Learning: A Critique of Traditional Schooling*. London: Routledge.

Gee, J. P. (2005) Semiotic social spaces and affinity spaces: From *The Age of Mythology* to today's schools. In D. Barton and K. Tusting (eds) *Beyond Communities of Practice: Language, Power and Social Context*, 214–32. Cambridge: Cambridge University Press.

Giddens, A. (1976) *New Rules of Sociological Method*. London: Hutchinson.

Giddens, A. (1984) *The Constitution of Society: Outline of the Theory of Structuration*. Cambridge: Polity Press.

Giddens, A. (1991) *Modernity and Self-identity: Self and Society in the Late Modern Age*. Stanford, CA: Stanford University Press.

Giddens, A. (1999) *Runaway World*. London: Profile Books.

Gleick, J. (1987) *Chaos: Making a New Science*. New York, NY: Penguin.

Gore, J. (1993) *The Struggle for Pedagogies: Critical and Feminist Discourses as Regimes of Truth*. New York and London: Routledge.

Grabois, H. (2008) Contribution and language learning: Service-learning from a sociocultural perspective. In J. P. Lantolf and M. E. Poehner (eds) *Sociocultural Theory and the Teaching of Second Languages*, 380–406. London: Equinox.

Gregg, K. R. (2006) Taking a social turn for the worse: The language socialization paradigm for second language acquisition. *Second Language Research* 22 (4): 413–42.

Gremmo, M. J. and Riley, P. (1995) Autonomy, self-direction and self-access in language teaching and learning: The history of an idea. *System* 23 (2): 151–64.

Grimmett, P. P., Fleming, R. and Trotter, L. (2009) Legitimacy and identity in teacher education: A micro-political struggle constrained by macro-political pressures. *Asia-Pacific Journal of Teacher Education* 37 (1): 5–26.

Gu, M. (2009a) College English learners' discursive motivation construction in China. *System* 37 (2): 300–12.

Gu, M. (2009b) *The Discursive Construction of Second Language Learners' Motivation: A Multi-level Perspective*. New York, NY: Peter Lang.

Gu, M. (2010) Identities constructed in difference: English language learners in China. *Journal of Pragmatics* 42 (1): 139–52.

Güemez Pineda, M. (2006) *Language, Culture and Indigenous Rights in Rural Yucatan*. Paper presented at the Conference on Mayab Bejlae: Yucatan Today, Kroeber Hall, University of California Berkeley, CA. 21–23 April 2006.

Gumperz, J. (1982) *Discourse Strategies*. Cambridge: Cambridge University Press.

Gunzenhauser, M. G. (2008) Care of the self in a context of accountability. *Teachers College Record* 110 (10): 2224–44.

Haenen, J. (1996) *Piotr Gal'perin: Psychologist in Vygotsky's Footsteps*. New York, NY: Nova Science Publishers.

Hall, S. (1981) Notes on deconstructing the popular. In R. Samuel (ed.) *People's History and Socialist Theory*, 227–40. London: Routledge.

Hammerly, H. (1982) *Synthesis in Language Teaching: An Introduction to Linguistics*. Blaine, WA: Second Language Publications.

Haneda, M. (2006) Classrooms as communities of practice: A reevaluation. *TESOL Quarterly* 40 (4): 807–17.

Hanson, J. (2009) Displaced but not replaced: The impact of e-learning on academic identities in higher education. *Teaching in Higher Education* (14) 5: 553–64.

Hawkins, M. R. (2005) Becoming a student: Identity work and academic literacies in early schooling. *TESOL Quarterly* 39 (1): 59–82.

Heller, M. (2008) Doing ethnography. In Li Wei and M. G. Moyer (eds) *The Blackwell Guide to Research Methods in Bilingualism and Multilingualism*, 249–62. Malden, MA: Blackwell.

Hellerman, J. (2008) *Social Actions for Classroom Language Learning*. Clevedon: Multilingual Matters.

Higgins, E. T. (1987) Self-discrepancy: A theory relating self and affect. *Psychological Review* 94 (3): 319–40.

Hill, D. (2007) Critical teacher education, new labour, and the global project of neoliberal capital. *Policy Futures in Education* 5 (2): 204–25.

Hodge, R. and Jones, K. (2000) Photography in collaborative research on multilingual literacy practices: Images and understandings of researcher and researched. In M. Martin-Jones and K. Jones (eds) *Multilingual Literacies*, 299–318. Amsterdam: John Benjamins.

Hoffman, E. (1989) *Lost in Translation: A Life in a New Language*. New York, NY: Dutton.

Holec, H. (1981) *Autonomy in Foreign Language Learning*. Oxford: Pergamon.

Holec, H. (ed.) (1988) *Autonomy and Self-directed Learning: Present Fields of Application*. Strasbourg: Council of Europe.

Holland, D. and Lachicotte, W. Jr. (2007) Vygotsky, Mead, and the new sociocultural studies of identity. In H. Daniels, M. Cole and J. V. Wertsch (eds) *The Cambridge Companion to Vygotsky*, 101–35. New York, NY: Cambridge University Press.

Holliday, A. (2003) Social autonomy: Addressing the dangers of culturism in TESOL. In D. Palfreyman and R. C. Smith (eds) *Learner Autonomy Across Cultures: Language Education Perspectives*, 110–26. Basingstoke: Palgrave Macmillan.

Holliday, A. (2005) *The Struggle to Teach English as an International Language*. Oxford: Oxford University Press.

Ilyenkov, E. A. (1974) *Activity and Knowledge*. Retrieved from http://www.marxists.org/archive/ilyenkov/works/activity/index.htm.

Infinito, J. (2003a) Ethical self-formation: A look at the later Foucault. *Educational Theory* 53 (2): 155–71.

Infinito, J. (2003b) Jane Elliot meets Foucault: The formation of ethical identities in the classroom. *Journal of Moral Education* 32 (1): 67–76.

Ivanic, R. (1998) *Writing and Identity: The Discoursal Construction of Identity in Academic Writing*. Amsterdam: John Benjamins.

Jenkins, R. (2008) *Social Identity*. Third edition. London: Routledge.

Jiménez Raya, M. (2008) Learner autonomy as an educational goal in modern language education. In M. Jiménez Raya and T. Lamb (eds) *Pedagogy for Autonomy in Modern Languages Education: Theory, Practice and Teacher Education*, 3–15. Dublin: Authentik.

Jiménez Raya, M., Lamb, T. and Vieira, F. (2007) *Pedagogy for Autonomy in Language Education in Europe: Towards a Framework for Learner and Teacher Development*. Dublin: Authentik.

Johnson, D., Johnson, B., Farenga, S. and Ness, D. (2005) *Trivializing Teacher Education: The Accreditation Squeeze*. Lanham, MD: Rowman and Littlefield.

Kalaja, P., Barcelos, A. M. F. and Menezes, V. (eds) (2008) *Narratives of Learning and Teaching EFL*. Basingstoke: Palgrave Macmillan.

Kanno, Y. and Norton, B. (2003) Imagined communities and educational possibilities: Introduction. *Journal of Language, Identity, and Education* 2 (4): 241–9.

Karpov, Y. V. (2003) Vygotsky's doctrine of scientific concepts: Its role for contemporary education. In A. Kozulin, B. Gindis, V. S. Ageyev and S. Miller (eds) *Vygotsky's Educational Theory in Cultural Context*, 65–82. Cambridge: Cambridge University Press.

Karpov, Y. V. (2005) *The Neo-Vygotskian Approach to Child Development*. Cambridge: Cambridge University Press.

Keating, M. C. (2005) The person in the doing: Negotiating the experience of self. In D. Barton and K. Tusting (eds), *Beyond Communities of Practice: Language, Power, and Social Context*, 105–38. Cambridge: Cambridge University Press.

Kelsky, K. (1999) Gender, modernity, and eroticized internationalism in Japan. *Cultural Anthropology* 14 (2): 229–55.

Kelsky, K. (2001) *Women on the Verge: Japanese Women, Western Dreams*. Durham, NC: Duke University Press.

King, B. W. (2008) 'Being gay guy, that is the advantage': Queer Korean language learning and identity construction. *Journal of Language, Identity, and Education* 7 (3–4): 230–52.

Kirschner, P. A., Sweller, J. and Clark, R. E. (2006) Why minimal guidance during instruction does not work: An analysis of the failure of constructivist, discovery, problem-based, experiential, and inquiry-based teaching. *Educational Psychologist* 41 (2): 75–86.

Kjisik, F. (2007) Ten years in autonomy: Reflections and research on the ALMS programme. In D. Gardner (ed.) *Learner Autonomy 10: Integration and Support*, 114–26. Dublin: Authentik.

Kozulin, A. (1998) *Psychological Tools: A Sociocultural Approach to Education*. Cambridge, MA: Harvard University Press.

Kozulin, A. (2003) Psychological tools and mediated learning. In A. Kozulin, B. Gindis, V. S. Ageyev and S. M. Miller (eds) *Vygotsky's Educational Theory in Cultural Context*, 15–39. Cambridge: Cambridge University Press.

Kramsch, C. (2007) From communicative competence to symbolic competence. *Modern Language Journal* 90 (2): 249–52.

Kramsch, C. (ed) (2002) *Language Acquisition and Language Socialization: Ecological Perspectives*. London: Continuum.

Kramsch, C. and Lam, E. (1999) Textual identities: The importance of being non-native. In Braine, G. (ed.) *Non-Native Educators in English Language Teaching*, 57–72. Mahwah, NJ: Lawrence Erlbaum Associates.

Kramsch, C. and Whiteside, A. (2008) Language ecology in multilingual settings: Towards a theory of symbolic competence. *Applied Linguistics* 29 (4): 645–71.

Lakoff, G. and Johnson, M. (1980) *Metaphors We Live By*. Chicago, IL and London: University of Chicago Press.

Lam, A. S. L. (2005) *Language Education in China: Policy and Experience from 1949*. Hong Kong: Hong Kong University Press.

Lamb, M. (2004) 'It depends on the students themselves': Independent language learning at an Indonesian state school. *Language, Culture and Curriculum* 17 (3): 229–45.

Lamb, M. (2007) *The motivation of junior high school pupils to learn English in provincial Indonesia*. Unpublished PhD thesis, University of Leeds.

Lamb, M. (2009) Situating the L2 Self: Two Indonesian school learners of English. In Z. Dörnyei and E. Ushioda (eds) *Motivation, Language Identity and the L2 Self*, 229–47. Bristol: Multilingual Matters.

Lamb, T. E. (2003) Individualising learning: Organising a flexible learning environment. In M. Jiménez Raya and T. Lamb (eds) *Differentiation in the Modern Languages Classroom*, 177–94. Frankfurt am Main: Peter Lang.

Lamb, T. E. and Reinders, H. (eds) (2007) Special issue on learners' voices. *Innovation in Language Learning and Teaching* 1 (2).

Langford, P. (2005) *Vygotsky's Developmental and Educational Psychology*. Hove: Psychology Press.

Lantolf, J. P. (1996) Second language acquisition theory-building: 'Letting all the flowers bloom!' *Language Learning* 46 (4): 713–49.

Lantolf, J. P. (2008) SLA, *I* + 1, SCT, the ZPD, and other things: A response to Evensen. *Journal of Applied Linguistics* 5 (2): 215–19.

Lantolf, J. P. (2011) Integrating sociocultural theory and cognitive linguistics in the second language classroom. In E. Hinkel (ed.) *Handbook of Research in Second Language Teaching and Learning.* Second edition. 303–18. New York, NY: Routledge.

Lantolf, J. P. and Pavlenko, A. (2001) (S)econd (L)anguage (A)ctivity theory: Understanding second language learners as people. In M. P. Breen (ed.) *Learner Contributions to Language Learning*, 141–58. Harlow: Longman.

Lantolf, J. P. and Poehner, M. E. (eds) (2008) *Sociocultural Theory and the Teaching of Second Languages*. London: Equinox.

Lantolf, J. P. and Thorne, S. L. (2006) *Sociocultural Theory and the Genesis of Second Language Development*. Oxford: Oxford University Press.

Lantolf, J. P. and Thorne, S. L. (2007) Sociocultural theory and second language learning. In B. Van Patten and J. Williams (eds) *Theories of Second Language Acquisition: An Introduction*, 201–23. Hillsdale, NJ: Lawrence Erlbaum.

Larsen-Freeman, D. (1997) Chaos/Complexity Science and second language acquisition. *Applied Linguistics* 18 (2): 141–65.

Larsen-Freeman, D. (2001) Individual cognitive/affective learner contributions and differential success in second language acquisition. In M. P. Breen (ed.) *Learner Contributions to Language Learning: New Directions in Research*, 12–24. London: Longman.

Larsen-Freeman, D. and Cameron, L. (2008a) *Complex Systems and Applied Linguistics*. Oxford: Oxford University Press.

Larsen-Freeman, D. and Cameron, L. (2008b) Research methodology on language development from a complex systems perspective. *Modern Language Journal* 92 (ii): 200–13.

Latomaa, S. and Nuolijärvi, P. (2005) The language situation in Finland. In R. B. Kaplan and R. B. Baldauf Jr. (eds) *Language Planning and Policy. Europe, Vol. 1. Finland, Hungary and Sweden*, 125–232. Clevedon: Multilingual Matters.

Lave, J. (1988) *Cognition in Practice: Mind, Mathematics, and Culture in Everyday Life*. New York, NY: Cambridge University Press.

Lave, J. and Wenger, A. (1991) *Situated Learning: Legitimate Peripheral Participation*. Cambridge: Cambridge University Press.

Layder, D. (1990) *The Realist Image in Social Science*. London: Routledge and Kegan Paul.

Layder, D. (1993) *New Strategies in Social Research*. Cambridge: Polity Press.

Layder, D. (1997) *Modern Social Theory: Key Debates and New Directions*. London: Routledge.

Lea, M. R. (2005) Communities of practice in higher education. In D. Barton and K. Tusting (eds) *Beyond Communities of Practice*, 180–97. Cambridge: Cambridge University Press.

Lee, B. (1985) Intellectual origins of Vygotsky's semiotic analysis. In J. V. Wertsch (ed.) *Culture, Communication and Cognition: Vygotskian Perspectives*, 66–95. Cambridge: Cambridge University Press.

Leki, I. (2001) 'A narrow thinking system': nonnative-English-speaking students in group projects across the curriculum. *TESOL Quarterly* 35 (1): 39–67.

Lemke, J. L. (1995) *Textual Politics: Discourse and Social Dynamics*. London: Taylor and Francis.

Leontiev, A. N. (1959/2004) *Los principios del desarrollo mental y el problema del retraso mental* [Principles of mental development and the problem of mental retardation, translation by JPL]. In M. Cecchini (ed.) *Luria, Leontiev, Vygotsky. Psicología y Pedagogía*, 81–98. Madrid: Ediciones Akal.

Leontiev, A. N. (1978) *Activity, Consciousness, and Personality*. Englewood Cliffs, NJ: Prentice-Hall.

Leppänen, S. and Nikula, T. (2007) Diverse uses of English in Finnish society: Discourse-pragmatic insights into media, educational and business contexts. *Multilingua* 26 (4): 333–80.

Leppänen, S., Pitkänen-Huhta, A., Nikula, T., Kytölä, S., Törmäkangas, T., Nissinen, K., Kääntä, L., Räisänen, T., Laitinen, M., Pahta, P., Koskela, H., Lähdesmäki, S. and Jousmäki, H. (2011) *National Survey on the English Language in Finland: Uses, Meanings and Attitudes. Studies in Variation, Contacts and Change in English*. Helsinki: Research Unit for Variation, Contacts and Change in English.

Leppänen, S., Pitkänen-Huhta, A., Piirainen-Marsh, A., Nikula, T. and Peuronen, S. (2009) Young people's translocal new media uses: A multiperspective analysis of language choice and heteroglossia. *Journal of Computer-Mediated Communication* 14 (4): 1080–107.

Lincoln, Y. S. and Guba, E. G. (1985) *Naturalistic Inquiry*. Beverly Hills, CA: Sage.

Lincoln, Y. S. and Guba, E. G. (2003) Paradigmatic controversies: Contradictions and emerging confluences. In N. K. Denzin and Y. S. Lincoln (eds) *The Landscape of Qualitative Research: Theories and Issues*, 191–215. Thousand Oaks, CA: Sage.

Lindley, R. (1986) *Autonomy*. London: Macmillan.

Little, D. (1991) *Learner Autonomy. 1: Definitions, Issues and Problems*. Dublin: Authentik.

Little, D. (1994) Learner autonomy: A theoretical construct and its practical application. *Die Neueren Sprachen* 93 (5): 430–42.

Little, D. (1995) Learning as dialogue: The dependence of learner autonomy on teacher autonomy. *System* 23 (2): 175–82.

Little, D. (1996) Freedom to learn and compulsion to interact: Promoting learner autonomy through the use of information systems and information technologies. In R. Pemberton, E. S. L. Li, W. W. F. Or and H. D. Pierson (eds) *Taking Control: Autonomy in Language Learning*, 203–18. Hong Kong: Hong Kong University Press.

Little, D. (2000) Strategies, counselling and cultural difference: Why we need an anthropological understanding of learner autonomy. In R. Ribé (ed.) *Developing Learner Autonomy in Foreign Language Learning*, 17–33. Barcelona: University of Barcelona.

Little, D. (2007a) Introduction: Reconstructing learner and teacher autonomy in language education. In A. Barfield and S. H. Brown (eds) *Reconstructing Autonomy in Language Education: Inquiry and Innovation*, 1–12. Basingstoke: Palgrave Macmillan.

Little, D. (2007b) Language learner autonomy: Some fundamental considerations revisited. *Innovation in Language Learning and Teaching* 1 (1): 14–29.

Long, M. (2007) *Problems in SLA*. Mahwah, NJ: Erlbaum.

Lope Blanch, J. M. (1987) *Estudios Sobre el Espanol de Yucatan*. Mexico: Universidad Nacional Autonoma de Mexico.

Lorenz, E. N. (2001) *The Essence of Chaos*. Washington, DC: University of Washington Press.

Luck, M. and d'Inverno, M. (1995) A formal framework for agency and identity. *Proceedings of the First International Conference on Multi-agent Systems*. AAAI Press/MIT Press, 254–60. Retrieved from <http://www.aaai.org/Library/ICMAS/icmas95contents.php>

Luke, A. (2006) Teaching after the market. In L. Weis, C. McCarthy and G. Dimitriadis (eds) *Ideology, Curriculum, and the New Sociology of Education: Revisiting the Work of Michael Apple*, 115–41. New York, NY: Routledge.

Macaro, E. (2008) The shifting dimensions of language learner autonomy. In T. E. Lamb and H. Reinders (eds) *Learner and Teacher Autonomy: Concepts, Realities and Responses*, 43–62. Amsterdam: John Benjamins.

MacIntyre, P. D., Clément, R., Dörnyei, Z. and Noels, K. A. (1998) Conceptualizing willingness to communicate in an L2: A situational model of L2 confidence and affiliation. *Modern Language Journal* 82 (4): 545–62.

Mackenzie, C. and Stoljar, N. (eds) (2000) *Relational Autonomy: Feminist Perspectives on Autonomy, Agency, and the Social Self*. New York, NY: Oxford University Press.

Mandelbrot, B. B. (1982) *The Fractal Geometry of Nature*. New York, NY: W. H. Freeman and Company.

Marginson, S. (1997) *Markets in Education*. St Leonards, NSW: Allen and Unwin.

Markus, H. R. and Nurius, P. (1986) Possible selves. *American psychologist* 41, 954–69.

Martins, A. C. S. and Braga, C. F. B. (2007) Caos, complexidade e Linguística Aplicada: Diálogos transdisciplinares. *Revista Brasileira de Linguística Aplicada* 7 (2): 215–35.

Massen, S. and Weingart, P. (2000) *Metaphors and the Dynamics of Knowledge*. London: Routledge.

May, T. (2006) *The Philosophy of Foucault*. Chesham: Acumen Publishing.

McAdams, D. (2007) The role of narrative in personality psychology today. In M. Bamberg (ed.) *Narrative: State of the Art*, 17–26. Amsterdam: John Benjamins.

McClelland, N. (2000) Goal orientations in Japanese college students learning EFL. In S. Cornwell and P. Robinson (eds) *Individual Differences in Foreign Language Learning: Effects of Aptitude, Intelligence, and Motivation*, 99–115. Tokyo: Japanese Association for Language Teaching.

McLelland, M. J. (2000) *Male Homosexuality in Modern Japan: Cultural Myths and Social Realities*. London: Routledge Curzon.

McMahill, C. (1997) Communities of resistance: A case study of two feminist English classes in Japan. *TESOL Quarterly* 31 (3): 612–22.

McMahill, C. (2001) Self-expression, gender, and community: A Japanese feminist English class. In A. Pavlenko, A. Blackledge, I. Piller and M. Teutsch-Dwyer (eds) *Multilingualism, Second Language Learning, and Gender*, 307–44. Berlin: Mouton de Gruyter.

McNeill, D. (2005) *Gesture and Thought*. Chicago, IL: University of Chicago Press.

Mead, G. H. (1934) *Mind, Self and Society*. Chicago, IL: University of Chicago Press.

Menezes, V. (2008) Multimedia language learning histories. In P. Kalaja, V. Menezes and A. M. F. Barcelos (eds) *Narratives of Learning and Teaching EFL*, 199–213. London: Palgrave Macmillan.

Menezes, V. (2011) Affordances for language learning beyond the classroom. In P. Benson and H. Reinders (eds) *Beyond the Language Classroom*, 59–71. Basingstoke: Palgrave Macmillan.

Mertens, D. M. (2005) *Research and Evaluation in Education and Psychology: Integrating Diversity with Quantitative, Qualitative and Mixed Methods*. Thousand Oaks, CA: Sage.

Miller, C. and Blackman, C. (n.d.) *The Shape of the Learning Curve: Trajectories of Workplace Learning*. Retrieved 18 November 2009 from http://www.conferencereview.com/papers/1192005_8178.doc

Mondada, L. and Pekarek Doehler, S. (2004) Second language acquisition as situated practice: Task accomplishment in the French second language classroom. *Modern Language Journal* 88 (4): 501–18.

Morgan, B. (2004) Teacher identity as pedagogy: Towards a field-internal conceptualisation in bilingual and second language education. *International Journal of Bilingual Education and Bilingualism* 7 (2–3): 172–88.

Morgan, J. (1996) A defence of autonomy as an educational ideal. *Journal of Philosophy of Education* 30 (2): 239–52.

Mori, K. (1977) *Polite Lies: On Being a Woman Caught between Cultures*. New York, NY: Fawcett Books.

Morita, N. (2004) Negotiating participation and identity in second language academic communities. *TESOL Quarterly* 38 (4): 573–603.

Murphey, T. and Carpenter, C. (2008) The seeds of agency in language learning histories. In P. Kalaja, V. Menezes and A. M. F. Barcelos (eds) *Narratives of Learning and Teaching EFL*, 17–34. Basingstoke: Palgrave Macmillan.

Murphey, T., Jin, C. and Li-Chin, C. (2005) Learners' constructions of identities and imagined communities. In P. Benson and D. Nunan (eds) *Learners' Stories: Difference and Diversity in Language Learning*, 83–100. Cambridge: Cambridge University Press.

Murray, G. (2008) Communities of practice: Stories of Japanese EFL learners. In P. Kalaja, V. Menezes and A. M. F. Barcelos (eds) *Narratives of Learning and Teaching EFL*, 128–40. Basingstoke: Palgrave Macmillan.

Murray, G. (2009) *Language, Learning, Life: Mature Learners' Stories*. Paper presented at the Independent Learning Association Conference, Hong Kong Polytechnic University, 3–5 June, 2009.

Nahmias, E. (2007) Autonomous agency and social psychology. In M. Marraffa, M. De Caro and F. Ferretti (eds) *Cartographies of the Mind*, 169–85. Dordrecht, The Netherlands: Springer.

Nakata, Y. (1995) New goals for Japanese learners of English. *The Language Teacher* 19 (5): 17–20.

Nedelsky, J. (1989) Reconceiving autonomy: Sources, thoughts and possibilities. *Yale Journal of Law and Feminism* 1 (7): 7–36.

Negueruela, E. (2003) *A sociocultural approach to the teaching-learning of second languages: Systemic-theoretical instruction and L2 development*. Unpublished doctoral dissertation. The Pennsylvania State University. University Park, PA.

Negueruela, E. (2008) Revolutionary pedagogies: Learning that leads (to) second language development. In J. P. Lantolf and M. E. Poehner (eds) *Sociocultural Theory and the Teaching of Second Languages*, 189–227. London: Equinox.

Nelson, C. (1999) Sexual identities in ESL: Queer theory and classroom inquiry. *TESOL Quarterly* 33 (3): 371–91.

Nelson, C. D. (2009) *Sexual Identities in English Language Education: Classroom Conversations*. New York, NY: Routledge.

Nelson, C. D. (2010) A gay immigrant student's perspective: Unspeakable acts in the language class. *TESOL Quarterly* 44 (3): 441–64.

Nikula, T. and Pitkänen-Huhta, A. (2008) Using photographs to access stories of learning English. In P. Kalaja, V. Menezes and A. M. F. Barcelos (eds) *Narratives of Learning and Teaching EFL*, 171–85. Basingstoke: Palgrave Macmillan.

Norton, B. (2000) *Identity and Language Learning: Gender, Ethnicity and Educational Change*. London: Longman.

Norton, B. (2001) Non-participation, imagined communities and the language classroom. In M. P. Breen (ed.) *Learner Contributions to Language Learning: New Directions in Research*, 159–71. Harlow: Longman.

Norton, B. and Toohey, K. (2001a) *Critical Pedagogies and Language Learning*. Cambridge: Cambridge University Press.

Norton, B. and Toohey, K. (2001b) Changing perspectives on good language learners. *TESOL Quarterly* 35 (2): 307–22.

Norton Peirce, B. (1995) Social identity, investment, and language learning. *TESOL* Quarterly 29 (1): 9–31.

Ochs, E. (1993) Constructing social identity: A language socialization perspective. *Research on Language and Social Interaction* 26 (3): 287–306.

Ockerman, C. (1997) Facilitating and learning at the edge of chaos: Expanding the context of experiential education. Proceedings from *1997 AEE International Conference*. Available at http://eric.ed.gov/ERICDocs/data/ericdocs2/content_storage_01/ 0000000b/80/23/71/61.pdf

O'Leary, T. (2002) *Foucault and the Art of Ethics*. London: Continuum.

Olssen, M. (2005) Foucault, educational research and the issue of autonomy. *Educational Philosophy and Theory* 37 (3): 365–87.

Olssen, M. (2006) *Michel Foucault: Materialism and Education*. Boulder, CO: Paradigm Publishers.

Oxford, R. L. (2003) Toward a more systematic model of L2 learner autonomy. In D. Palfreyman and R. C. Smith (eds) *Learner Autonomy Across Cultures: Language Education Perspectives*, 75–91. Basingstoke: Palgrave Macmillan.

Paiva, V. L. M. (2011) Identity, motivation and autonomy in second language acquisition. In G. Murray, X. Gao and T. Lamb (eds) *Identity, Motivation and Autonomy in Language Learning*, 57–72. Bristol: Multilingual Matters.

Palfreyman, D. (2003) Introduction: Cultural and learning autonomy. In D. Palfreyman and R. C. Smith (eds) *Learner Autonomy Across Cultures: Language Education Perspectives*, 1–19. Basingstoke: Palgrave Macmillan.

Paradis, M. (2009) *Studies in Bilingualism 40: Declarative and Procedural Determinants of Second Languages*. Amsterdam: John Benjamins.

Passel, J. S., Randall, C. and Fix, M. E. (2004) *Undocumented Immigrants: Facts and Figures.* Retrieved 15 July 2005 from http://www.urban.org/url.cfm?ID=1000587

Pavlenko, A. (2001) Bilingualism, gender and ideology. *International Journal of Bilingualism* (5) 2: 117–51.

Pavlenko, A. and Blackledge, A. (eds) (2004) *Negotiation of Identities in Multilingual Contexts*. Clevedon: Multilingual Matters.

Pavlenko, A. and Lantolf, J. P. (2000) Second language learning as participation and the (re)construction of selves. In J. P. Lantolf (ed.) *Sociocultural Theory and Second Language Learning*, 155–77. Oxford: Oxford University Press.

Pennycook, A. (1997) Cultural alternatives and autonomy. In P. Benson and P. Voller (eds) *Autonomy and Independence in Language Learning*, 35–53. London: Longman.

Pennycook, A. (2007) *Global Englishes and Transcultural Flows*. London: Routledge.

Peters, M. (2007) Educational research: 'Games of truth' and the ethics of subjectivity. In M. Peters and C. Belsey (eds) *Why Foucault? New Directions in Educational Research*, 181–91. New York, NY: Peter Lang.

Pfeiler, B. (1996) 'Yan difereensia waye' yeetel maaya yukataan' (un estudio dialectal). In U. Hostetler (ed.) *Los Mayas de Quintana Roo: Investigaciones antropologicas recientes Vol. 14*, 7–13. Bern: Arbeitsblatter des Instituts fur Ethnologie der Universitat Bern.

Phillips, L. and Jørgensen, M. (2002) *Discourse Analysis as Theory and Method*. Thousand Oaks, CA: Sage.

Ratner, C. (2006) *Cultural Psychology: A Perspective on Psychological Functioning and Social Reform*. Mahwah, NJ: Erlbaum.

Raz, J. (1986) *The Morality of Freedom*. Oxford: Oxford University Press.

Resnick, L. B., Levine, J. M. and Teasley, S. D. (eds) (1991) *Perspectives on Socially Shared Cognition*. Washington, DC: American Psychological Association.

Ribé, R. (2003) Tramas in the foreign language classroom: Autopoietic networks for learner growth. In D. Little, J. Ridley and E. Ushioda (eds) *Learner Autonomy in the Foreign Language Classroom: Teacher, Learner, Curriculum and Assessment*, 11–28. Dublin: Authentik.

Richards, K. (2006) 'Being the teacher': Identity and classroom conversation. *Applied Linguistics* 27 (1): 51–77.

Riley, P. (2003) Self-access as access to 'self': Cultural variation in the notions of self and personhood. In D. Palfreyman and R. C. Smith (eds) *Learner Autonomy Across Cultures: Language Education Perspectives*, 92–109. Basingstoke: Palgrave Macmillan.

Riley, P. (ed.) (1985) *Discourse and Learning*. London: Longman.

Rogoff, B. (1995) Observing sociocultural activity on three planes: Participatory appropriation, guided participation, and apprenticeship. In J .V. Wertsch, P. del Rio and A. Alvarez (eds) *Sociocultural Studies of Mind*, 139–65. Cambridge: Cambridge University Press.

Rogoff, B. (1998) Cognition as a collaborative process. In D. Kuhn and R. S. Sieger (eds) *Cognition, Perception and Language. Vol 2 of Handbook of Child Psychology. Fifth edition*, 679–744. New York, NY: John Wiley and Sons.

Ryan, S. (2006) Language learning motivation within the context of globalization: A L2 self within an imagined global community. *Critical Inquiry in Language Studies* 3 (1): 23–45.

Ryan, S. (2009) Self and identity in L2 motivation in Japan: The ideal L2 self and Japanese learners of English. In Z. Dörnyei and E. Ushioda (eds) *Motivation, Language Identity and the L2 Self*, 120–44. Bristol: Multilingual Matters.

Sabatini, Y. (2007) Case study of a female educator: Gender and learning to teach. *Journal of Engaged Pedagogy* 6: 33–43.

Sade, L. A. (2008) *Complexity and Identity Reconstruction in Second Language Acquisition*. Symposium paper presented at AILA 2008 – 15th World Congress of Applied Linguistics, Essen/Germany, August.

Sade, L. A. (2009) *Identidade e aprendizagem de inglês sob a* ótica *do caos e dos sistemas complexos*. Doctoral dissertation. Universidade Federal de Minas Gerais, Brazil.

Salomon, G. (ed.) (1993) *Distributed Cognition*. New York, NY: Cambridge University Press.

Sasaki, M. (2004) A multiple-data analysis of the 3.5-year development of EFL student writers. *Language Learning* 54 (3): 525–82.

Sasaki, M. (2007) Effects of study-abroad experiences on EFL writers: A multiple-data analysis. *Modern Language Journal* 91 (4): 602–20.

Sato, G. and Yoshitani, T. (2005) *Hitoo wakerumono tsunagumono* [Things that separate people and those that connect them]. Kyoto: Nakanishiya.

Saunston, H. and Kyratzis, S. (2007) Introduction: Language, sexualities and desires. In H. Saunston and S. Kyratzis (eds) *Language, Sexualities and Desires: Cross-cultural Perspectives*, 1–16. Basingstoke: Palgrave Macmillan.

Scheurich, J. and McKenzie, K. (2005) Foucault's methodologies: Archaeology and genealogy. In N. K. Denzin and Y. Lincoln (eds) *Handbook of Qualitative Research*, 841–68. Thousand Oaks, CA: Sage.

Schmenk, B. (2005) Globalizing learner autonomy. *TESOL Quarterly* 39 (1): 107–18.

Schwandt, T. A. (1994) Constructivist, interpretivist approaches to human inquiry. In N. K. Denzin and Y. S. Lincoln (eds) *Handbook of Qualitative Research*, 118–34. Thousand Oaks, CA: Sage.

Scollon, R. and Scollon, S. W. (2004) *Nexus Analysis: Discourse and the Emerging Internet*. London: Routledge.

Sealey, A. (2007) Linguistic ethnography in realist perspective. *Journal of Sociolinguistics* 11 (5): 641–60.

Sealey, A. and Carter, B. (2004) *Applied Linguistics as Social Science*. London: Continuum.

Sfard, A. (1998) On two metaphors for learning and the dangers of choosing just one. *Educational Researcher* 27 (2): 4–13.

Sheerin, S. (1997) An exploration of the relationship between self-access and independent learning. In P. Benson and P. Voller (eds) *Autonomy and Independence in Language Learning*, 54–65. London: Longman.

Siegal, M. (1996) The role of learner subjectivity in second language sociolinguistic competency: Western women learning Japanese. *Applied Linguistics* 17 (3): 356–82.

Simmel, G. (1997) The metropolis and mental life. In D. Frisby and M. Featherstone (eds) *Simmel on Culture: Selected Writings*, 174–85. London: Sage. (First published 1903 as Die Grossstädte und das Geistesleben, *Jahrbuch der Gehe-Stiftung* 9: 185–206).

Skehan, P. (1991) Individual differences in second language learning. *Studies of Second Language Acquisition* 13: 275–98.

Skutnabb-Kangas, T. (2000) *Linguistic Genocide in Education – Or Worldwide Diversity and Human Rights?* Mahwah, NJ: Lawrence Erlbaum.

Sleeter, C. (2008) Equity, democracy, and neoliberal assaults on teacher education. *Teaching and Teacher Education* 24 (8): 1947–57.

Sleeter, C. (ed.) (2007) *Facing Accountability in Education: Democracy and Equity at Risk*. New York, NY: Teachers College Press.

Slobin, D. I. (1996) From 'thought and language' to 'thinking for speaking'. In J. J. Gumperz and S. C. Levinson (eds) *Grammatical Constructions? Their Formation and Meaning*, 195–220. Oxford: Clarendon Press.

Smith, L. (2007) *Chaos: A Very Short Introduction*. Oxford: Oxford University Press.

Smith, R. C. (2001) Group work for autonomy in Asia: Insights from teacher research. *The AILA Review* 15: 70–81.

Smith, R. C. (2003) Pedagogy for autonomy as (becoming)-appropriate methodology. In D. Palfreyman and R. C. Smith (eds) *Learner Autonomy Across Cultures: Language Education Perspectives*, 129–46. Basingstoke: Palgrave Macmillan.

Solsken, J. (1993) *Literacy, Gender and Work: In Families and in School*. Norwood, NJ: Ablex Publishing Company.

Speidel, G. and Nelson, K. E. (eds) (1989) *The Many Faces of Imitation in Language Learning*. New York, NY: Springer Verlag.

Stetsenko, A. and Arievitch, I. (2000) The quality of cultural tools and cognitive development: Gal'perin's perspective and its implications. *Human Development* 43: 69–92.

Stetsenko, A. and Arievitch, I. (2004) Vygotskian collaborative project of social transformation: History, politics and practice in knowledge construction. *Journal of Critical Psychology* 12 (4): 58–80.

Stone, C. M. (1990) Autonomy, emotions and desires: Some problems concerning R. F. Dearden's account of autonomy. *Journal of Philosophy of Education* 24 (2): 271–83.

Street, B. V. (1984) *Literacy in Theory and Practice*. Cambridge: Cambridge University Press.

Stroud, C. and Wee, L. (2007) Identity and English language literacy: Exploring liminalities in social positioning. *TESOL Quarterly* 41 (1): 33–54.

Sunagawa, H. (2006) The social situation facing gays in Japan. Translated by M. McLelland. *Intersections* 12. Retrieved from http://wwwsshe.murdoch.edu.au/intersections/issue12/sunagawa1.html

Swain, M. (2006) Languaging, agency, and collaboration in advanced second language proficiency. In H. Byrnes (ed) *Advanced Language Learning. The Contribution of Halliday and Vygotsky*, 72–94. London: Continuum.

Swain, M. and Deters, P. (2007) 'New' mainstream SLA theory: Expanded and enriched. *Modern Language Journal* 91 (1): 820–36.

Taavitsainen, I. and Pahta, P. (2008) From global language use to local meanings: English in Finnish public discourse. *English Today* 24 (3): 25–38.

Taniguchi, H. (2006) The legal situation facing sexual minorities in Japan. *Intersections* 12. Retrieved from http://wwwsshe.murdoch.edu.au/intersections/issue12/taniguchi.html

Tharp, R. and Gallimore, R. (1988) *Rousing Minds to Life: Teaching, Learning and Schooling in Social Context*. Cambridge: Cambridge University Press.

Thorne, S. (2006) Epistemology, politics, and ethics in sociocultural theory. *Modern Language Journal* 89 (3): 393–409.

Tomasello, M. (2003) *Constructing Language: A Usage-Based Theory of Language Acquisition*. Cambridge, MA: Harvard University Press.

Tomlinson, B. (2000) Talking to yourself: The role of the inner voice in language learning. *Applied Language Learning* 11 (1): 123–54.

Toohey, K. (2000) *Learning English at School: Identity, Social Relations and Classroom Practice*. Clevedon: Multilingual Matters.

Toohey, K. (2007) Conclusion: Autonomy/agency through socio-cultural lenses. In A. Barfield and S. H. Brown (eds) *Reconstructing Autonomy in Language Education: Inquiry and Innovation*, 231–42. Basingstoke: Palgrave Macmillan.

Toohey, K. and Norton, B. (2003) Learner autonomy as agency in sociocultural settings. In D. Palfreyman and R. C. Smith (eds) *Learner Autonomy Across Cultures: Language Education Perspectives*, 58–72. Basingstoke: Palgrave Macmillan.

Toohey, K., Day, E. and Manyak, P. (2007) ESL learners in the early school years. In J. Cummins and C. Davison (eds) *International Handbook of English Language Teaching*, 625–38. Boston, MA: Springer.

Torfing, J. (1999) *New Theories of Discourse: Laclau, Mouffe and Zizek.* Oxford: Blackwell.

Torikai, K. (2011) *Kokusai kyotsugotoshiteno eigo* [English as a lingua franca for international communication]. Tokyo: Kodansha.

Trent, J. (2006) A reader responds: Speaking in a foreign language academic community of practice: Toward a holistic understanding. *TESOL Quarterly* 40 (2): 430–35.

Tsui, A. (2007) Complexities of identity formation: A narrative inquiry of an EFL teacher. *TESOL Quarterly* 41 (4): 657–80.

Turner, J. C. and Patrick, H. (2008) How does motivation develop and why does it change? Reframing motivation research. *Educational Psychologist* 43 (3): 119–31.

Tusting, K. (2003) A review of theories of informal learning. *Working Paper No 2*. Lancaster: Lancaster Literacy Research Centre.

Ushakova, T. (1994) Inner speech and second language acquisition: An experimental–theoretical approach. In J. P. Lantolf and G. Appel (eds) *Vygotskian Approaches to Second Language Research*, 135–56. Norwood, NJ: Ablex.

Ushioda, E. (1996) *Learner Autonomy 5: The Role of Motivation*. Dublin: Authentik.

Ushioda, E. (2006) Language motivation in a reconfigured Europe: Access, identity, autonomy. *Journal of Multilingual and Multicultural Development* (27) 2: 148–61.

Ushioda, E. (2009) A person-in-context relational view of emergent motivation, self and identity. In Z. Dörnyei and E. Ushioda (eds) *Motivation, Language Identity and the L2 Self*, 215–28. Bristol: Multilingual Matters.

van Lier, L. (1997) Observations from an ecological perspective. *TESOL Quarterly* 31 (4): 783–7.

van Lier, L. (2000) From input to affordance: Social-interactive learning from an ecological perspective. In J. P. Lantolf (ed.) *Sociocultural Theory and Second Language Learning*, 245–59. Oxford: Oxford University Press.

van Lier, L. (2002) An ecological-semiotic perspective. In C. Kramsch (ed.) *Language Acquisition and Language Socialization: Ecological Perspectives*, 140–264. London: Continuum.

van Lier, L. (2004) *The Ecology and Semiotics of Language Learning: A Sociocultural Perspective*. Dordrecht: Kluwer Academic Publishers.

van Lier, L. (2007) Action-based teaching, autonomy and identity. *Innovation in Language Learning and Teaching* 1 (1): 46–65.

van Lier, L. (2008) Agency in the classroom. In J. P. Lantolf and M. E. Poehner (eds) *Sociocultural Theory and the Teaching of Second Languages*, 163–88. London: Equinox.

van Manen, M. (1990) *Researching Lived Experience.* Albany, NY: State University of New York Press.

Varghese, M., Morgan, B., Johnston, B. and Johnson, K. A. (2005) Theorizing language teacher identity: Three perspectives and beyond. *Journal of Language, Identity and Education* 4 (1): 21–44.

Voller, P. (1997) Does the teacher have a role in autonomous learning? In P. Benson and P. Voller (eds) *Autonomy and Independence in Language Learning*, 98–113. London: Longman.

Vygotsky, L. S. (1978) *Mind in Society: The Development of Higher Psychological Processes*. Cambridge, MA: Harvard University Press.

Vygotsky, L. S. (1987) *The Collected Works of L. S. Vygotsky Volume 1: Problems in General Psychology, Including the Volume Thinking and Speech* (R. W. Rieber and A. S. Carton eds). New York, NY: Plenum.

Vygotsky, L. S. (1997) *The Collected Works of L. S. Vygotsky Volume 3: Problems of the Theory and History of Psychology* (R. W. Rieber and J. Wollock eds). New York, NY: Plenum.

Wain, K. (2007) Foucault: The ethics of self-creation and the future of education. In M. Peters and T. Belsey (eds) *Why Foucault? New Directions in Educational Research*, 163–80. New York, NY: Peter Lang.

Waldrop, M. M. (1993) *Complexity: The Emerging Science at the Edge of Order and Chaos*. New York, NY: Touchstone.

Weedon, C. (1997) *Feminist Practice and Poststructuralist Theory*. Second edition. Malden, MA: Blackwell.

Wellman, B. (2002) Little boxes, glocalization, and networked individualism. In M. Tanabe, P. Besselaar and T. Ishida (eds) *Digital Cities II: Computational and Sociological Approaches*, 10–25. Berlin: Springer.

Wenden, A. (2002) Learner development in language learning. *Applied Linguistics* 23 (1): 32–55.

Wenger, E. (1998) *Communities of Practice: Learning, Meaning and Identity.* Cambridge: Cambridge University Press.

Wertsch, J. V. (2007) Mediation. In H. Daniels, M. Cole and J. V. Werstch (eds) *The Cambridge Companion to Vygotsky*, 178–92. New York, NY: Cambridge University Press.

Wertsch, J. V., Tulviste, P. and Hagstrom, F. (1993) A sociocultural approach to agency. In E. A. Forman, N. Minick and C. A. Stone (eds) *Contexts for Learning. Sociocultural Dynamics in Children's Development*, 336–56. New York, NY: Oxford University Press.

White, C. (1999) Expectations and emergent beliefs of self-instructed language learners. *System* 27 (4): 443–57.

White, S. H. and Siegel, A. W. (1984) Cognitive development in time and space. In B. Rogoff and J. Lave (eds) *Everyday Cognition: Its Development and Social Context*, 238–77. Cambridge, MA: Harvard University Press.

Whiteside, A. (2006) *'We are the explorers': Transnational Yucatec Maya-speakers negotiating multilingual California*. Unpublished PhD dissertation. University of California Berkeley, CA.

Whitley, M. S. (1986) *Spanish/English Contrasts*. Washington, DC: Georgetown University Press.

Williams, M., Burden, R. L. and Al-Baharna, S. (2001) Making sense of success and failure: The role of the individual in motivation theory. In Z. Dörnyei and R. Schmidt (eds) *Motivation and Second Language Acquisition*, 171–86. Honolulu, HI: University of Hawai'i Press.

Yáñez-Prieto, C. (2008) *On literature and the secret art of invisible words: Teaching literature through language*. Unpublished doctoral dissertation. The Pennsylvania State University. University Park, PA.

Yang, J. (2006) Learners and users of English in China. *English Today* 22: 3–10.

Yaroshevsky, M. (1989) *Lev Vygotsky*. Moscow: Progress Press.

Yashima, T. (2000) Orientations and motivations in foreign language learning: A study of Japanese college students. *JACET Bulletin* 31: 121–33.

Yashima, T. (2002) Willingness to communicate in a second language: The Japanese EFL context. *Modern Language Journal* 86 (1): 54–66.

Yashima, T. (2004) *Dainigengo komyunikeshonto ibunkatekio* [Second language communication and intercultural adaptation]. Tokyo: Tagashuppan.

Yashima, T. (2009) International posture and the ideal L2 self in the Japanese EFL context. In Z. Dörnyei and E. Ushioda (eds) *Motivation, Language Identity and the L2 Self*, 144–64. Bristol: Multilingual Matters.

Yashima, T. (2010) The effects of international volunteer work experiences on intercultural competence of Japanese youth. *International Journal of Intercultural Relations* 34 (3): 268–82.

Yashima, T. and Tanaka, T. (1996) Sosharusukiru kunreno toriireta eigokyoiku [English teaching for intercultural adjustment using social skill training techniques]. *Intercultural /Transcultural Education* 10: 150–66.

Yashima, T. and Zenuk-Nishide, L. (2008) The impact of learning contexts on proficiency, attitudes, and L2 communication: Creating an imagined international community. *System* 36 (4): 566–85.

Yashima, T., Zenuk-Nishide, L. and Shimizu, K. (2004) The influence of attitudes and affect on willingness to communicate and second language communication. *Language Learning* 54 (1): 119–52.

Young, R. (1986) *Personal Autonomy: Beyond Negative and Positive Liberty*. London: Croom Helm.

Zembylas, M. and Lamb, T. (2008) Interrogating the notion of autonomy in education: Tensions and possibilities. In M. Jiménez Raya and T. Lamb (eds) *Pedagogy for Autonomy in Modern Languages Education: Theory, Practice and Teacher Education*, 21–35. Dublin: Authentik.

Zhao, J. and Guo, J. (2002) The restructuring of China's higher education: An experience for market economy and knowledge economy. *Educational Philosophy and Theory* 34 (2): 207–21.

Zuengler, J. and Miller, E. R. (2006) Cognitive and sociocultural perspectives: Two parallel SLA worlds? *TESOL Quarterly* 40 (1): 35–58.

Index

action research 155–57, 162
affective repertoire 48, 58
affinity space 10, 13, 115
age 32, 85–6, 108–9, 134, 144, 176
agency 7, 41–2, 55–6, 58, 64–6, 69, 133, 148–51
    autonomy vs. 7–8, 18–19, 80, 183–5
    individual 3, 13, 15, 104–6, 126–7, 154
    post-structural theory and 136
    socially-oriented 2, 92, 104–6
    Sociocultural Theory and 17–31
    Social Realism and 138
    structure and 8–11, 14, 135, 179
    teacher 165, 177
alignment 36–7, 43, 48, 52, 55, 119–20, 123, 130–31, 137, 154
anthropology 13, 34
Applied Linguistics 1–9, 11–16, 33–4, 35, 45–9, 58–62, 71, 75, 79, 81, 83, 85, 119, 136–7, 141, 150, 152, 176–81, 183–6
aptitude 32, 46
articulation 57–8, 164, 178–9
Asia 46–58, 85, 99, 157
athletics 108, 113
attractor 70–3
authentic concern 83, 86
authenticity 82–4
autonomy 7–8, 42–4, 64–6, 75–89, 90–103
    agency vs. 7–8, 18–19, 80, 183–5
    classroom 77–8
    personal 79–81, 84
    philosophy of 80–4
    relational 81–4
    Sociocultural Theory and 17–31
    teacher 78, 165, 177

ballroom dancing 108, 111–2
behavioural repertoire 48, 56, 58
belief 1, 10, 51, 69, 90–103, 126, 166, 168, 170, 173–5
bilingual 108, 156
biography 135, 165
biological 3, 12, 18, 19, 153, 163
border-crossing 137–8
Brazil 59–74

Canada 26, 40–1, 48, 53
care of the self 164–77
case study 2, 107, 155, 157–8, 162
Chaos Theory 14, 59–74, 154
China 119–34
Chinese 61–2, 74, 119, 120–1, 127, 130, 132
code-switching 110
cognition
    cognitive development 19
    cognitive repertoire 48, 58
    cognitivism 92
    distributed 4
coherence 82–4, 86, 88, 126
collaborative role-play games 10
communicative repertoire 55, 59
community 3, 10, 13–4, 20–1, 28, 32–7, 39–41, 43–58, 66, 69, 81, 92, 96, 99, 112, 121, 123–6, 130–3, 147–8, 144–50, 153, 155–6, 162, 178
Community of Practice (CoP) 1, 13–4, 16, 32–45, 48, 50, 53, 55, 61, 92, 105, 109–134, 138, 182, 185
Complexity 26, 32, 59–60, 62, 65, 105, 128, 131, 158
Complexity Theory 1, 11, 14–6, 62, 152–5, 157, 162–3, 179
constructivism 22–3, 28, 126, 168
    epistemology 22

Conversation Analysis 33, 36, 45, 155–6, 158–62
counselling 76
creation myth 61
culture
  cultural capital 135, 137
  determination of 3, 10, 12, 37, 53, 65, 79, 80, 82, 93, 128, 133, 152, 154, 163, 166, 179–82, 185
  historical 46–7, 90, 106, 134
diary 122
discourse
  discourse analysis 1, 33, 45
  Critical Discourse Theory 16
  discourse theory 33, 104–18
disengagement 35
dynamic system 15, 60
Dynamic Systems Theory 14, 59, 152–63

elitism 8–9
email correspondence 122–3
emergence 1, 5, 23, 29–30, 43–44, 64–5, 68, 73, 81, 94, 101, 104, 107, 109, 115, 131, 136–7, 146, 150–1, 153–5, 157–8, 181–4
engagement 5, 13–4, 34–6, 42–5, 48–50, 53, 55, 84, 104–5, 110, 117–20, 123, 131, 165, 169, 170–71, 174–5, 177, 182
English 10, 26, 30, 40–2, 44, 49, 50–2, 54–5, 57–8, 61, 64–6, 68–72, 79, 84–8, 94–100, 102, 104, 106–17, 120–30, 132, 134–4, 139, 140–2, 145–51, 153, 156–8, 169
  attitudes towards 54, 112, 116
  as a Foreign Language (EFL) 33, 38, 40, 44, 46–54, 56, 64, 100, 141, 139
  as a Second Language (ESL) 33, 35, 38, 40–1, 48–9, 141
  for Academic Purposes (EAP) 90, 94
  for Speakers of Other Languages (ESOL) 44
  language learning histories 84
environmentalism 61
ethical self-formation 164–77
  ethnography 6, 38, 53, 104–7, 117, 155–6
Experientialism 60

fashion 108, 111, 125, 169
feminism 51, 81, 139
Finland 79, 104–118
Finnish sign language 108
flexible control 82–4, 86–7
Foucault 81, 177
  ethics 16

gay men 129, 136–45
gender 51, 57, 82 134, 139, 181, 184
globalization 10–1, 46–9, 58, 95–6, 108, 116, 120, 186
grammar 29, 30, 55, 70, 87–88, 97, 111, 114–5, 160, 181

Hong Kong 53, 71–2, 85, 109, 170–2

ice-hockey 108–9
identity 5–7, 37–40, 64–6, 73, 98–100, 135–51, 181–3
  classroom participation and 38–40
  Second Language 1, 88
  sexual 135–51
  L2 119–34
  teacher 164–77
  group 110
  identity work 50–3, 112, 136, 143, 171
imagination 10, 14, 36, 43, 46–58, 60, 119–20, 123, 126–9
Imagined Community 10, 13–6, 35, 46–58, 73, 92, 97, 99, 111–2, 139, 149, 183
Imagined
  future self 90, 100
  L2 community 50–1, 55, 137
independence 8–10, 83–4
independent learners 46
interview 52–3, 94, 98, 101, 122–3, 129, 140, 142–3, 146, 151, 158, 162

individual 1–16, 45, 75–89, 150–1
  autonomy and 7–8, 75–89
  biological 3, 12, 18–19
  conceptions of 3–5, 21
  individual difference 5, 32, 120, 132, 185–6
  social 4, 75–89
  social and 1–16, 18, 33, 115–7
  individualism 2, 3, 75, 80–81, 178
  individuality 18, 104, 116, 131, 133, 185–6
  individualization 10, 50, 75–7
  view of language learning 1
  individual identity 9
Indonesia 40
inner speech 24–6
interaction 1, 12, 38, 44, 46, 55, 60, 62–3, 65, 78, 93, 120, 123, 136, 157, 163, 178, 181
interdependence 8, 66, 75, 77–8, 81, 83, 86, 88, 167, 185
international posture 58, 96, 138, 150
investment 2, 65, 92, 96, 112, 137, 138, 140, 185

Japan 39, 41, 46–58, 62, 72, 79, 94–8, 99–100, 102, 129, 135–51, 157–8
joint enterprise 34–5, 40–1, 43–5, 49
Journal of Applied Linguistics 11
L2 (see also language, second) 22, 24–7, 30, 38–9, 41, 43, 46–7, 51–6, 58, 119–20, 123, 128–34, 137–9, 145 148
  identity formation 120, 131, 134
  learner 25, 38, 47–50, 120, 133–4
language
  aptitude 32
  ecology (see Social-ecological Theory)
  first 25–6, 61, 63, 88, 139, 149
  foreign (FL) 9–11, 21, 24, 38, 47–50, 52, 104, 108, 121
  language learning history (LLH) 59, 62, 64, 67, 70–3, 79, 86, 90, 102
  language proficiency 21–4
  second (see also L2) 9, 24–5, 47, 52, 58–9, 62–4, 74, 92, 102, 122, 138, 183
learner
  Learner Development 94–5, 98, 102
  Learner reflection 21–2
  learner training 44, 75
  learner-centred 37, 75–6, 178
  learner contract 76
learning
  active and passive 37
  acquisition and participation metaphor 45, 47, 50, 55–6, 105
  differentiated 79, 185
  discovery 28
  experiential 27
  informal 116
  learning history 70, 73, 79, 85, 119, 121, 134
  learning strategy 1, 2, 39, 75, 94
  learning style 1, 45, 75
  out-of-class 78
legitimate peripheral participation (LPP) 34, 39–40, 42
lexis 30, 33
longitudinal 54, 57, 134
Marxism 27, 179–80
  post-Marxism 9, 184
media 48–9, 108, 111, 130, 143–44, 149
  new media 108
memory 4, 18, 24, 62, 69, 85, 113–4, 163
mentalist 61
metaphor 20, 47, 50, 54–5, 59–61, 67, 73, 75, 98, 100, 103, 154
Mexican migrant 152
Model United Nations (MUN) 50
modernity 11, 116, 121
motivation 2, 4, 10, 20, 32, 38, 40–1, 45–6, 49–50, 54, 65, 67, 69, 71, 75–6, 79, 86, 90, 92, 94, 96, 101–2, 107, 126, 137–8, 147, 149–50, 162, 165, 172–3, 175
  motivational 'push' 150
multilingual 10, 40, 105, 152, 158, 162

music 44, 63, 65, 73, 87, 108, 111, 113, 115
mutual engagement 34, 45
myth 59–62, 73

narrative 1, 6, 53, 62, 68
neoliberal ideologies 164
networked individualism 10
New Zealand 90–103

objective 59, 91, 101, 132
objectivity 12, 23, 60, 138, 142
online 10, 11, 35
  communication 10, 137, 138
  learning 62
  social networks 44, 122, 170, 172
ontology 8

Pangu/Chinese myth 74
participant observation 155–6
participation 10, 13–4, 18, 33–40, 42–5, 47, 50, 52–8, 92–3, 97, 100–1, 104–5, 112, 123, 133, 139, 149
pedagogical dialogue 22
peer mediation 22
peer relationship 124
peripheral 34, 36, 41, 55
personality 39, 46, 53, 109, 145, 173
Piaget 20–1
Poland 26, 182
popular culture 111, 115
Portuguese migrant 13
post-structuralism 46–7, 119, 136, 150, 154, 176, 179–80
power 7, 9, 41, 42, 49, 53, 57–8, 107, 124, 135, 138, 148, 167–8
  power relation 37, 39, 47, 53, 56, 132, 167, 177
Pragmatics 1, 30, 121
private speech 22, 24–5
psychobiography 135, 151
psycholinguistics 1
reading 13, 22, 27, 42, 70, 86–7, 95, 108, 113–4, 129
reflection 21–2
research
  empirical 3, 5, 11, 16, 28–9, 31, 42, 154–5, 162–3, 179
  qualitative 2, 5, 45, 79, 167
  quantitative 5, 45, 79
Romany 108

Sámi 108
scout 113
Second Language Acquisition (SLA) 2, 5, 11–2, 15, 24, 27, 32, 45–7, 59, 61–4, 66–74, 119, 138, 140, 151, 153
self
  future 49, 99–101
  ideal 49, 51, 137, 139, 145, 147, 149, 150, 183
  ideal sexual 135–51
  imagined self 47, 49, 50, 53, 99
  L2 53, 58, 137, 139, 147, 149–50
  Motivational Self System 137–8, 145, 150
  ought-to 49, 99
  possible 49–50, 101, 137–8, 149
self-access 75–6, 78
self-determination 80, 82–3, 163
self-dialogue 22
self-directed learning 75–6
self-instruction 75, 77, 87
self reflection 84
self-regulation 46, 92, 94–5, 101, 185
shared repertoire 34–5, 43, 45
Singapore 40
Situated Learning Theory (SLT) 1, 11, 13–5, 32–45, 177, 179, 182–3
skateboarding 109–10, 112
snowboarding 108–9
social
  individual and 3, 6, 15, 75, 89
  social construction 4, 93
  social determination 8
  social dialogue 22
  social interaction 1, 11–4, 78, 89, 114, 181
  social networking 11
  structure 8, 131, 135–8, 149–50, 180, 184
  turn 1, 4, 14, 32, 46–7
Social-Ecological Theory 1, 14, 33, 60, 62, 74, 91, 93, 102, 152–63

Social Realism 1, 16, 42, 135–51
socialization 10, 12–3, 15, 30, 53, 80, 82, 116–7, 162, 178, 180, 182–4
society 10, 19, 21, 56, 76, 80, 108, 115–8, 120, 129–30, 132, 134, 143–4, 148, 163, 166–7, 184
sociocultural
  approach 46, 104–5
  community 28
Sociocultural Theory (SCT) 1, 11–16, 17–31, 33, 46, 90–3, 176–7, 179–90, 182–3
Sociolinguistics 153, 156
Soviet Union 25
Spanish (language) 18, 21, 25, 29–30, 68–9, 71, 74, 156–8, 162
Spanish (speaker) 156
Spanish/Maya bilingual 153
statistical method 76
structuralist 61, 179
study abroad 38, 50, 52–4, 56, 94–5, 100
subjectivity 57, 60, 133, 154, 160, 165–6, 168–9
Swedish 108, 113

teacher 164–77
  strategy 171, 173, 175
textbook 29, 114
transnational migrant 152
television 87, 108, 110–1, 113, 143

United Arab Emirates (UAE) 33, 35–6, 165, 169, 172–5
United States of America 26, 41, 52–3, 55–7, 85–6, 110, 127, 129, 146, 152–63, 165–66, 183

vocabulary 55, 63, 97, 111, 160, 181
Vygotsky 1, 11–2, 14–5, 18–22, 24–5, 27–8, 31, 185

western 3, 9, 18, 52, 85, 121, 127, 139, 145, 153
Willingness to Communicate 53, 56, 138

Yucatan 152–63
Zone of Proximal Development (ZPD) 20

CPSIA information can be obtained
at www.ICGtesting.com
Printed in the USA
BVHW041051200920
589231BV00005B/58